To Celia,
our much missed daughter and sister

To Billy,
our much loved husband and father

To Sara,
dearly loved mother and grandmother

And to Lois,
our special friend

Acknowledgements

Special gratitude is extended to:

Frank and Rose Ciccone, Mary Fudge, Mariette and Claude Gagne, Pam Green, Keith Josefiak, Pamela Lanier, Amy Moreno, Jackie and Lee Morrison, Bill Pinson, Diane Polk, Patsy Rach, Becky and John Robinson, Brent Savage, Christian Simard, Sandy Soule, Marcia Thompson, Johannes Tromp, Lois Ward, recipe contributors and testers, special friends who believed "we could and we would"—and who provided supportive encouragement from beginning to end. We extend heartfelt thanks to each of you.

Recipe Testers

Eva Avery, GA	Nellie Hodges, GA	Joanne Ohlman, FL
Kirk Blaine, GA	Celia Hilliard, IL	Joanne Pemberton, AL
Gail Bosley, GA	Linda & Mike Johnson, GA	Malyssa Pinson, GA
Ashlee Brady, NC	Helen Jungmann, GA	Maxine Pinson, GA
Patti Burgener, GA	Jeff Leggett, GA	Diane Polk, GA
Jason Chervenak, GA	Sharon & Jim Mahanes, SC	Patsy Rach, AL
Rose & Frank Ciccone, NY	"Sam" Miles, GA	Jennifer & David Price, SC
Amanda & Morgan Colburn, MD	Jane Miller, GA	Martha Rowe, VA
"Sis" Cook, GA	Marsha Moore, GA	Lynda Salisbury, AL
Marian English, VA	Mary Moore, FL	Debbie Shealy, GA
Mary Fudge, GA	Jackie Morrison, SC	Lesley Simmons, GA
Elilzabeth Gibson, GA	Margie Morken, MS	Lyn Springer, SC
Mariette Gagne, NC	Judy Nelson, TX	Sara Willis, GA
Lawson Hardee, SC	Donna Nichols, GA	Vikki Woods, TN

Note: Frank Ciccone, the food consultant for *Lowcountry Delights*, has trained at the Culinary Institute of America in Hyde Park, NY. In addition to providing willing assistance to us, concerning numerous questions while editing and testing the recipes, he also did a final proofing of the recipe pages (assisted by his wife, Rose, Associate Editor of *BedandBreakfast.com Report*). Thanks to their untiring efforts, the recipes in this book are much easier to follow than they would have been otherwise. To read some special tips from Frank (or to e-mail recipe-related questions to him), see page 221.

Credit for Photographs & Quotes

Cover Photograph
Maxine Pinson

Authors' Photograph
Jason Chervenak

Middleton Place
for permission to use photograph of Middleton Oak

The Lodge at Little St. Simons Island
for permission to use aerial photograph of the island

Beaufort Chamber of Commerce
for permission to use photograph of Beaufort
on back cover

Charleston Area Convention and Visitors Bureau
for permission to use photograph of Charleston
on back cover

Savannah Area Convention
and Visitors Bureau
for permission to use quotes on Savannah

Lowcountry Delights

Cookbook & Travel Guide

Third Edition
2004

A collection of recipes from
Favorite Bed and Breakfast Inns, Historic Inns, and Restaurants
in The Lowcountry

Beaufort, South Carolina
Charleston, South Carolina
Savannah, Georgia
St. Simons Island, Georgia
plus
Selected Lowcountry Barrier Islands

Maxine Pinson & Malyssa Pinson

SSD, Inc.
d/b/a
The INNside Scoop
www.innsidescoop.com
The Food Scoop
www.thefoodscoop.com
Savannah Restaurants Online
www.eatinginsavannah.com

Savannah, Georgia

Published by
SSD, Inc.
22 W. Bryan St.— PMB 202
Savannah, GA 31401

Cover/Layout Design: Maxine Pinson **Food Consultant:** Frank Ciccone
Publishing Consultant: Christian Simard **Copy Editors:** Malyssa Pinson
Rose Ciccone

Original Artwork

Amy Cullings Moreno
(dearlake@aol.com)
www.illustrationsbyamy.com
(pages 26, 28, 38, 44, 52, 64, 66, 68, 70, 72, 74, 86, 88, 92, 94, 98,
110, 112, 114, 120, 122, 132, 136, 142, 147, 158, 160, 166, 170)

Theron Wallis
(pages 25, 43, 96, 105, 128, 140)

First Printing	May 2002	4,000
Second Printing	July 2003	3,000
Third Printing	September 2004	13,000

Library of Congress Control Number: 2003093167

An order form for *Lowcountry Delights*
(including a special "Value-pack")
is available on page 223.
One may also be printed from: www.thefoodscoop.com/lcd.html

Disclaimer and Limits of Liability

While the authors and publisher have used their best efforts to insure the accuracy of all information at press time; changes do transpire, especially when there is a change of management or ownership. There-fore, SSD, Inc. does not guarantee the accuracy or completeness of any information and is not responsible for any errors or omissions or the results obtained from use of such information. This book is sold as is without any warranty of any kind, either expressed or implied. Neither the authors nor SSD, Inc. or its distributors shall be liable to the purchaser or any other person or entity with respect to any liability, loss, or damage caused or alleged to be caused directly or indirectly by this book.

ISBN 0-9716662-3-7
PRINTED IN CANADA

Table of Contents

Lowcountry Recipes

Beaufort, SC

B&Bs and Historic Inns

Restaurants

Charleston, SC

B&Bs and Historic Inns

Restaurants

Other Cowcountry B&Bs and Historic Inns

Other Cowcountry Restaurants

Savannah, GA
B&Bs and Historic Inns

Savannah Restaurants

The Lowcountry's Barrier Islands
Cumberland Island, GA

Other Recipes

The Scoop on Cowcountry Delights

The selection of the B&Bs and Historic Inns, included in *Lowcountry Delights,* is based upon the following criteria:

- Hospitality and personal warmth of innkeepers
- Willingness to accommodate the requests of guests, when possible
- Professionalism of innkeepers
- Appearance of exterior and interior of inn
- Furnishings, style/design, room decor
- Attention-to-detail
- Distinctive features
- The quality and presentation of breakfast
- Amenities and conveniences
- Availability and upkeep of grounds or garden area
- Location of inn and consideration of area attractions
- Private baths
- Respect for the privacy of guests
- Telephones in room, preferred but not mandatory
- Value of accommodations and services received
- Historical significance, when applicable
- Honesty and congruency in marketing
  (Web site and brochure *accurately* represent the inn)
- The integration of each of the 5 senses (sight, sound, taste, touch, smell) into a unique inn experience

---

Authors' notes: *No payment was received for any inclusion in this book. Each inn and restaurant featured, listed, or photographed has been personally experienced by either one or both of the authors; featured inns and restaurants have been visited since 2001. Some of the inns and restaurants are big-time operations, others are family-run and operate on a smaller scale. The inns range from private homes, where the innkeepers live with their family, to urban mansions filled with museum-quality antiques. The restaurants range from a 5-Diamond dining room to one located on the ground level of a 19th century townhouse where guests participate in communal dining. There is an inn and restaurant in this book to suit every taste!*

The selection of the restaurants, included in *Lowcountry Delights*, is based upon the following criteria:

- Selection and uniqueness of menu
- Service and food knowledge by server
- Timely delivery of meal
- Presentation of meal

- Decor and ambience
- Friendliness of staff
- Location
- Value of meal for price paid

The Selection and Testing of Recipes included in *Lowcountry Delights*

The recipes included in this book were either requested, specifically, by the authors or chosen by the contributor in accordance with the authors' guidelines. An attempt was made to select a wide range of Lowcountry cuisine as well as recipes that are quick 'n easy for novice (and "don't-like-to-cook") cooks and challenging recipes for gourmet cooks with advanced culinary skills. Each place included has been experienced, by one of authors, since 2001.

Maxine says, "While editing the recipes, Malyssa (as a beginner cook) made certain each recipe was clear enough so she would feel comfortable preparing it alone. She brought to my attention ingredients and/or terminology needing clarification. It was through the testing of these recipes—alone and with me—that Malyssa learned to cook. She now enjoys cooking more than I do. It has been a fun, learning, and rewarding experience for each of us."

All recipes, included in this cookbook, have been tested in a non-commercial kitchen. They were tested either by one of the authors or a member of *Lowcountry Delights'* testing team (see listing on page 4)—individuals ranging from a ten-year-old to an octogenarian. The majority of the recipes have been double-tested, and a number of the recipes have been triple-tested. Notes or suggestions are included, at the end of many recipes, to assist in easier preparation of the dish or ideas for variations of the recipe. In addition, pronunciation is provided for most of the non-English words and notes of historical interest (about a recipe or an ingredient) are included with selected recipes. Substitutions are included for hard-to-find ingredients or guidance is provided for locating the item.

Why *Lowcountry Delights* is one-of-a-kind cookbook/travel guide

Our research reveals *Lowcountry Delights* is the only cookbook/travel guide available including *all* of the following features:

- No payment for inclusion

- Basic information provided, at a quick glance, about each inn and restaurant

- Favorite local dining establishments recommended in locations of B&Bs/ Historic Inns

- The inclusion of a sketch or photograph of each inn/restaurant featured, enabling one to get a feel for its style and ambience in advance

- A section on dining etiquette addressing basic questions one may have prior to dining out (especially at an upscale restaurant) or having breakfast at a B&B

- A comprehensive Q&A section, for inn-goers (laced with "inntertaining" inn-related anecdotes) familiarizing guests with the B&B concept before making a visit to one

"Lowcountry Delights isn't just another cookbook. It's a whole lot more!"

Introduction

by Pamela Lanier

❧❧❧❧❧❧❧❧❧❧❧❧❧❧❧❧❧❧❧❧❧❧❧❧❧❧❧❧❧❧❧❧

*W*hen Maxine asked me to write the introduction to her cookbook I was thrilled — not only because Maxine is a wonderful supporter of bed and breakfasts, but also because Southern cooking (especially Lowcountry cooking) is one of my very favorite cuisines. It's only natural, I guess, since I grew up in Tennessee and have spent many happy summers visiting family members on Lowcountry beaches. The whole area from Beaufort, South Carolina, to "the marshes of Glynn" resonate strongly throughout my family due, in part, to my forbear, the poet Sidney Lanier, whose poems so beautifully capture the magic of the area.

Beauty and magic abound in the Lowcountry, and the inns Maxine has chosen are perfect reflections of the area. What is most delightful about this book is that you have the opportunity to bring some of the inns' atmosphere home. Preparing these wonderful dishes in your own kitchen can fill your heart and home with the same warmth and pleasure kindled at the inn's table.

The warmth and pleasure of bed and breakfasts and country inns have fascinated me ever since I returned from a post-college trip to Europe where I stayed in B&Bs and small inns. I was so captivated that I wrote a guidebook entitled *The Complete Guide to Bed & Breakfasts, Inns & Guesthouses*. I've just completed its 19th edition. What is it about these lodgings that I find so compelling? Why am I still enthralled after so many years in the industry?

Well, first of all, like a snowflake each inn is unique, shaped by the building's architecture and décor, the innkeepers' personalities, and the region in which it is located. With no two being alike, I am assured of distinctly different and inspiring experiences at each inn I visit. Secondly, I love being pampered—and, for me, breakfast in bed or tea served in my room is the ultimate in pampering. Just to lean back into the pillows sipping my tea and nibbling on a freshly baked muffin, perusing a magazine or gazing out a window at the surrounding countryside—to me this is heaven.

And I do not think I am very different from most inngoers. After a hectic week at the office, they arrive at an inn ready for that pampering, enveloping environment—a unique experience that lets them know they are somewhere special, a place where they can shed the week and rejuvenate. Nothing says "change of pace" more for the average working person than to wake up ensconced in a feather bed surrounded by a beautiful, romantic ambience with the smell of coffee wafting upstairs. Here they can savor breakfast, the one meal of the day most busy folks do not have the luxury of enjoying. An assembly-line bagel, scoffed down on the way to an early-morning meeting, can hardly compare to the lavish, relaxing repast spread before them at a country inn.

Which brings me to the third reason I am still passionately involved in this industry—country inn cuisine. Being a great breakfast fan, the thrill of a new breakfast every morning in itself is enough to keep me going! As the cuisine an inn serves is as unique as the inn itself, each meal is a new and exciting celebration of local ingredients and ambience. A successful inn cannot be separated from the region in which it is located, and the most successful inn cuisine reflects this regional character.

Sharing—recipes, stories, family photographs—is what brings guests and innkeepers together. Who can forget conversations around a gorgeous breakfast table amidst heaping platters of fresh fruit, home-baked breads, and fragrant egg dishes? What makes these meals so memorable is sharing joy and laughter with other guests and the innkeepers themselves. At that table, in that special inn, no one is a stranger; ages and occupations are not significant, and barriers melt away as easily as warm butter on a stack of flapjacks.

Have I become jaded by bed and breakfasts? Never!

I hope you enjoy the beautiful and delicious recipes from Lowcountry inns—and imagine yourself nestled by the warmth of their hearths.

Bon Appétit!

Pamela Lanier
www.TravelGuides.com

Pamela Lanier is the author of The Complete Guide to Bed & Breakfasts, Inns and Guesthouses (currently in its 21st anniversary edition), host of the Yahoo! Gold Star recipient web site TravelGuides.com, and editor of four bed and breakfast cookbooks. She also serves as director of Bed & Breakfast Inns and Guesthouses International, with a membership of over 7,000 inns.

Georgia's & South Carolina's Lowcountry

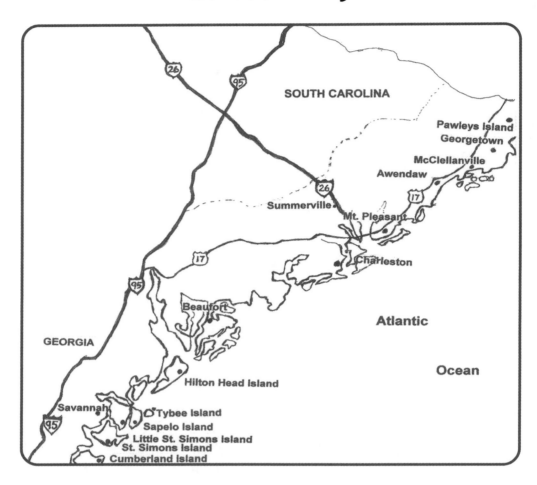

*The lay-of-the-land in The Lowcountry (sometimes spelled Low Country)
is defined by its name. It is flat land, barely above sea level. It is also a region
impassioned with a sense-of-place which embodies a spirit as high as the land is low.*

Approximate Mileage between Lowcountry Destinations

Beaufort to Charleston: 69 miles
Beaufort to Pawleys Island: 139 miles
Beaufort to Savannah: 41 miles
Beaufort to Summerville: 78 miles
Charleston to Awendaw: 26 miles
Charleston to Beaufort: 69 miles
Charleston to Georgetown: 58 miles
Charleston to Mt. Pleasant: 6 miles

Charleston to Pawleys Island:70 miles
Charleston to Savannah: 108 miles
Charleston to Summerville: 23 miles
Savannah to Beaufort: 41 miles
Savannah to Charleston: 108 miles
Savannah to Georgetown: 166 miles
Savannah to Pawleys Island: 178 miles
Savannah to Summerville: 101 miles

Selected Barrier Islands
of Georgia & South Carolina

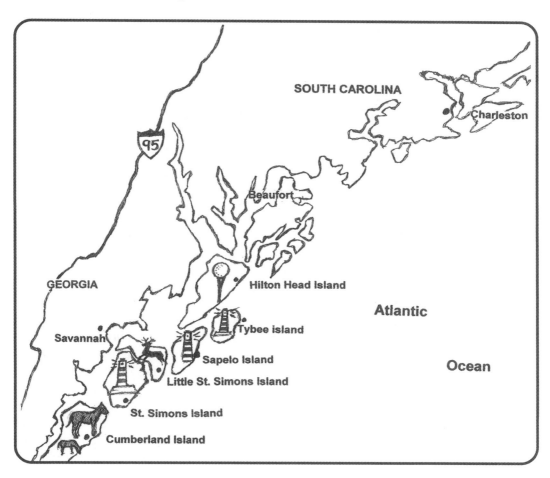

Cumberland, Little St. Simons, and Sapelo Islands are not connected to the mainland. However, each is accessible via ferry or special arrangements. Ferry schedules are available online or information can be provided by the inn on your island destination.

Approximate Mileage to Lowcountry's Barrier Islands

Beaufort to Cumberland Island: 155 miles
Beaufort to Hilton Head Island: 42 miles
Beaufort to St. Simons Island: 123 miles
Beaufort to Little St. Simons Island: 135 miles
Beaufort to Sapelo Island: 96 miles
Beaufort to Tybee Island: 46 miles
Charleston to Cumberland Island: 217miles
Charleston to Hilton Head Island: 118 miles
Charleston to St. Simons Island:185 miles

Charleston to Little St. Simons Island: 200 miles
Charleston to Sapelo Island: 158 miles
Charleston to Tybee Island: 114 miles
Savannah to Cumberland Island: 118 miles
Savannah to Hilton Head Island: 40 miles
Savannah to St. Simons Island: 86 miles
Savannah to Little St. Simons Island: 101 miles
Savannah to Sapelo Island: 59 miles
Savannah to Tybee Island: 10 miles

About Cover Photograph

Laurel Hill Plantation Bed and Breakfast
(1991 - 2001)

When the original Laurel Hill Plantation house was constructed in 1850, Richard Tillia Morrison (the current owner's great-great-grandfather) owned more than 20,000 acres in the area. Laurel Hill was a turpentine plantation that produced lumber and naval stores. The Morrison family sold Laurel Hill in the 1950s, and the new owners used the land for truck farming. Except for short periods, when migrant workers stayed in the house, it was vacant.

For over 20 years, Jackie Morrison longed to own the abandoned house and begged the owners to sell it. They finally agreed to sell the house, but not the land. A stipulation was made that the house had to be moved, in its entirety, and the site had to be left in pristine condition.

In January 1983, Jackie and Lee Morrison moved the Laurel Hill Plantation House from Highway 17 to its present location on another part of the original plantation tract. Restoration of the dilapidated house moved slowly, but the results were remarkable. In May of 1985, Laurel Hill was listed on the National Register of Historic Places. A year later, Laurel Hill was featured in *Country Living* magazine. In July 1986, the Morrisons opened their country home as a bed and breakfast inn—a true Lowcountry delight.

On September 21, 1989, Hurricane Hugo hit the South Carolina coast with a twenty foot tidal surge and 200 m.p.h. winds. The house at Laurel Hill was destroyed—nothing was left. The Morrisons refused to give up their dreams and set about designing a replacement house, based upon the plan of their lost home (see page 20).

On July 1, 1991, Laurel Hill Plantation Bed and Breakfast was re-opened in the new structure. The Morrisons operated Laurel Hill as a B&B for fourteen years. During that time, Jackie also served as president of the South Carolina Bed and Breakfast Association (2000-2002). Jackie and Lee retired from innkeeping in January 2002; however, they continue sharing their idyllic Lowcountry home with friends on a regular basis. Jackie is a wonderful cook and compiled a cookbook of her own favorite recipes during her innkeeper years. To order a copy of Jackie's cookbook, *Laurel Hill Plantation Cookbook*, print out the order form online at www.thefoodscoop.com/LHPcookbook.html.

A conservation easement on Laurel Hill Plantation has been granted to The Nature Conservancy by the Morrisons.

Preface

$\mathcal{L}$iving in The Lowcountry, for the past thirty-two years, has been a highlight of my life. No matter where I go—in this country or abroad—when I say I am from Savannah, there is usually instant recognition. Positive comments follow, and I feel proud and privileged to live where I do. The Lowcountry—boasting the low lands of Beaufort, Charleston, and Savannah—is an uncommon place. And the uniqueness of The Lowcountry is no longer a secret.

After publishing a parenting publication in Savannah, GA for five rewarding years (1990-1994), I expanded to Beaufort and Charleston, SC. My newsmagazine, *Savannah Parent*, became *Low Country Parent*. It was during this time that I became enchanted with Beaufort and Charleston and began recommending area restaurants to my readers. It was also when I re-discovered B&Bs and began writing travel articles for my publication. Bed and breakfasts inns were making a strong entry into the U.S. travel industry, and delightful ones were popping up throughout the country.

Due to a series of crisis-level personal circumstances, I discontinued my parenting publication in the fall of 1995. At that point-in-time, I could no longer meet the demands of publishing *Low Country Parent* without compromising the high quality and service to which I was committed. To give less than my best was something I was unwilling to consider. However, by then, publishing was in my blood; I knew I would never be able to give it up completely. Writing ideas—including experiences I wished to share and stories I felt needed telling—were swirling in my head. Some of my editorials, from *Savannah Parent* and *Low Country Parent*, remain online at www.the-innside-scoop.com/mpeditorials.htm.

The last issue of my parenting publication came out in October 1995; the first issue of *The INNside Scoop* (a B&B newsletter "Dedicated to the Discovery of Bed & Breakfast Getaways") made its debut in December 1995. Since that time, I have reviewed inns in over thirty states and Canada. I had no concept, when I first began, of the joys awaiting me as I moved forward into the next chapter of my life. I continue to be amazed, and I continue to be grateful.

For the first five years, *The INNside Scoop* was a 4-page quarterly newsletter featuring bed and breakfast inns in Georgia and the Carolinas; it then became an 8-page bi-annual newsletter featuring inns in Georgia, the Carolinas, plus four additional states. The newsletter now has a new format which I plan to use indefinitely. Each January and July issue includes reviews of B&Bs in five states in addition to 12 inns recommended throughout the U.S. and, occasionally, Canada. Each newsletter also features favorite recipes from B&Bs I have previously visited. A photograph is shown of each inn, and area dining suggestions (in over 25 states and Canadian provinces) are included. My dining recommendations are also available online at www.thefoodscoop.com. Each inn and restaurant, appearing in *The INNside Scoop* Bed & Breakfast newsletter, is rated upon criteria I use in determining how highly I feel I can conscientiously recommend the property to others. I only recommend inns/restaurants personally experienced by me, and payment is not accepted for any of my reviews or recommendations. See page 181 for subscription information for the newsletter (e-subscriptions are free).

I first became hooked on bed and breakfasts (see page 176) during 1971 when my husband, Bill, and I spent the summer in Europe. Since that time, I have had the opportunity of experiencing hundreds of inns—large, small, and in-between—in all parts of this country, Canada, and abroad. I cherish each of my trips to other countries and consider travel abroad an invaluable cultural and educational experience. However, the more I travel within our own country, the more appreciative I become of the magnificent beauty and offerings we have right here at home. The more of the U.S.A. I see, the more of it I want to see.

How It Happened: "The Tracks of Max"

On August 3, 1998, at the end of what I refer to as my "decade of hell," Bill and I lost our first child, Sara Cecilia, to a rare and vicious form of cancer (mycosis fungoides). We shall always be grateful for the time God entrusted our beautiful daughter to us, a child doctors once told me I was incapable of conceiving. Unwilling to give up hope for a child, I petitioned, begged, and nagged the Great Physician to grant me the blessing of motherhood. My pleas for a child were finally answered. God sent us Celia, but only for a short time. Our daughter was just 23-years-old when she died, so young and full of promise. Yet, the legacy she left continues to inspire individuals who knew Celia as well as those who never met her (see www.innsidescoop.com/Celia.htm). Her inimitable spirit will live forever.

Maxine and Celia during a visit to a B&B
September 1992

When Celia died, a big part of me died with her. I survived, emotionally, by staying busy. And, yes, I confess: my busyness tends to be obsessive, but it channels my restless energy into productivity and keeps me afloat. Five months after losing Celia, I started thinking about a message of hope which impacted me at another low point in my life, and I decided to enroll in the extended campus program (ECP) at Union Theological Seminary-Presbyterian College of Christian Education (Union-PSCE) in Richmond, Virginia. I submitted my application, along with my statement of faith, and I was accepted into the program in early 1999. I remained in the ECP program at Union-PSCE through 2003 learning more about the Christian faith and the difference between genuine spirituality versus pharisaical religiosity (see www.the-innside-scoop.com/unhealthy.html). Importantly, I wanted to receive instruction in an environment where I would not be exposed to an indoctrinational form of learning and where questioning was encouraged, not discouraged. I wanted to hone my writing skills so I could pursue a writing ministry providing hope, encouragement, and comfort for individuals whose suffering I could personally relate to and vicariously understand.

Jackie and Lee Morrison, "innkeepers emeritus," know about hope and the encouragement it provides. The story of their twenty year struggle to acquire their home (cover photo of this book), only to have it decimated by Hurricane Hugo, may be read on page 18. The Morrisons were devastated, understandably, by their loss. But Jackie and Lee did not permit their unfortunate circumstances to wash away their lives or zest for living. Instead, they rebuilt and started anew. The house they reconstructed is even better, stronger, and more charming than the original structure. Even though other ferocious storms have thundered through the Morrisons' property since Hugo, requiring déjà vu evacuations, their new home has survived these storms with minimal damage. In addition, The Morrisons have discovered that they are now better equipped, in more ways than one, to weather the inevitable tempests of life as well as those of coastal living—and Jackie says they now place less value on material things.

I have always felt that good can evolve from evil, and this conviction has brought me to where I am today. If it had not been for a personal trauma I experienced in 1989 (to be addressed in a forthcoming book, see page 215), I never would have returned to my college alma mater to enroll in journalism, speech, and technical writing classes. Little did I know how helpful each of these courses would prove to be in the years ahead. I only knew that taking these courses was something I felt inexplicably compelled to do at the time, and I have learned to trust my instincts. Seldom do they mislead me.

A few months after completing my courses, I was contacted by a publisher in Atlanta requesting that I become editor for a new parenting publication, *Savannah Parent*. He had met me through Celia, who was a staff writer for a teen newspaper published by him. I was totally intimidated by the idea of editing a newspaper, and so I refused—adamantly. However, a few weeks after my second refusal, 20,000 copies of the new publication were shipped to Savannah. I was listed as editor, even though I had absolutely nothing to do with that edition. After overcoming my initial annoyance, I began feeling pleased that someone had that degree of confidence in me and my potential. Holding my breath, I accepted editorship of *Savannah Parent*. The decision was one I never regretted, and it led to the beginning of a new career.

After three months (during which time I was working 60-plus-hour weeks), I still had not received my promised compensation for editing *Savannah Parent*. Finally, two checks arrived on the same day. Each bounced. Long story made short: after making a few phone calls, consulting an attorney, and writing the publisher, "Max made tracks" by bouncing into the position of owner, publisher/editor/ad representative/marketing director for *Savannah Parent* newsmagazine. In less than two years, the free community service publication went from zero advertisers to advertisers in over thirty states.

I am not known to be a silent sitter—just not my modus operandi. I discovered early in life, especially as a woman reared in the Deep South, that being "nice and sweet" does *not* always produce positive results; sometimes untraditional tactics are required for grievances to be heard and addressed. When one is taught (directly or indirectly) to suppress thoughts and feelings, rather than feeling free to express them without fear of retribution, a destructive cycle spirals into motion. The pattern continues until it is recognized and broken. Mustering the courage to stand up and confront an unacceptable situation can have unpleasant consequences, but it can also be liberating and self-affirming.

People often ask how I "got started" with *The INNside Scoop*. Now you have it—the inside scoop on *The INNside Scoop! Savannah Parent* is the grandparent of *The INNside Scoop*, which is the parent of *Lowcountry Delights Cookbook & Travel Guide*. Today some of my dearest and most cherished friends are innkeepers. I consider them a special "breed." As much as I love staying in their incomparable bed and breakfasts and historic inns, what I cherish most are the relationships formed as a result of a snoop named Max trying to get the facts—the *innside scoop* on their bed and breakfast or historic inn. I hope you know, my friends, how much I care about and appreciate you.

Life has taken me on many journeys during these past years, and not all paths have led to pampering bed and breakfast inns. During my years as a travel writer/restaurant reviewer, I have enjoyed fine dining at its best. I have also gleaned "food for thought"—lessons in life allowing me to see human beings, from varied backgrounds, and material stuff through clearer lenses. However, of all the memorable trips I have taken, my most meaningful journey has been an inner one that has forever forged my faith and made me acutely aware of my personal dependence upon God for daily guidance and perseverance in all that I do.

It is my hope that *Lowcountry Delights* will guide you to delightful and memory-making journeys, introduce you to delectable new dishes, and maybe even provide a little "food for thought" en route to whatever your final destination in life may be. May each of your sojourns leave you with a reservoir of delightful and lasting memories, and may all the calories consumed evaporate as you travel to your next adventure!

—*Maxine Pinson*
September 2004

We hope you enjoy our book!

Maxine   *Malyssa*

Malyssa and Maxine Pinson
at one of their first book signings
during the summer of 2002.

Notes

Recipes

from

Favorite Inns & Restaurants
in
The Lowcountry

Good food and gracious hospitality
flow through The Lowcountry like a tidal creek.

"It's a place where fresh water meets salt and where creeks, marshes, and rivers meld with sunshine, tides, and sea breezes."
—*Southern Living* magazine (April 2003)

Beaufort lands a coveted spot on the *2001 National Trust for Historic Preservation* list of "12 Distinctive Destinations"—
travel treasures providing "striking alternatives to Anyplace, USA."

USA Today names Beaufort, SC as "one of 10 great places to honeymoon—or renew nuptial bliss—for romantics seeking an All-American destination." The article refers to Beaufort as a "sleeper hit, a sweet coastal gem filled with sweet B&Bs and the sweeping verandas of antebellum mansions."
—*USA Today* (October 22, 2001)

Beaufort is one of 50 towns chosen for inclusion in the 2001 edition of *The 50 Best Small Southern Towns*. The guidebook selects small southern towns portraying a "gentler way of life." According to the authors: "Beaufort exudes charm. The many historic homes, built in the late 1800s and early 1900s, gracefully enhance the town's color-ful character. Live oak trees, draped with Spanish moss, grace the brick walkways and narrow streets; the town commands spectacular water views in three directions. No wonder several movies have been filmed in Beaufort."
—Gerald Sweitzer and Kathy Fields

Web Site for Beaufort, SC
(pronounced "Bew-fort")

www.beaufortsc.org

Beaufort

"Beauty by the Bay"

*Typical scene in the enchanting moss-draped,
history-filled community of beautiful Beaufort, SC*

The Beaufort Inn

*Located in the center of Beaufort's Historic Landmark District,
The Beaufort Inn offers an impeccable sense of style
where great expectations are quietly met.*

Address: 809 Port Republic Street
Beaufort, SC 29902
(Historic District)
Telephone: (843) 521-9000
E–mail: bftinn@hargray.com

Web Site: www.beaufortinn.com
Category: Historic Inn
General Manager: David Boyd
Rates: $160-$285 (year-round)

Scrambled Egg and Cheese Casserole

12 tablespoons butter, divided
6 tablespoons all-purpose flour
2 cups half-and-half
2 cups Cheddar cheese, grated
Salt and pepper, to taste
Pinch of nutmeg

1½ cups fresh button mushrooms,
  stemmed and quartered
½ cup green onions, sliced
1½ cups tasso or good quality ham, diced
12 eggs, lightly beaten
¾ cup dried plain bread crumbs

In a heavy saucepan, melt 6 tablespoons of butter over medium heat. Remove from heat and add flour; stir until smooth. Return to low heat and cook 5 minutes. Gradually, add the half-and-half and cook over medium heat, stirring constantly, until thickened. Remove from heat and add the cheese, stirring until melted and smooth. Season with salt, pepper, and nutmeg. Set aside. In a medium pan, heat 2 tablespoons butter over high heat. Add mushrooms and cook until tender, about 5 minutes. Add next 2 ingredients and continue cooking until just warmed. Season with salt and pepper. Add mixture to the reserved cheese sauce. In a non-stick pan, over medium-high heat, melt 2 tablespoons butter. Add eggs and cook until they begin to set. Stir with a spatula to form large curds until eggs are thickened. Add eggs to the cheese sauce and stir lightly to combine. Pour egg mixture into a 12 x 9-inch buttered casserole dish. Melt remaining 2 tablespoons butter and mix with bread crumbs until coated; spread evenly over casserole. Cover and refrigerate overnight. Remove from refrigerator one hour before baking. Bake, uncovered, at 350° for 30 to 45 minutes or until heated through.

Yield: 6-8 servings

Poppy Seed Waffles

1½ cups all-purpose flour
6 tablespoons sugar
3 tablespoons poppy seeds
1½ teaspoons baking powder
¼ teaspoon salt

3 large eggs
1¼ cups buttermilk
¼ cup (½ stick) unsalted butter, melted
2 teaspoons vanilla

In large bowl, mix first 5 ingredients until combined. In a small bowl, whisk eggs and add next 3 ingredients to blend. Add buttermilk mixture, all at once, to flour mixture and whisk until just blended. Let mixture sit 15 minutes. Preheat waffle iron according to manufacturer's instructions. Spoon batter onto waffle iron; cover and cook until golden and cooked through-out, about 7 minutes (cooking time varies, depending on waffle iron). Repeat with remaining batter. Serve immediately with warm Papaya Orange Chutney.

Yield: 6 servings (using approximately ¾ cup of batter per pancake)

Papaya Orange Chutney

4 papayas, peeled, seeded, and thinly sliced
½ cup orange juice

1 cup orange marmalade
½ teaspoon Chinese five-spice powder

Combine all ingredients in a medium saucepan. Simmer, stirring occasionally, until papaya is tender and mixture slightly thickens, about 10 minutes.

Editors' Notes: *Chinese five-spice powder can be found in the Oriental section of upscale grocery stores, in an Asian food market, or ordered online (see page 220). To serve this dish, we suggest dusting the waffles with powdered sugar and spooning the Chutney directly onto center of waffle. Garnish with a sprig of fresh mint.*

"One of the Top Ten Most Romantic Inns in The USA"
—*The Road Best Traveled*, 1998

Named one of the "Top Ten Inns in the Country"
by American Historic Inns.

"From check-in to check-out,
the Beaufort Inn is a haven of wonderful experiences."
—Karen Lingo, *Southern Living* magazine

The Craven Street Inn

*This lovely Victorian home, built as a private residence in 1870,
creates a new standard for casual, affordable elegance.*

Address: 1103 Craven Street
Beaufort, SC 29902
(Historic District)
Reservations: 1-888-522-0250
Telephone: (843) 522-1668

E-mail: cravenstinn@hargray.com
Web Site: www.thecravenstreetinn.com
Category: B&B
Innkeeper: June Spinelli
Rates: $125-$215 (seasonal)

Spinach and Leek Quiche

1½-2 tablespoons olive oil or butter
1 medium leek (white and green parts),
   trimmed and chopped
½ small onion
4 eggs
1 cup heavy cream
½ teaspoon salt

¼ teaspoon freshly ground pepper
A generous pinch of nutmeg
Dash of red pepper flakes
1 (6-ounce) bag fresh spinach,
   coarsely chopped
4 ounces sharp Cheddar cheese, grated
1 pre-baked pie crust

Preheat oven to 375°. In sauté pan, sauté leek and onion in oil or butter. In a large bowl, whisk eggs with cream and next 4 ingredients. When the leek and onions are translucent (not brown), add spinach and cook until just wilted. Add leek and spinach to egg mixture. Place the grated Cheddar into pie shell and cover with egg and spinach mixture. Bake until quiche (KEESH) is puffed and golden (about 30 to 40 minutes).

Yield: 6 servings

Editors' Note: *Frozen onions and spinach may be substituted for fresh vegetables.*

Chocolate Walnut Brownies

2 sticks plus 3 tablespoons butter
3 cups sugar
4 eggs
1½ cups cocoa powder, sifted
2 teaspoons vanilla

2¼ cups all-purpose flour
½ teaspoons salt
½ teaspoons baking soda
½ cup chocolate chips
½ cup walnuts, chopped

Preheat oven to 350°. Melt butter in a large saucepan; when completely melted, add sugar and blend well. Set aside. In a large mixing bowl, beat eggs; reduce speed and slowly add cocoa powder and vanilla. Blend in butter mixture. In a separate bowl, mix together the next 3 ingredients and add to wet mixture. Blend well, but do not overmix. In another bowl, combine chocolate chips and walnuts. Add to brownie mixture and spoon into a greased 9½ x 13½-inch glass pan. Cook approximately 25 to 30 minutes or until firm (even though brownies may still appear wet). Let brownies sit for 3 hours before cutting and serving.

Yield: 16-20 brownies

Chunky Chocolate Chip Cookies

1¼ cups all-purpose flour
½ teaspoon baking powder
¼ teaspoon salt
½ cup butter, room temperature
½ cup granulated sugar

¼ cup light brown sugar, packed
1 egg
1 teaspoon vanilla extract
¾ cup chocolate chunks
½ cup walnuts, chopped

Preheat oven to 325°. Combine first 3 ingredients and set aside. Cream butter and sugars in a mixer bowl, at high speed, until creamy (do not over mix). Beat in egg and vanilla until thoroughly blended. Reduce mixer speed to low and gradually blend in flour mixture. Using a wooden spoon, stir in chocolate chips and walnuts. Drop dough by rounded teaspoons onto ungreased baking sheets spaced about 2 inches apart. Bake for 16 to 20 minutes until golden brown. Cool cookies on baking sheets for one minute before transferring to wire racks (do not leave on baking sheet to cool or cookies will break into pieces when removed).

Yield: 2 dozen cookies

Editors' Note: *For tasty variations to this delicious cookie, substitute ¾ cup of white chocolate chips and ½ cup of Macadamia nut halves* **or** *¾ cup of Heath bar chips and ½ cup of chopped pecans for the chocolate chunks and walnuts. Chocolate chips (instead of chunks) and pecans (instead of walnuts) may be used in the original recipe.*

Built as a single family residence in 1870, the house served as the residence of the Lipton family for almost 75 years. Mr. Lipton was the cobbler at Parris Island who made all the boots for the Marine Corps recruits.

The Rhett House Inn

A place full of history, romance, and relaxation
providing the simple pleasures of an authentic plantation house

Address: 1009 Craven Street
Beaufort, SC 29902
(Historic District)
Reservations: 1-888-480-9530
Telephone: (843) 524-9030
E-mail: info@rhetthouseinn.com

Web Site: www.rhetthouseinn.com
Category: Historic Inn
Owners/Innkeepers:
Steve & Marianne Harrison
Rates: $145-$325 (seasonal)

Southern Grits

1 cup coarse, stone-ground grits
4 cups water
2-4 tablespoons chicken-base paste

2-4 tablespoons butter
Milk or half-and-half, as needed

Combine all ingredients. Cook over low heat for about an hour, stirring occasionally. Cover and put into refrigerator overnight. The next morning, resume cooking. Add milk/half–and–half until desired consistency is reached or as needed. Cook over low heat for about an hour.

Yield: 6-8 servings

Editors' Notes: *Stone-ground grits and chicken-base paste may be purchased at gourmet and specialty food stores or ordered online (see page 220). No substitute for either of these ingredients is recommended. Use less chicken-base paste for a less salty taste and more if you prefer a saltier taste; 3 tablespoons was just the right amount for us. We also prefer using half-and-half (about 2 cup) instead of milk. The result is creamier and richer. We did not find it necessary to continue cooking grits an additional hour the next morning. They just need warming up. These grits are definitely more time-consuming than instant grits, but they are about the best grits we G.R.I.T.S. ("Girls raised in the South") have ever tasted.*

Cheese Hot Bites

1 cup flour	¼ teaspoon salt
2 cups Cheddar cheese, shredded	½ teaspoon cayenne pepper
½ cup butter	1 cup pecans, chopped

Cream all ingredients, except pecans, together by hand. Stir in pecans until well mixed; roll into logs. Wrap logs in wax paper and chill in refrigerator overnight. Thinly slice and bake on an ungreased baking sheet 10 to 15 minutes in a 325° oven; do not brown. Sprinkle salt on wafers while still warm. Logs may be frozen.

Yield: 4 logs

Editors' Notes: *Before baking, sprinkle with sesame seeds and paprika. Store in an air-tight container.*

Pecan Pie
Filling

1¼ cups dark brown sugar	4 eggs
¾ cup light corn syrup	2 cups pecans
¼ cup melted butter	2 teaspoons vanilla

Blend all ingredients. Pour into 9 or 10-inch pie dish lined with unbaked pie shell. Bake at 400 degrees for 10 minutes. Finish baking at 325° for 30 minutes or until set. Cool.

Crust

¾ cup shortening	2 cups flour
1 cup boiling water	1 teaspoon salt
1 tablespoons milk	

Whip shortening into boiling water until fluffy; whip in milk. Add remaining ingredients, blending until moist. Form into a ball and roll out onto a floured surface. Place into a pie pan and prick bottom with a fork.

Yield: 6 servings

Editors' Note: *For 12 individual tarts, half pie filling recipe. After rolling out dough for crust, use a biscuit cutter to cut out 3-inch circles. Place dough in a muffin tin and spoon in filling. Bake same as for pie. Serve pie or tarts with vanilla ice-cream or cool whip.*

"Set a block inland from the waterfront, The Rhett House Inn occupies a photogenic 1820s residence outlined by classic fluted white columns and a double-tiered porch that conjures up an idealized vision of the Old South."

—Andrew Harper's *Hideaway Report*, June 2004

Two Suns Inn

By far the best view in Beaufort

Address: 1705 Bay Street
Beaufort, SC 29902
(Historic District)
Reservations: 1-800-532-4244
Telephone: (843) 522-1122
E-mail: info@twosunsinn.com

Web Site: www.twosunsinn.com
Category: B&B
Owners/Innkeepers:
Henri & Patricia Safran
Rates: $130-$168 (seasonal)

Filled Shaken Omelet

4 large eggs
Salt and pepper, to taste
4 teaspoons water
2 teaspoons butter

1 cup finely cut smoked salmon
1 tablespoon sour cream, to taste
Chopped fresh dill to garnish

Break eggs in small bowl; season with salt and pepper. Add water and beat no more than 30 strokes or until minimal amount of foam develops. Melt butter in an 8-inch non-stick skillet (hold skillet at a 45 degree angle to burner). Rapidly shake pan back-and-forth so egg mixture is thrown against the pan's sides; using a spatula helps with distribution of eggs. Return pan to burner. Rotate pan so any uncooked egg in center moves to perimeter of pan. Cook evenly 20 to 40 seconds. Quickly place salmon and sour cream in center of omelet. Fold omelet over filling by tilting pan a little higher off the burner and using a spatula to fold it over. Turn omelet onto a plate. Sprinkle with dill and serve.

Yield: 2 servings

Editors' Note: *The key to success is speed and heat. Smoked ham (sliced and cubed) or another meat may be substituted, if desired, for the salmon. Chopped chives provide a good alternate garnish for this dish.*

୬-୬

Prune Clafouti

½ cup sugar

1½ cups pitted prunes

3 eggs

1 tablespoon vanilla extract

¼ cup all purpose flour

1 cup milk

1 cup heavy cream

Preheat oven to 375°. Butter a quiche pan (approximately 2 inches deep) or a 2 quart casserole dish. Sprinkle 2 tablespoons of sugar over bottom of cooking container; scatter prunes (or other fruit) on top. In a blender, combine eggs, vanilla, and remaining sugar; blend until smooth. Add flour and blend briefly. Add remaining ingredients and blend until all ingredients are incorporated. Pour mixture over fruit and bake about 45 minutes or until puffed and browned. Set aside to cool for 15 minutes before serving. Serve warm.

Yield: 6 servings

Editors' Notes: *Another fruit (pitted cherries, plums, nectarines, peaches, pears, blueberries, or strawberries) may be substituted in the clafouti (kla-foo-TEE) for the prunes. A wonderful way to begin breakfast, especially during the cooler months.*

Mini Apple Tarte Tatin

1 cup sugar

¼ cup water

4 tablespoons unsalted butter

½ cup fresh cranberries, chopped

½ cup walnut halves, chopped

12 Lady Apples, peeled and cored
   from the bottom, stems intact

1 sheet frozen puff pastry, defrosted

Preheat oven to 400°. Whisk together sugar and water. Without stirring, cook mixture over medium heat until an amber-colored caramel (320° to 350° on a candy thermometer). Pour 1 tablespoon of the caramel into the bottom of each cup of a 12-cup muffin pan. Add 1 teaspoon of butter to each cup and set aside. Combine cranberries and walnuts; fill each apple with mixture. Place apples, stem side down, into caramel. Roll out puff pastry to a 12-inch square. Cut out 12 (2½-inch) circles and place over apples, tucking pastry around apples. Bake until golden brown and puffed, 30 to 35 minutes. Invert immediately, onto a serving plate, and serve (stem side up with pastry on bottom) while warm.

Yield: 12 servings

Editors' Notes: *Lady Apples have a sweet-tart flesh and are brilliant red to yellow (with red blushing) in color. If Lady Apples are unavailable for the tarte Tatin (tah-TAN), Fuji or Braeburn apples may be used instead. Use dried cranberries if fresh ones are not in season.*

> "Perched atop the highest spot in historic Beaufort,
> the bayview from Two Suns mesmerizes the onlooker."
> —*The INNside Scoop,* June 1996

Bateaux Restaurant

Fine dining overlooking picturesque Lowcountry marshlands

Address: White Hall Landing
Lady's Island, SC 29902
Telephone: (843) 379-0777
Web site: www.bateauxrestaurant.com

Cuisine: Fine Southern Cuisine
Executive Chef: Dean Dupuis
Price Range: Lunch/$5-$14
Dinner/$20-$28

Seared Sea Scallops Au Poivre
Scallops

2-3 tablespoons canola oil
8 sea scallops, with muscle removed

Salt, to taste
Freshly cracked black pepper

Heat sauté pan until extremely hot; add oil. Lightly season scallops with salt on both sides, then press some cracked peppercorns into one side. Sear scallops on the peppered side for 45 seconds or until nicely browned. Turn scallops over, adding more oil if necessary, and cook an additional 45 seconds.

Smoky Collard Greens

4 cups collard greens
 (stem removed & thinly sliced)
5 pieces bacon, diced

½ yellow onion, sliced
2 tablespoon garlic, minced
Salt and pepper, to taste

Bring one-half gallon salted water to a boil and blanch collards until tender (approximtately 5 minutes). Drain collards and place in ice water to cool quickly. Sauté bacon in butter until crispy, then add onion and garlic; season with salt and pepper. Add collards and let cook together until warmed through. Adjust seasoning with salt and pepper.

Spicy Tomato Oil

2 Roma tomatoes, diced
1 teaspoon garlic

½ cup extra virgin olive oil
½ teaspoon cayenne pepper

1 tablespoon chopped fresh herbs (such as basil, thyme, parsley, chives)

Roast tomatoes in a 450° oven until lightly charred; remove from oven. Purée tomatoes in blender, with remaining ingredients, until smooth. Adjust seasoning with salt and pepper. To serve, place 2 small piles of Smoky Collard Greens on each plate (save extra greens to serve as a side dish later). Put one scallop on top of collards and drizzle with Spicy Tomato Oil.

ᔰᔰᔰᔰᔰᔰᔰᔰᔰᔰᔰᔰᔰᔰᔰᔰᔰᔰᔰᔰᔰᔰᔰᔰᔰᔰᔰ

Grilled Flatiron Steak with Balsamic Butter
Balsamic Butter

| 1 stick unsalted butter | 2 tablespoons balsamic vinegar | Salt and pepper |

Let butter sit out until room temperature. Using a mixer or a wooden spoon, whip butter together with vinegar. Season with salt and pepper to taste. Set aside.

Steaks

1 tablespoon garlic, minced	4 (8-ounce) Flatiron steaks
1/2 cup olive oil	(ask for top blade shoulder chuck
1 tablespoon black pepper	N.A.M.P. #1114D or substitute 2 pounds
1/4 cup parsley, chopped	of boneless sirloin, flank, or "skirt" steak)

Combine first 4 ingredients and rub into each side of steak(s) and let sit a few hours, preferably overnight, in refrigerator. When ready to serve, season steaks with salt on both sides and grill to desired doneness (medium rare to medium works best). Once grilled, let steaks rest 5 to 6 minutes; slice thinly against the grain. Place a pile of Smoky Collard Greens (page 34) on serving plate and stack sliced steak on top of collards; place a dollop of Balsamic Butter on top of steak. Serve with Garlic Grits "Fries."

Yield: 4 servings

Roasted Garlic Grits "Fries"

2 cups chicken broth	2 tablespoons Parmesan cheese, grated
1/2 cup heavy cream	3 eggs, plus 1/4 cup water
1/2 stick unsalted butter	1 cup all-purpose flour,
1 tablespoon garlic, roasted or minced	seasoned with salt and pepper
1/2 cup stone ground grits	2 cups panko (Japanese) bread crumbs
Salt and pepper, to taste	Canola oil, for deep-frying

Bring first 4 ingredients to a boil. Whisk in grits, turn down heat to low, and simmer approximately 45 minutes (stirring every few minutes). Taste and adjust seasoning with salt and pepper; stir in cheese. Coat a shallow pan (7 x 10-inch) with a non-stick spray and pour grits into pan. Refrigerate and allow grits to set (at least 4 hours, but preferably overnight). Once thoroughly chilled, dump the solid block of grits onto counter and cut into thin sticks, approximately 1/2-inch x 1/2-inch x 4-inches. Whisk eggs (together with water and seasoned with a pinch of salt and pepper) and place in a bowl. Put flour in another bowl and season lightly with salt and pepper. Place bread crumbs into a third bowl; season with salt and pepper. To bread the "fries," roll them in the flour; be sure to coat each one evenly. Dip each "fry" into egg wash and then into the crumbs; press crumbs onto "fries" so each is completely covered. Repeat. Store breaded "fries" in refrigerator until ready to cook. Fry in canola oil at 365° until crisp and lightly golden brown. Drain and serve hot.

Yield: 4 servings

Newly opened, Bateaux Restaurant is well on its way to becoming Beaufort's premier dining spot.

The Beaufort Inn

Offering three exceptional dining experiences

Address: 809 Port Republic Street
Beaufort, SC 29902
(Historic District)
Telephone: (843) 521-9000

Web Site: www.beaufortinn.com
Cuisine: Contemporary Southern
Executive Chef: Keith Josefiak
Price Range: Dinner/$16-$29

Beaufort Inn She Crab Soup

¼ pound unsalted butter
½ small yellow onion, diced
½ tablespoon fresh garlic, chopped
½ cup flour
1 bay leaf
½ teaspoon fresh thyme, chopped
¼ teaspoon nutmeg
½ tablespoon Worcestershire sauce
½ cup dry sherry

2 cups whole milk
1 cup heavy cream
½ cup crab stock, clam juice,
   or 2 tablespoons commercial crab base
½ pound crab (blue, preferred) claw meat,
   picked clean of shell
⅛ cup crab roe, cleaned
Salt and fresh black pepper, to taste

Melt butter in a heavy-bottomed stockpot; sauté the onion and garlic for 5 minutes until softened. Stir in flour and whisk until smooth, creating a roux which will thicken the soup. Cook for 5 minutes. Add remaining ingredients, except for crab and roe; whisk thoroughly to remove all lumps. Bring to a boil and stir until thickened. Season to taste, using lots of black pepper and salt. After puréing crab and roe in a food processor, gently stir it into the soup mixture. Adjust consistency, if needed, by adding more milk.

Yield: 4-5 servings

Editors' Notes: *Crab stock is sometimes available already prepared in specialty shops, where crab base may also be found. These items may also be ordered online (see page 220). Fresh crab roe is only available in the spring.*

Restaurants
Beaufort, South Carolina

જ⁓જ⁓જ⁓જ⁓જ⁓જ⁓જ⁓જ⁓જ⁓જ⁓જ⁓જ⁓જ⁓જ⁓જ⁓જ

Shrimp and Grits

1 pound large shrimp, peeled and deveined
¼ cup olive oil
1 tablespoon garlic, chopped
½ cup smoked tasso ham, diced fine
½ cup sun-dried tomatoes
  (soaked, drained, and minced)
½ cup dry white wine

2 cups heavy cream
2 tablespoons butter
Salt and pepper, to taste
1 cup grits, cooked
  (according to directions)
Parmesan cheese

In a very hot sauté pan, sear shrimp in olive oil; stir constantly. Add next 3 ingredients and continue stirring. Deglaze with wine and add cream. Cook an additional 2 to 3 minutes. Remove shrimp to a serving dish; cover to keep warm. Continue cooking sauce until thickened. Add butter and adjust seasoning. Pour sauce over shrimp and serve over cooked grits flavored with Parmesan cheese.

Yield: 2 servings

Editors' Note: *Tasso ham is sometimes available at upscale grocery stores or delicatessens. It may also be ordered by calling 1-800-392-2266. Italian cappacola, prosciutto, or slices from a country ham may be substituted, but the taste is not the same.*

Molasses Pecan Butter

1 pound unsalted butter, room temperature
½ cup toasted pecans, finely ground
½ cup maple syrup

⅛ cup molasses
½ tablespoon salt

Cream butter in mixer, add remaining ingredients. Blend well. Roll into tubes of wax paper and freeze. Use as needed.

Yield: 1¼ pounds

Editors' Note: *This delicious butter, wonderful on biscuits, molds beautifully!*

"Top Inn Dining" —*Country Inns Magazine*

"A *must* dining experience"—*The Atlanta Constitution*

"Four Stars Outstanding" —*Savannah News* restaurant review

Featured on "Dining Around" —The Television Food Network

Featured on "Great Chefs of the South"
—Public Broadcasting Television Network

Magnolia Bakery Cafe

A refreshing neighborhood eatery with patio dining under the magnolias

Address: 703 Congress Street
Beaufort, SC 29902
(Historic District)
Telephone: (843) 524-1961

Web site: www.thefoodscoop.com/mbc.html
Cuisine: Contemporary American
Executive Chef: Dana Johnsrude
Price Range: Lunch only/$4.25-$11.50

Curried Yellow Squash Soup

1 tablespoon unsalted butter
1 medium onion, diced
1 leek, washed and rinsed (white part only, diced)
1-2 teaspoons curry powder, to suit taste
Salt and white pepper, to taste

2 pounds yellow squash, diced
1 medium carrot, diced
2 cups chicken or vegetable stock
1 cup whipping cream
Cilantro and scallions, chopped

Melt butter in a heavy soup pot; sweat onion and leek over medium heat, until softened. Add seasonings, then stir and cook mixture until leeks are softened. Stir in next 3 ingredients and simmer for 25 minutes (or until vegetables are tender). Add whipping cream and purée mixture in a blender until smooth. Serve soup hot or chilled; garnish with chopped cilantro and scallions.

Yield: 4-6 servings

Editors' Notes: *Use a Vidalia onion, if available. For a tasty variation of this recipe, use two onions instead of one; omit the curry and leek. Grated carrots (about ¼ cup) may also be added to vary the recipe while adding color.*

❧❧❧❧❧❧❧❧❧❧❧❧❧❧❧❧❧❧❧❧❧❧❧❧

Baked Ham and Cheese Strata

5 large eggs
2½ cups whole milk
½ teaspoon onion powder
¼ teaspoon ground black pepper
½ teaspoon salt

5 ounces fresh bread crumbs
  (cut into ½-inch cubes)
¾ cup Cheddar cheese, shredded
7 ounces baked Virginia ham,
  finely chopped (use a food processor)

Beat together eggs and milk; stir in next 3 ingredients. Spray or butter sides and bottom of a 1 quart soufflé or casserole dish. Spread bread crumbs evenly in bottom of dish. Sprinkle ½ cup of cheese over the bread and put remaining cheese aside; pour in liquid mixture. Refrigerate overnight. Top with ham and bake in a 350° oven 45 to 55 minutes. The strata should be golden brown with a puffy appearance. Top with remaining cheese and let rest 10 minutes before serving.

Editors' Note: *Use your imagination to create different variations of this delicious strata. Excellent combinations include spinach and feta, tomato and dill (or basil), broccoli and Cheddar, Monterey Jack cheese and chorizo (a highly-seasoned pork sausage used in Mexican and Spanish cookery).*

Lemon Squares

1 cup unsalted butter (2 sticks)
¼ cup powdered sugar
1 cup plus 2 tablespoons
  all-purpose flour
4 large eggs
2 cups granulated sugar

2½ tablespoons all-purpose flour
1 teaspoon baking powder
2 tablespoons lemon zest,
  grated
½ cup fresh lemon juice
  (2 lemons)

To make the crust: beat together first 3 ingredients in a large mixing bowl until fluffy. Scrape mixture into a greased 6 x 8½-inch sheet pan, patting into place with dampened fingers. Bake in a preheated 325° oven for 15 minutes. In a medium bowl, beat together eggs and sugar. Using a whisk, blend in remaining 4 ingredients and pour into the crust. Bake at 325° for 30 to 40 minutes or until the filling is set. Cool before cutting and garnish with powdered sugar.

Yield: 12-15 large Lemon Squares

Featured in *Carolina Morning News* (1999).

"Best Bakery"—First Place
2001 Reader's Choice Award
The Beaufort Gazette's Reader's Choice Awards

Plum's Waterfront Cafe

Casual dining on Beaufort's waterfront

Address: 904½ Bay Street
Beaufort, SC 29902
(Historic District)
Telephone: (843) 525-1946

Cuisine: Eclectic American
Executive Chef: Joshua J. McLean
Price Range: Lunch/$5-$10
Dinner/$13-$26

Lowcountry Shrimp Salad

1½ pounds "popcorn-size" shrimp
  (peeled, tail removed, cooked and drained)
2 stalks celery, diced into ⅛-inch pieces
1 rounded teaspoon Lawry's garlic salt

½ teaspoon dry dill weed
4-5 tablespoons Hellmann's mayonnaise
¾ teaspoon lemon juice,
  freshly squeezed with seeds removed

Mix together first 5 ingredients. Stir in lemon juice and chill until ready to serve. Serve over lettuce.

Yield: 4-6 servings

Editors' Notes: Simple to prepare and a Lowcountry summer favorite!

Plum's Turkey Apricot Nut Salad

2 cups smoked turkey breast, chopped
¼ cup golden raisins
¼ cup dried apricots, roughly chopped
¼ cup toasted almonds (chopped)

½ cup medium onion, diced
½ cup Hellmann's mayonnaise
Salt and pepper to taste
Lettuce

Combine all ingredients, chill, and serve over lettuce.

Yield: 4-6 servings

Editors' Notes: Chopped chicken breast and mandarin oranges may be used as a substitute for the turkey and apricots.

Grilled Filet with Brandied Chèvre

Sautéed Onions and Artichoke Hearts

Olive oil
1 medium onion, thinly sliced

8 fresh garlic cloves
Small can of artichoke hearts, drained

Oil a sauté pan and bring to medium-high heat. Add sliced onion and sauté, cooking and stirring until the onion begins turning a golden brown. Allow onion to attain a dark brown color to fully release its natural sugars into the pan. Continue cooking until caramelization is reached. Submerge garlic cloves in olive oil and cook in a 450° oven until tender. Squeeze excess water out of artichoke hearts by taking handfuls and squeezing each handful individually. Lay the hearts onto a sheet pan and season with salt and pepper. Bake at 250° until artichokes become crispy and golden around the edges.

Brandy Blue Chèvre Sauce

1 cup heavy cream
¼ cup brandy

¼ cup Maytag blue cheese
¼ cup chèvre (goat cheese)

Add all ingredients together in a sauce pan and bring to medium heat, stirring constantly. When sauce begins to thicken, it is ready. Adjust the taste with salt, if needed.

Grilled Filets

2 (8-ounce) filet mignons

Salt and pepper, to taste

Season filets (fih-LAYS) with salt and pepper. Grill over charcoal, wood, or a stove-top grill. Top each filet with caramelized onions, artichoke hearts, and garlic. Top with the chèvre (SHEHV) sauce.

Yield: 2 servings

Chosen as Beaufort's "Best All-Round Restaurant"
by *Lowcountry Weekly* (1999 & 2000)

"A crowded little place with a waterfront deck that seems to do almost everything well." —*Washington Post*, October 2000

"The bustling Plum's Cafe boasts creative casual cuisine and a prime waterfront location." —*Atlanta Constitution Journal*, May 2001

For the ninth consecutive year, readers of *Condé Nast Traveler* name Charleston as "One of the Top 10 Travel Destinations in North America." (2001)

❧❧❧❧❧❧❧❧❧❧❧❧❧❧❧❧❧❧❧

The Charleston, SC area receives distinction
in the October 2001 issue of *National Geographic Traveler*,
as one of the "Top 50 Places of a Lifetime: America."

❧❧❧❧❧❧❧❧❧❧❧❧❧❧❧❧❧❧❧

Bride's Magazine honors the Charleston area as a "Top U.S. Destination"
in its 2001 Worldwide Honeymoon Guide

❧❧❧❧❧❧❧❧❧❧❧❧❧❧❧❧❧❧❧

"Charleston will turn the head of the most arrogant modernist. The brick-paved street lined with cast-iron lamps, the rows of pastel-colored houses—all conspire to make the city one huge antique: British colonial with a warm Southern breeze."
—*Conde Nast Traveler*

❧❧❧❧❧❧❧❧❧❧❧❧❧❧❧❧❧❧❧

Charleston claims the top spot for the eighth consecutive year
on Marjabelle Young Stewart's "Most Mannerly" list. (2000)

❧❧❧❧❧❧❧❧❧❧❧❧❧❧❧❧❧❧❧

'Suddenly, a warm fresh breeze turns up our collars and causes the swags of moss to sway gracefully, like billowing curtains. There is something in the air. It is not the familiar tang of the sea or the perfume of Confederate jasmine, nor is it the pealing of church bells or the delicate rustle of palmetto fronds. It is romance."
—Stephanie Fletcher for *The Buffalo News*

❧❧❧❧❧❧❧❧❧❧❧❧❧❧❧❧❧❧❧

"Everything living has to change with the times, and I, for one, am as glad Charleston is a living city as I am that it remembers the past. As long as it can hold on to both, it will always be a place we want to go."
—Mel White for *National Geographic Traveler*

Web Site for Charleston, SC
www.charlestoncvb.com

Charleston
"Champion of Character and Charm"

The Battery captures the charismatic charm of Charleston

21 East Battery B&B

One of the first dwellings constructed along the High Battery

Address: 21 East Battery
Charleston SC 29401
(Historic District)
Reservations: 1-800-543-4774
Telephone: (843) 556-0500

E-mail: info@21eastbattery.com
Web Site: www.21eastbattery.com
Category: Historic Inn
Manager: Mindy Crawford
Rates: $195-$395 (seasonal)

East Battery Banana and Pecan Muffins

1 cup sugar
½ cup butter
2 large eggs
2¾ cups mashed bananas
¼ cup milk
2 teaspoons vanilla extract
1 teaspoon cinnamon

1 teaspoon nutmeg
2½ cups flour
2 teaspoons baking powder
¾ teaspoon salt
½ teaspoon baking soda
1¼ cups pecans, chopped
   (reserve ¼ cup for top of muffins)

Preheat oven to 350°. In a large bowl, mix first 3 ingredients. Once combined, stir in the the next 5 ingredients; fold in remaining ingredients. After thoroughly mixing, pour or spoon mixture into greased muffin tins. Sprinkle reserved pecans on top and bake 40 to 45 minutes until done.

Yield: Approximately 24 medium-sized muffins.

Editors' Note: *We also like to bake these tasty muffins in mini-muffin pans and lightly sprinkle the tops with 10-X sugar.*

Pecan Butter

1 cup butter, softened
⅓ cup pecans, chopped

1 teaspoon brown sugar
1 teaspoon vanilla extract

Combine all ingredients and mix at a low speed until mixed well. Keep refrigerated in a tightly covered container. This butter also molds well in plastic butter molds and may be frozen until ready to use.

Yield: 1 cup butter spread

Strawberry Muffins

¼ cup soft butter
1¼ cups sugar
2 eggs
½ teaspoon vanilla
1½-2 cups flour

2 teaspoon baking powder
½ cup milk, approximately
2 cups fresh strawberries,
 hulled and cut into medium-
 sized pieces

Preheat oven to 375°. In a large bowl, cream together butter and sugar. Add next 2 ingredients and beat mixture well. In a separate bowl, combine the next 2 ingredients. Once mixed, stir in butter mixture. Next, stir in milk until mixture is just moist. In a food processor, add half of strawberries to muffin batter; lightly purée. Add remaining strawberries to the batter and mix lightly. Bake in greased muffin tins for about 20 minutes or until done.

Yield: 6 large (or 12 small) muffins

Editors' Note: *Frozen strawberries, thawed and drained, may be substituted for fresh ones.*

Nestled within Charleston's historic Edmondston-Alston House, one of the first dwellings constructed along the High Battery facing Charleston Harbor, 21 East Battery was built in 1825. The rear dependency, now part of the bed and breakfast, originally served as a stable and livery for the wealthy rice planter's fine horses and handsome town carriages. The quarters, where the bed and breakfast's guest rooms are now located, once housed the servants who worked to maintain this grand home.

Ashley Inn

A true taste of The South set in a charming architectural treasure

Address: 201 Ashley Avenue
Charleston SC 29403
(Historic District)
Reservations: 1-800-581-6658
Telephone: (843) 723-1848

E-mail: ashleyinnbb@aol.com
Web Site: www.charleston-sc-inns.com
Category: Historic Inn
Owner/Innkeeper: Barry Caroll
Rates: $89-$250 (seasonal)

Tut's Toffee

35 saltine crackers
2 sticks butter, softened
1 cup brown sugar

1 (12-ounce) package
semi-sweet chocolate chips
1½ cups pecans, chopped

Preheat oven to 350°. Line a (10 x 15-inch) jelly-roll pan or a shallow baking dish with waxed or parchment paper. Place saltines (7 down and 5 across) in pan. Combine next 2 ingredients in a microwave-safe bowl. Microwave on high 2 to 3 minutes; stir thoroughly and pour mixture over crackers. Bake at 350° for 20 minutes. Remove from oven and cover with chocolate chips. Smooth with spatula and sprinkle with nuts. Chill and break into bite size bits.

Yield: 4 dozen pieces

Editors' Note: *Easy and delicious! Store in airtight container. We've served this recipe at many of our book signings, and everyone loves it.*

Peaches 'n Cream Stuffed Waffles

Peaches

2 fresh peaches, peeled and thinly sliced—save some for garnish

Waffle Batter

2 cups waffle mix	2 eggs
¾ cup milk	1 teaspoon vanilla
¾ cup water	1 teaspoon orange extract

Mix together all ingredients together and prepare waffles on a preheated waffle iron.

Filling

6 ounces cream cheese, softened	¼ cup powdered sugar
½ teaspoon orange extract	

Whip all ingredients together with an electric mixer. Spread 1½ tablespoons filling on one-half of waffle. Top with peach slices and fold over. Keep warm.

Praline Sauce

1 cup brown sugar	½ cup whole pecans
½ stick butter	¼ cup sour cream
¼ cup water (or maple syrup)	Sprigs of mint, optional

Combine first 2 ingredients and melt in a saucepan. Add next 2 ingredients. Top stuffed waffles with Praline Sauce. Garnish with a dollop of sour cream, more peach slices, and a sprig of mint.

Yield: 4 servings

Editors' Note: *If time is short, use frozen waffles.*

"Charleston's Gourmet Breakfast Place"

Recipient of prestigious "1997 Carolopolis Award"

Featured in the nationally televised
"Country Inn Cooking with Gail Greco" on PBS.

Built in 1832 by Alexander Black,
an inventor of rice and cotton processing equipment

Cannonboro Bed & Breakfast

A place to be pampered with very special Southern hospitality

Address: 184 Ashley Ave.
Charleston, SC 29403
(Historic District)
Reservations: 1-800-235-8039
Telephone: (843) 723-8572

E-mail: cannonboroinn@aol.com
Web Site: www.charleston-sc-inns.com
Category: Historic Inn
Owner/Innkeeper: Barry Caroll
Rates: $89-$250 (seasonal)

Sausage Turnovers

Cheese Sauce

1½ cups of a basic white sauce
½ cup Cheddar cheese, shredded
¼ Parmesan cheese, grated

⅛ teaspoon oregano
Pinch of cayenne pepper

Make sauce using a basic white sauce recipe, a white sauce mix (prepared as directed), or a prepared white sauce. Stir in remaining ingredients. Keep warm.

Turnovers

1 pound sausage
½ red pepper, chopped
½ green pepper, chopped
½ onion, chopped

Frozen puff pastry sheets
¾ cup Cheddar cheese, shredded
1 egg

Cook first 4 ingredients together and drain. Thaw pastry sheets and cut into individual squares. Put ¼ cup of sausage mixture in center of each square and top with 2 tablespoons of cheese; fold over, making a triangle. Crimp edges of turnover and press together with prongs of a fork. Brush with egg wash (1 egg whisked with a drop of water and a pinch of salt) and prick holes in top of turnover with a fork. Bake at 425 degrees 15 to 18 minutes. Top with cheese sauce.

Yield: 4-6 servings

Editors' Note: *Instead of pricking top of turnover with a fork, a simple design (see example at right) can be "carved" into top of pastry with tip of a knife.*

Bacon and Tomato Dip

½ pound bacon
8 ounces sour cream

8 ounces cream cheese, softened
½ large tomato, chopped

Cook bacon (in frying pan or microwave) until crisp; drain and crumble. Mix together next 2 ingredients (adjusting amount of sour cream, if desired). Stir in bacon, tomatoes, and desired seasonings. Chill until ready to use and serve with crackers.

Yield: Approximately 2 cups

Editors' Note: *Also makes a nice spread on an open-faced tea sandwich.*

Kit Kat Bars

1½ cups graham cracker crumbs
¾ cup brown sugar
1 cup granulated sugar
¾ cup butter
⅓ cup milk

Butter crackers (such as Waverly)
1 cup butterscotch chips
1 cup semi-sweet chocolate chips
¾ cup peanut butter

Put first 5 ingredients into a saucepan and bring to a boil. Boil for 5 minutes, being careful not to burn. Set aside. Place a layer of crackers in a greased 9 X 13-inch pyrex dish and cover with one-half of sugar mixture. Top with another layer of crackers and cover with remaining mixture. Add a third layer of crackers on top. Make topping by melting last 3 ingredients together in a saucepan over low heat. Spread mixture over top layer of crackers and let cool. Cut into squares.

Yield: 24-30 squares

A Charleston single house, built in the Victorian style, the home was built in 1853 by a wealthy rice planter. The house is particularly noted for its two circular piazzas featuring twenty-two massive columns.

Governor's House

*One of the most elegant and historically significant homes in Charleston,
a city whose past is part of its soul.*

Address: 117 Broad Street
Charleston, SC 29401
(Historic District)
Reservations: 1-800-720-9812
Telephone: (843) 720-2070
E-mail: governorshouse@aol.com

Web Site: www.governorshouse.com
Category: Historic Inn
Owners/Innkeepers: Karen Spell Shaw
Robert Hill Shaw, III
Rates: $165-$330 (seasonal)

Sherried Baked Grapefruit

Brown sugar
1 red grapefruit (ripe, but firm)
Sherry, 1 tablespoon per grapefruit half

Preheat oven to 350°. Cut grapefruit in half and section with a grapefruit knife. Brush tops of grapefruit with sherry and sprinkle with brown sugar. Bake for 15 to 20 minutes until warm.

Yield: 2 servings

Editors' Note: *A wonderful first-course breakfast dish during the fall and winter months. Garnish with a maraschino cherry or an edible flower.*

Broad Street Olive Cheese Spread

Dash of Texas Pete hot sauce
1 (8-ounce) block of cream cheese, softened

16 black olives, pitted and chopped
12 green olives (with pimientos), chopped

Sir hot sauce into cream cheese. Stir in the olives and chill for at least one hour. Serve at room temperature with wheat or buttered crackers.

Yield: 1½ cups

Editors' Notes: *This mixture may also be formed into a ball and rolled in crushed, toasted pecans. It also makes a delicious spread for party sandwiches. If Texas Pete hot sauce is unavailable, use another hot sauce or Tabasco.*

Summer Peach Schnapps Cake

1 cup pecans, chopped (optional)
1 small package instant vanilla pudding
½ cup cold water
½ cup Peach Schnapps

1 package yellow cake mix
5 eggs
½ cup Crisco oil

Preheat oven to 325°. Grease and flour a 10-inch Bundt or tube pan; sprinkle nuts over bottom of pan. Mix remaining ingredients well with an electric beater. Pour batter over nuts. Bake for 50 minutes or until a toothpick, inserted in center of cake, comes out clean. Set cake on a wire rack to cool and then invert onto a serving plate. Prick top and drizzle or pour glaze evenly over top of cake while still hot.

Glaze

¾ cup powedered sugar
¼ cup lemon juice

2 teaspoons butter, melted
1 teaspoon Peach Schnapps

Mix all ingredients together until blended and smooth; add more sugar, if needed, to thicken glaze.

Yield: 1 cake

Editors' Notes: *Our tester suggests leaving the pecans out of this recipe when preparing the cake in a Bundt pan; she found them to be "too concentrated in the grooves of the pan." If pecans are desired, she recommends either using an angel food cake pan or stirring the nuts directly into the batter. Peach Schnapps (SHNAPS) is a strong, dry spirit which is produced by using the distillation of peaches.*

"Check into Charleston's Governor's House,
and you may never want to check out."
— *Southern Living,* September 1999

Hayne House B&B

An oasis of character and charm near The Battery

Address: 30 King Street
Charleston, SC 29401
(Historic District)
Telephone: (843) 577-2633
E-mail: haynehouse@yahoo.com

Web Site: www.haynehouse.com
Category: B&B
Owners/Innkeepers: Brian & Jane McGreevy
Rates: $135-$285 (seasonal)

Robie's Sausage and Egg Casserole

¼ pound bulk sausage (mild or spicy)
¾ tablespoon butter
2 tablespoons chopped mushrooms
¼ cup cream or half-and-half

4 eggs
¼ cup New York sharp Cheddar
cheese, grated

Brown sausage in skillet; crumble and drain. Spread sausage in bottom of a casserole dish. Sauté mushrooms in butter; drain and mix with cream in a separate dish. Soft scramble eggs and layer on top of sausage. Spread mushroom/cream mixture over eggs. Sprinkle grated cheese over top. Cook at 350° for 20 minutes or until cheese is melted and casserole is bubbly.

Yield: 4 servings

Editors' Note: *An egg substitute product may be used instead of fresh eggs. Garnish with fresh basil.*

❦❦❦❦❦❦❦❦❦❦❦❦❦❦❦❦❦❦❦❦❦❦❦

Mrs. Lacey's Pound Cake

3 sticks Country Morning Blend
   butter (or margarine)
3 cups sugar
6 eggs

3 cups cake flour
1 (8-ounce) carton sour cream
1 teaspoon vanilla

Do not preheat oven. Thoroughly grease and flour Bundt pan. Cream butter and sugar together. Add eggs one at a time, beating well after each. Alternately, add flour and sour cream. Add vanilla. Place pan in oven. Turn oven on and bake at 325° for 1½ hours.

Yield: 1 pound cake

Editors' Notes: *For variety, other flavorings (i.e., almond, lemon, orange, rum) may be substituted for the vanilla. Very good served at breakfast with fruit.*

Hayne House Pumpkin Bread

4 eggs
2½-3 cups sugar
   (depending on personal taste)
1 cup oil
1 cup cold water
1 (15-ounce) can pumpkin

2 teaspoons pumpkin pie spice
1 teaspoon salt
1 teaspoon cinnamon
2 teaspoons baking soda
1 teaspoon baking powder
3⅓ cups all-purpose flour

Beat eggs and stir in next 4 ingredients. Sift together dry ingredients and add to pumpkin mixture. Mix well. Divide into 2 large or 3 medium-sized loaf pans. Bake at 350° for 60 to 75 minutes until done.

Yield: 2 or 3 loaves

Editors' Notes: *Muffins offer another variation of this recipe (lessen the cooking time) and are delicious served chilled with cream cheese. This popular recipe can also be baked in a jar for a unique gift presentation. Pour mixture into a greased wide-mouth pint jar and fill half-full. Place filled jars on cookie sheet and bake at 325° for 45 minutes. When done, remove one jar at a time and wipe sealing edge with a paper towel. Screw cap on tightly, and the heat will vacuum-seal jar. Bread will keep up to one year in sealed jar.*

Selected as one of the top three inns in Charleston
and the only one with a top-rated breakfast.
— *Travel Holiday* (February 2002)

"This converted Georgian-style single house—true native architecture—
on the residential (read: "Old Money") part of King Street
is pure Charleston." —Sherri Eisenberg, *Travel Holiday* (February 2002)

John Rutledge House

America's most historic inn

Address: 116 Broad Street
Charleston, SC 29401
(Historic District)
Telephone: (843) 723-7999
Reservations: 1-800-476-9741

Web Site: www.charminginns.com/
rutledgehouse.html
Category: Historic Inn
Innkeeper: Kathy Leslie
Rates: $165-$375 (seasonal)

Rutledge Biscuit with Hot Sherried Fruit

Sherried Fruit

1 (8-ounce) can pineapple, juice reserved
1 (8-ounce) can of peaches, cut into chunks,
   juice reserved
1 (8-ounce) can of pears, cut into chunks,
   juice reserved

¼ cup light brown sugar, firmly packed
⅛ teaspoon ground cinnamon
¼ cup cream sherry (or to taste)
1 teaspoon cornstarch
2 tablespoons water

In a 2-quart saucepan, combine first 3 ingredients and their juices. Add next 2 ingredients and heat through. Stir in cream sherry. In a small bowl or cup, mix corn starch and water. Stir mixture into hot fruit. Cook, stirring occasionally, until thickened.

Biscuits

1 cup self rising flour
⅛ teaspoon baking soda

3 tablespoons shortening
¼ cup buttermilk

In a large bowl, combine first 2 ingredients. Cut shortening into flour mixture with a pastry blender. Add buttermilk and mix just until combined. Turn out onto a floured surface. Knead about 5 minutes or until dough is no longer sticky. Pat or roll to about a ¾-inch thickness and cut with a biscuit cutter. Place on a hot greased baking pan, with sides of biscuits touching. Bake on an ungreased baking pan in a 450° oven until lightly browned (8 to 10 minutes). Serve with hot Sherried Fruit.

Yield: 4 biscuits with fruit

Curried Chicken Salad

1 cup chopped or shredded chicken
2-3 teaspoons curry powder
½ cup cream cheese, softened
½ cup mayonnaise

1 large tablespoon Ranch
   Peppercorn dressing
1 teaspoon sugar
Grapes (purple, green, or both),
   chopped or whole

Combine and chill first two ingredients. Combine and chill next three ingredients. Combine sugar with remaining ingredients and blend everything together. Serve with crackers or pita bread.

Yield: 4 servings

Editors' Notes: *Mandarin oranges, chopped pecans, chopped dates, chopped celery, golden raisins, toasted coconut, and/or pineapple bits make a nice addition to this salad. Pineapple-flavored cream cheese provides still another variation. Add more mayonnaise if too dry.*

Rutledge House Inn's Fudge

1 stick (4-ounce) butter
½ stick (2-ounce) margarine
1 small (5-ounce) can evaporated milk
3 cups sugar

1 (12-ounce) bag semi-sweet chocolate chips
½ teaspoon vanilla
1 jar (8-ounce) marshmallow cream

In a 2-quart, heavy sauce pan, heat first 4 ingredients to 234° on a candy thermometer. Add chocolate chips. Allow to soften, then stir in vanilla and marshmallow cream until glossy. Pour into buttered 9 x 13-inch pan. After cool, cut into squares.

Yield: approximately 3 dozen squares

Editors' Note: *This is absolutely the best fudge we have ever sampled! For a mocha-flavored fudge, add 1 teaspoon of instant coffee when sugar is added.*

"Charleston's Classiest Inn"
—Andrew Harper's *Hideaway Report,* 1996

Named "Top-rated place to stay in Charleston" by
—*Conde' Nast Traveler,* 1999

John Rutledge, one of the fifty-five signers of the U.S. Constitution, built his home in 1763. Now an exquisitely restored inn, it is the only home of one of these signers which now accommodates overnight guests.

Lowndes Grove Plantation

Overlooking The Ashley River, Lowndes Grove Plantation
proffers 18th century living at its finest

Address: 266 St. Margaret Street
        Charleston, SC 29403
Telephone: (843) 723-8438
E–mail: info@lowndesgrove.com

Web Site: www.lowndesgrove.com
Category: B&B
Owners/Innkeepers: Lex & Tina Opoulos
Rates: $125-$165 (year-round)

Muesli with Fruit

2 cups mixed seasonal fruit (assorted berries,
    bananas, apples, pineapples, orange
    sections, pears, nectarines, etc.)
2 cups vanilla low-fat yogurt

1 cup muesli
2 teaspoons honey
2 tablespoons slivered almonds
    or cashews, toasted

Wash and cut mixed fruit into bite-sized pieces. Sprinkle with sugar (or sweetener) to taste. Place prepared fruit in a large cereal bowl, add yogurt, and top with the muesli. Drizzle with honey; sprinkle with almonds or cashews.

Yield: 3-4 servings

Editors' Note: *Muesli ((MYOOS-lee) is a cereal found in most food and health food stores; if desired, granola may be substituted for muesli. Raspberries and blueberries make a tasty and colorful fruit combination. When serving this dish for breakfast, place yogurt and fruit mixture into individual bowls and refrigerate the night before. The next morning, you will just need to top mixture with muesli (or granola), drizzle with honey, and sprinkle with almonds.*

Peanut Butter and Banana French Toast

3 eggs, beaten
¼ cup cool water
½ teaspoon vanilla extract
2 teaspoons peanut butter
4 slices egg bread (challah)

1 tablespoon margarine
2 bananas, peeled and sliced
   into ½-inch chunks (reserve
   some for garnish)
2 tablespoons real maple syrup

In a shallow bowl, beat water and vanilla into eggs until well-mixed. Spread a teaspoon of peanut butter onto two slices of bread and dip into egg mixture. Then take the other two slices and dip them into egg mixture. Heat margarine in a large frying pan over medium-high heat. When margarine starts bubbling, add the peanut butter slices into the skillet with peanut butter side up. Quickly place banana pieces onto the peanut butter and top with a slice of egg-dipped bread. Squish the sandwich together with a spatula. Let cook about 3 minutes on first side; flip and cook for another few minutes on other side. After 6 or 7 minutes of cooking, if sandwich seems too moist, cover pan with a lid and let cook an additional minute or two. Turn out French toast sandwiches onto big plates and garnish with extra banana slices. Serve with maple syrup.

Yield: 2 servings

Editors' notes: *Challah (KHAH-lah), a traditional Jewish yeast bread, has a light texture and is rich with eggs. For a delicious, crunchy variation, roll sandwich in Corn Flakes before browning.*

"Offers closest thing you will find to experiencing what life must have been like for the spoiled planter class that ruled the antebellum South.
— Steve Bailey, *The Boston Globe* (1999)

Lowndes Grove Plantation was selected in 2001 as the setting for a photo-shoot by Tiffany and Company, headquartered in New York City, to convey the lifestyle of Tiffany's clientele.

The only surviving plantation on the historic Charleston penisula, Lowndes Grove Plantation is listed in the National Register of Historic Places and known as one of "Charleston's 62 most famous homes."

Two Meeting Street

Charleston's oldest and most renowned inn

Address: 2 Meeting Street
Charleston, SC 29401
(Historic District)
Telephone: (843) 723-7322

Web Site: www.twomeetingstreet.com
Category: Historic Inn
Owners/Innkeepers: Jean & Pete Spell
Rates: $165–$310

Baked Pears with Mango Chutney

9 pears
2 sticks butter
1 (8-ounce) jar mango chutney

1 cup raisins
1 teaspoon cinnamon

Cut pears in half and core. Mix remaining ingredients in a bowl. Stuff 1 teaspoon of butter mixture into each pear. Bake at 350° for 20 minutes. Serve warm.

Yield: 9 pears

Editors' Note: *This mixture may also be used for stuffing apples (leave whole and core). Fruit used may be microwaved until tender and then baked in oven; baste with liquid. Serve stuffed fruit with dairy topping for a tasty dessert.*

Ambrosia

4 oranges, sectioned
3 pink grapefruits, sectioned
1 small can chunk pineapple

1 (4-ounce) jar red cherries, drained
½ cup coconut, shredded
½ cup pecans, chopped

Mix all ingredients together, chill, and serve.

Yield: 4-6 servings

Editors' Note: *Add green cherries, along with the red ones, for a festive look at Christmas time. Good served with pound cake (see page 53).*

Cucumber Spread

1 medium cucumber
   (peeled, seeded, and grated)
½ teaspoon garlic power

1 (8-ounce) block of cream cheese,
   softened
1 stick butter

Combine all ingredients. Place in a small glass bowl and serve with crackers or assorted vegetables.

Yield: 1-1½ cups

"Best in the South"
—*Southern Living* magazine poll
(1999 & 2000)

Featured in *Southern Accents, Southern Living, Travel and Leisure, Country Living,* Andrew Harper's *Hideaway Report, Country Inns and Gourmet,* and served as host for The Discovery Channel's "Great Country Inns of America" series.

---

*The beautiful Queen Anne mansion,
completed in 1892 and given as a wedding gift,
has welcomed guests from all over the world for over 68 years.*

Wentworth Mansion

To step through its doors is to step into a world of refinement

Address: 149 Wentworth Street
Charleston, SC 29401
(Historic District)
Reservations: 1-888-466-1886
Telephone: (843) 853-1886

Web Site: www.wentworthmansion.com
Category: **Historic** Inn
Innkeeper: **Bob Seidler**
Rates: $315-$695 (seasonal)

Cheese Sticks

1¼ cups all-purpose flour
1 teaspoon baking powder
1 teaspoon salt
¾ teaspoon gumbo filé
¼ teaspoon black pepper
¾ teaspoon cayenne pepper

¾ teaspoon granulated garlic
½ cup unsalted butter,
　(cut into small pieces)
1¼ cups white Cheddar cheese,
　shredded
¼ cup grated Parmesan cheese

Mix first seven ingredients together. Whip butter and cheese together; add flour mixture, incorporating it until dough forms a ball. Wrap in plastic wrap and chill 30 minutes or up to 2 days. Preheat oven to 325°. Roll dough into a rectangle (approximately ⅛–inch thick) on a lightly floured surface. Cut dough into strips and transfer them to an ungreased baking sheet spaced 1½ inches apart. Bake for 12 to 16 minutes or until golden brown. After cheese sticks cool, serve immediately.

Yield: 10 servings

Editors' Note: *Gumbo filé ((FEE-lay), made from the leaves of a sassafras tree, is used in Creole cooking and can be found in the spice section of most supermarkets. Top cheese sticks with toasted sesame seeds and sprinkle with paprika. Dough may be frozen and used later.*

Bed & Breakfasts and Historic Inns
Charleston, South Carolina

Sticky Buns

Buns

1½ ounces yeast	Pinch of salt	5 cups bread flour
1 cup water	1 ounce of Carnation	½ cup cake flour
4 ounces butter	non-fat dry milk	½ cup sugar
½ cup sugar	3 eggs	2 tablespoons cinnamon

All ingredients should be room temperature. Place yeast in a small amount of the water using a separate container. In a mixer, combine next 4 ingredients until well-creamed. Add eggs, one at a time, until incorporated; add water and mix briefly. Add flour and then yeast mixture to the bowl; mix until smooth. Cover dough with plastic wrap and allow to rise for 1½ hours. Pre-heat oven to 375°. Scale dough into equal parts. On a floured work surface, roll each piece of dough into a 9 x 12-inch rectangle about ¼-inch thick. Brush off any excess flour. Next, brush surface of dough with softened butter and sprinkle with a mixture of sugar and cinnamon. Roll dough up into a 12-inch long log. Cut log roll into 1-inch circular rolls and place on a greased pan with the honey pan glaze and pecan pieces smeared onto the bottom of it. Bake for 12 to 15 minutes or until golden brown. Allow buns to cool before inverting them onto a plate to be served. If they are not completely cool, the glaze will run when inverted.

Honey Pan Glaze

10 ounces brown sugar	2½ ounces corn syrup
4 ounces butter	1 ounce water
2½ ounces honey	

Cream together first four ingredients in a mixer. Add enough water to bring mixture to a spreadable consistency.

Yield: 12 buns

Editors' Note: *This excellent glaze can also be used when baking a ham or to make glazed pecans.*

"Hideaway of the Year" —Andrew Harper's *Hideaway Report*, December 1999

One of the "50 Best Secrets" —*Travel Holiday's* Insider Awards, September 1999

"Inn of the Month" —*Travel & Leisure*, November 1998

―――――――――――――

Built in 1886 and designed in the Second Empire style as an opulent private residence by a wealthy cotton merchant, the Wentworth Mansion is now one of the world's finest and most unique inns—a pristine example of America's Gilded Age.

82 Queen

Eleven dining areas and a picturesque garden courtyard

Address: 82 Queen Street
Charleston, SC 29414
(Historic District)
Telephone: 1-800-849-0082
(843) 723-7591
Web Site: www.82queen.com

Cuisine: Authentic Lowcountry cuisine
Executive Chef: Stephen Stone
Price Range: Lunch/$8-$13
Dinner/$16-$22
Cookbook: *The Best of Lowcountry Cuisine*

McClellanville Crab Cakes

1 pound lump crabmeat,
   picked clean of shell
½ cup mayonnaise
2 green onions, chopped fine
2 dashes of Tabasco sauce

1 dash of Worcestershire sauce
½ cup coarse bread crumbs
½ ounce fresh lemon juice
½ teaspoon ground thyme

Combine ingredients thoroughly. Form into desired cake size (about 4 ounces each).

Egg Wash

2 eggs   ¼ cup of half-and-half

Make egg wash by combining eggs with half-and-half. Dip crab cakes into egg mixture, then roll into more bread crumbs. Sauté cakes in butter or olive oil until golden brown. Serve with Roasted Red Pepper Cream Sauce.

Roasted Red Pepper Cream Sauce

4 ounces butter
½ cup flour
2 cups milk
2 cups fish stock
¼ cup sherry

2 red bell peppers (seeded, peeled, roasted, puréed)
¼ teaspoon cayenne pepper
Salt and white pepper, to taste
1 teaspoon paprika
¼ cup bacon fat

In a saucepan, melt butter over low heat. Add flour and whisk until a roux is formed. Add next 3 ingredients and bring to a boil. Reduce heat and simmer. Add peppers and remaining ingredients. Simmer 10 minutes; strain through a strainer. Add more milk, if too thick.

Yield: 6 servings

Grilled Portabello Mushrooms

2 cups oil
2 sprigs rosemary
1 teaspoon salt
1 teaspoon black pepper
1 teaspoon garlic

4-6 portabello mushrooms
  (5" diameter with stems removed)
Chèvre (goat's cheese)
Gourmet greens

Mix first 5 ingredients (for marinade) in a shallow pie pan. Place mushrooms in pan and cover with marinade; marinate for 1 to 2 hours or overnight. Mushrooms will absorb most of the marinade. Grill mushrooms 5 to 8 minutes per side, cook until tender. Remove, slice, and top with Vinaigrette. Garnish with chèvre (SHEHV-ruh) and serve on a bed of gourmet greens.

Yield: 4-6 servings

Vinaigrette

6 teaspoons balsamic vinegar
2 teaspoons olive oil

2 teaspoons brown sugar
Salt and pepper, dash of each

Mix all ingredients. Keep chilled until ready to use.

Shrimp Gazpacho
(gahz-PAH-choh)

¼ pound small shrimp
1 pound fresh tomatoes, peeled
  and diced (2-3 medium tomatoes)
½ small onion, chopped
½ green pepper, chopped
½ large cucumber, chopped
1 cup tomato juice

1 tablespoon cider vinegar
1 tablespoon sugar
½ teaspoon garlic, minced
¼ teaspon oregano
2 bay leaves
¼ tespoon salt
¼ teaspoon black pepper

Poach shrimp; chill and peel. Purée next 3 ingredients in a blender. Stir remaining ingredients into mixture and chill for 12 hours. Serve cold.

Yield: 4 servings

"Readers' Choice Awards – Best City Restaurant"
—*Southern Living* magazine (1997, 1998, 1999)

Blossom

A high-energy, contemporary space that perfectly complements the fresh seafood cuisine

Address: 185 E. Bay Street
Charleston, SC 29401
(Historic District)
Telephone: (843) 722-9200 x 1
Web Site: www.magnolias-blossom-cypress.com

Cuisine: Lowcountry cuisine with an Italian flair
Executive Chef: Aaron Siegel
Price Range: Lunch/$9-$13
Dinner/$16-$27

Pan-Seared Mahi with Tomato Basil Couscous

Caper Butter Sauce

1 tablespoon lemon juice
1 shallot, diced
1 tablespoon capers, chopped

¼ cup heavy cream
8 ounces butter, room temperature
Salt and pepper, to taste

Place first 3 ingredients in a small sauce pan over medium-low heat. Allow mixture to reduce until liquid is almost gone. Next, add cream and reduce mixture until thick. Lower heat and add butter (cut in ½-inch cubes); whisk constantly. Season with salt and pepper. The sauce may be made an hour or two before serving, but hold it at room temperature. Do not reheat as sauce will separate and become unusable.

Couscous

2 cups strong vegetable stock
 (chicken stock may be substituted)
½ cup couscous

2 tablespoons diced tomato
2 tablespoons fresh basil
Salt and pepper, to taste

Bring the stock to a boil in a medium saucepan. Add remaining ingredients and stir; remove from heat and allow to sit for 3 to 5 minutes. Fluff with a fork. Set aside, but keep warm.

Mahi Mahi

Olive oil (about 2 tablespoons)
½ cup all-purpose flour

Salt and pepper
2 (6-ounce portions) mahi mahi

Cover bottom of a heavy, oven-proof frying pan with olive oil. Season flour with salt and pepper. Lightly dust fish in seasoned flour and sauté in olive oil until golden brown (make sure fish are not touching as they cook). After turning the fish, place pan in a 350° oven for 5 minutes. Serve fish over couscous (KOOS-koos) and cover with Caper Butter Sauce. Yield: 4 servings

Editors' Note: *Tilapia or cod may be substituted for mahi mahi (MAH-hee MAH-hee).*

Scallopini of Veal with Marsala Wine Sauce

1½-2 pounds veal top round or pounded scallopini
   (3 pieces per person, 1¾ ounces per piece)
Salt and pepper, as needed

½ cup flour
Olive oil blend, as needed

Slice veal into 1¾-ounce pieces; cover with plastic and pound with a mallet to tenderize and flatten. Do not pulverize (over-pound with mallet). Season veal with salt and pepper. Dredge in flour, shaking off excess. Sauté in oil blend 3 to 4 pieces at a time, cooking (over even heat) just until done. Be careful not to burn caramelized bits that may accumulate on bottom of pan. Place veal on a plate until all is cooked.

Marsala Wine Mushroom Sauce

3 tablespoons olive oil blend
½ cup shallot, minced
2 teaspoons garlic, minced
½ cup shiitake mushroom caps, julienned
½ cup crimini mushrooms, quartered

1 cup Marsala wine
2 cups browned, veal stock, reduced
¼ cup basil, fresh, julienned
⅓ cup dried tomatoes, julienned
Salt and black pepper, to taste

Add oil to pan used for cooking veal. Sauté shallots with garlic until translucent; add mushrooms and cook another minute. Deglaze with wine, reducing by two-thirds. Add remaining ingredients. Reduce by one-third over medium high heat. Add cooked veal to sauce, with all juices, until heated through.

Herbed Pasta

8 ounces angel hair pasta, fresh
3 tablespoons whole butter
1 teaspoon chopped garlic

3 tablespoons assorted chopped herbs (parsley, basil, chives, chervil, oregano)

Toss the just-cooked pasta with remaining ingredients. Place a nest of pasta at top of the plate and shingle 3 pieces of veal in front of it. Coat with sauce.

Yield: 4 servings

Editors' Note: *If shiitake (shee-TAH-kay) or crimini (cri-MEE-nee) mushrooms are unavailable, substitute common white mushrooms (the flavor will be less intense, so a few more mushrooms will need to be used). Veal stock may be ordered online (see page 220). Marsala (mahr-SAH-lah) is an Italian wine important to producing the flavor needed for creating this dish. Do not use cooking Marsala wine, sold at supermarkets, as these wines are usually too salty. Chicken may be substituted, for the veal, to create Chicken Marsala.*

"For a big night out on the town, pick one of the flowers of Charleston's restaurant garden . . .Blossom."
—*Southern Living* magazine

Charleston Chops

Friendly fine dining, a piano bar, and a classy Southern style

Address: 188 East Bay Street
Charleston, SC 29401
(Historic District)
Telephone: (843) 937-9300
Web Site: www.charlestonchops.net

Cuisine: Steak, seafood, and
wild game specialties
Executive Chef: Jeffrey Gibbs
Price Range: Dinner/$18-$26

Bourbon and Ginger Tenderloin Salad

½ cup bourbon
¼ medium red onion
1½ cups soy sauce
1½ tablespoons fresh ginger, peeled and grated

½ tablespoon crushed red pepper
1 cup brown sugar
½ pound beef tenderloin

Combine first 6 ingredients and bring to a boil. Let cool. Add beef and marinate for one hour. Sear over medium-high heat until evenly browned. Let stand for five minutes.

Pear and Ginger Vinaigrette

½ cup fresh pear, peeled and chopped
¾ cup rice vinegar
1 tablespoon Dijon mustard
2 tablespoons fresh, grated ginger
2 tablespoons chopped shallots
1 tablespoon chopped garlic
3 tablespoons soy sauce

Salt and pepper, to taste
1 cup olive oil
4 cups arugula,
washed and sliced
½ medium red onion, sliced
1 pear, cored and sliced

Combine first 8 ingredients in blender. Blend until smooth, slowly adding olive oil. Mix remaining ingredients and let sit for five minutes. Place in center of plates and top with sliced beef.

Yields: 4 servings

Editors' Note: *Arugula (ah-ROO-guh-lah), a mustard-flavored green also known as Italian cress, may be substituted with any green you like; another meat may be substituted for the tenderloin.*

Smoked Gouda Potato Gratin

½ stick butter
½ small onion, diced
½ tablespoon fresh garlic, minced
3 Yukon gold (boiling) potatoes,
    thinly sliced

1 cup heavy cream
1 cup Gouda (GOO-dah)
    cheese, shredded
2 eggs
Salt and pepper, to taste

Melt butter in skillet and caramelize onion with garlic. Mix onion and garlic with potatoes; pour into a shallow 9 x 13-inch pan. Mix remaining ingredients together and pour evenly over potatoes. Cover with topping and bake at 350° for 25 minutes.

Topping

¼ cup ground smoked bacon
1 cup panko (Japanese) bread crumbs
¼ cup shredded gouda

Salt and pepper, to taste
⅛ pound melted butter

Cook bacon until crisp; drain and grind in a food processor. Mix bacon with next 4 ingredients. Slowly mix in melted butter.

Yields: 2-4 servings

Beef Tartare

2 tablespoons garlic
1 tablespoon anchovy paste
2 tablespoons horseradish
2 tablespoons Dijon mustard
2 tablespoons minced capers

1 tablespoon Worcestershire sauce
½ teaspoon Tabasco sauce
Salt and pepper, to taste
1 pound filet mignon
Brioche, crackers, or toast points

Combine first 8 ingredients. Cut filet into finely diced pieces and mix with mustard mix thirty minutes before serving. Tightly wrap and refrigerate. Serve with brioche (BREE-ohsh), crackers, or toast points.

Yields: 4 servings

Editors' Notes: *Use only top-quality beef for this dish. Beef/Steak Tartare (tar-TAR) is served, uncooked, in the tradition of the Tartars who inhabited the Baltic provinces of medieval Russia. This dish is often offered, as an appetizer, at fine dining steak houses. For an impressive presentation, prepare tartare in a ring mold and garnish with capers, chopped parsley, sliced red onions, and Asiago cheese.*

"A first-class steakhouse."—*Post & Courier,* February 1998

"A jazzy interior with Southern style."—*Post & Courier,* April 2003

Cypress Lowcountry Grille

Charleston's hottest new place to dine

Address: 167 East Bay Street
Charleston, SC 29401
(Historic District)
Telephone: (843) 727-0111 x 1
E-mail: reservations@magnolias-blossom-cypress.com
Web Site: www.magnolias-blossom-cypress.com

Cuisine: Classic American
cuisine with an Asian flair
Executive Chef: Craig Deihl
Price Range: Dinner/$17-$36

Tuna and Oysters on Half Shell with Cilantro

2 tablespoons chopped cilantro
¼ cup freshly-squeezed lime juice
3 tablespoons rice wine vinegar
3 tablespoons honey
1 teaspoon salt

10 fresh oysters in shell
 (scrubbed free of dirt and debris)
½ pound sashimi-grade tuna
1 cup rock salt
Cilantro leaves

Combine the first five ingredients in a small mixing bowl and incorporate evenly. Place in the refrigerator to chill. Using an oyster knife, shuck oysters and remove top shell. Leaving the oyster in the half shell, rinse with water to remove any remaining grit. Using a sharp knife, cut tuna into 10 thin strips (approximately ⅛-inch thick) and place on top of the oysters. Place 1 teaspoon of refrigerated glaze on top of each oyster. On a plate, place 1 cup of rock salt and top with cilantro leaves (the rock salt keeps the oysters from sliding around). Place oysters on top of cilantro and rock salt; serve immediately.

Yield: 2 servings

Editors' Notes: *Placing meat (such as tuna in this recipe) in a freezer for up to 20 minutes makes it easier to slice thin. Sashimi (sah-SHEE-mee) is a fish served raw with condiments.. Since it is served raw, it must be fresh and top-quality. It may be ordered, along with the oysters, by calling 1-800-556-2783. Cilantro, also known as coriander and Chinese parsley, can usually be found year-round in most supermarkets. Rice wine vinegar can be found with other vinegars in a supermarket, at an Asian market, or ordered online (see page 220).*

༄‑༄

Seared Wahoo Over Truffle Grits

Wahoo

10 ounces fresh wahoo
   (can substitute grouper, snapper, or halibut)
Salt and pepper, to taste
2 ounces olive oil
2 ounces butter
6 large local white shrimp (peeled and deveined)
2 tablespoons thinly sliced garlic cloves
3 tablespoons thinly sliced shallots

1 cup asparagus tips
3 ounces white wine
3 ounces butter (cold)
½ cup grape tomatoes, sliced in half
3 tablespoons fresh basil, chopped
1 teaspoon salt
Pinch of white pepper

Cut fish into 2 equal-size pieces; season with salt and pepper. Sear wahoo (in hot olive oil in a sauté pan) over medium-high heat 2 to 3 minutes. Flip fish and add next 4 ingredients. Continue to cook 2 to 3 minutes, then remove fish from pan. Add asparagus to pan and cook 1 to 2 minutes. Remove shrimp from pan and deglaze pan with white wine; reduce liquid by half (takes approximately 2 minutes). Over low heat, stir in butter until melted and creamy. Add remaining ingredients. To assemble, place wahoo on top of a serving of Truffle Grits and surround with three shrimp. Next, place equal amounts of asparagus and tomato mixture on top of fish. Spoon sauce around the fish.

Yield: 2 servings

Editors' Note: *Grape tomatoes are baby Roma tomatoes.*

Truffle Grits

3 cups of water
1 cup white grits, preferably stone ground
3 tablespoons butter
¼ cup heavy cream

1-2 teaspoons truffle oil
1½ tablespoons salt
½ teaspoon ground white pepper
1½ tablespoons honey

Bring water to boil. Stir in grits and cook 25 to 30 minutes over medium-low heat until water is absorbed; grits should be slightly creamy. Add remaining ingredients and cook another 5 to 10 minutes.

Yield: 2-4 servings

Editors' Notes: *Truffles, an edible fungi considered a delicacy, have been proclaimed (since ancient times) to have therapeutic and aphrodisiac powers. Truffle oil and stone ground grits can usually be found in gourmet or specialty shops; they may also be ordered online (see page 220). The flavor of truffle oil is strong, so only add a little at a time.*

> "In opening Cypress, they have raised the bar
> for Charleston restaurants. This is a special place."
> —Charleston's *Post & Courier,* 2002

Hominy Grill

Charleston's favorite neighborhood restaurant

Address: 207 Rutledge Avenue
Charleston, SC 29403
(Historic District)
Telephone: (843) 937-0930
Web Site: www.hominygrill.com

Cuisine: Southern cooking
Executive Chef: Robert Stehling
Price Range: Breakfast/$2.75-$5.75
Lunch/$3.25-$6.75
Dinner/$8.50-$17.25

Southern Fried Chicken

1 (3-pound) chicken, cut up
1 cup buttermilk
2 cups peanut oil

1 cup all-purpose flour
2 teaspoons salt
Freshly ground black pepper

Marinate chicken in buttermilk 2 to 24 hours. Preheat peanut oil in cast-iron skillet. While oil is preheating, combine dry ingredients in a paper bag; drop chicken pieces into the bag, tossing to coat evenly (be careful not to over-flour). Hold each piece up and shake off excess flour. Place chicken in hot skillet, skin side down, with about one-half inch of oil. Add dark pieces to skillet first, followed by white pieces. Chicken should start frying immediately. After a minute or so, turn heat down to medium low. Leave chicken alone, agitating it only enough to make sure it is not sticking to the pan. When chicken starts turning white and juices are oozing out, flip to cook other side. It should be about two-thirds cooked at this time. If the heat is too high and the chicken is flipped too soon, the crust will fall off. Finish frying and set chicken pieces on a platter to rest for 5 minutes. After checking doneness, by making a small cut in bottom of chicken, remove chicken to paper towels to drain.

Yield: 5-6 servings

Editors' Notes: *We used skinless, boneless chicken breasts, and they were excellent!*

Restaurants
Charleston, South Carolina

Okra Beignets

½ cup jasmine rice, cooked
2 cups fresh okra, sliced
½ green pepper, diced
1 onion, diced

1 egg
¼ cup heavy cream
½ cup all-purpose flour
Canola oil, enough for deep frying

Cook rice, according to directions. Let cool. Combine next 6 ingredients and let set for at least 20 minutes. Mixture will become slimy from okra. Add drained rice to ingredients. Spoon mixture into frying pan, with hot canola, and deep fry until brown on each side. Drain well and serve.

Yield: 12-15 beignets

Editors' Notes: *Jasmine rice can be found at most supermarkets or at an Asian food market. Beignets (ben-YAYS) is a derivative of the French word meaning "fritter" and are especially popular in New Orleans in other variations. Cooked, chopped shrimp is also excellent added to the beignets. If shrimp is desired, stir in after adding the rice.*

Saffron Rice Croquettes

White Sauce

Use your favorite white sauce recipe and season (to taste) with 1 bay leaf, red pepper flakes, nutmeg, butter, salt and white pepper. Stir in ½ cup onion, julienned.

Croquettes

1½ cups jasmine rice
Pinch of saffron
½ cup white sauce, chilled
2½ tablespoons fresh parsley,
    chives, and/or basil (finely chopped)
¼ cup Parmesan cheese, grated

⅛ cup sweet red pepper,
    sautéed till tender
Salt, white pepper, and
    Tabasco sauce, to taste
½ cup plain bread crumbs
Peanut oil for frying

Cook rice, according to directions, with saffron. Drain rice and stir in white sauce, fresh herbs, Parmesan cheese, and red pepper. Season with salt, pepper, and Tabasco. Roll mixture into walnut-sized nuggets, dredge in bread crumbs, and deep fry until brown and crispy. Drain and serve hot.

Yield: 8-10 croquettes

"Where the Biscuits Meet the Gravy."
—*New York Times*, April 2000

"If you want to have an excellent meal in a cozy inviting Charleston single house where you can hold a conversation, Hominy Grill is the place."

Joseph's

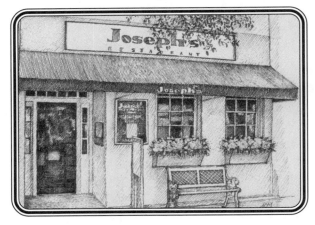

Family-operated and a favorite with the locals

Address: 129 Meeting Street
Charleston, SC 29401
(Historic District)
Telephone: (843) 958-8500
Web Site: www.josephsofcharleston.com

Cuisine: American eclectic
Executive Chef: Joseph Passarini
Price Range: Breakfast/$5.50-$8.95
Lunch/$5-$12

Joseph's Famous Tomato Soup

1 teaspoon butter
½ heaping tablespoon minced garlic
¼ cup onion, diced
1 (46-ounce) can tomato juice
1 (46-ounce) can V-8 juice

1 cup chicken broth
Roux (see page 220)
1 cup heavy cream
Salt and pepper, to taste

In a sauce pot, melt butter and sauté next 2 ingredients until onions are soft. Pour in next 3 ingredients. Bring to a rapid boil and boil for 10 minutes; reduce to a simmer. Slowly stir in roux until soup has reached desired thickness. Simmer for 15 minutes, stirring frequently. Add last ingredients and remove from heat.

Yield: 8 servings

Editors' Note: This is an excellent soup to supplement with additional ingredients (fresh crab meat, Romano cheese and fresh basil, or cooked chicken and curry) once the basic soup is prepared. Just add as much or as little as you desire. Our food consultant and his wife tested this recipe and decided to flavor it with sautéed mushrooms and basil. They reported that it was "very good." A friend also tested this recipe and shared a batch with us. We agree, it is a "very good" recipe.

❦❦❦❦❦❦❦❦❦❦❦❦❦❦❦❦❦❦❦❦❦❦❦

Fried Green Tomatoes with Sweet Citrus Rémoulade

Dust

2 cups all-purpose flour	½ teaspoon cayenne pepper
1 teaspoon salt	1 teaspoon garlic powder
1 teaspoon black pepper	1 teaspoon onion powder

Blend together and set aside.

Tomatoes

4 large green tomatoes, cut into thick slices	3 whole eggs, beaten
1 cup flour	4 cups dust
	Vegetable oil, for frying

Dust tomatoes in plain flour, in eggs, then into dust. Fry at 350° until golden brown. Drain on paper and serve hot with rémoulade.

Editors' Note: *Green tomatoes are seasonal and available during the spring and summer months.*

Sweet Citrus Rémoulade

2 cups mayonnaise	1 tablespoon green sweet relish
1 teaspoon Worcestershire sauce	Handful of fresh parsley
Pinch of salt and pepper	1 tablespoon grained mustard
2 tablespoons lemon juice	1 tablespoon capers
1 teaspoon paprika	

Put all ingredients into food processor and blend for about 30 seconds. Chill.

Yield: 4 servings

"Unpretentious...superb."
—*The New York Times*

"Breakfast and lunch never tasted so good."
—*The Post and Courier*

Featured on the *Food Network*, October 2002

The Passarini family takes great pride in the quality, consistency, and honesty of their food and service.

Magnolia's

A unique blend of historic charm and contemporary excitement

Address: 185 E. Bay Street
Charleston, SC 29402
(Historic District)
Telephone: (843) 577-7771
Web Site: www.magnolias-blossom-cypress.com

Cuisine: New Southern cuisine
Executive Chef: Donald Drake
Price Range: Lunch/$7-$16
Dinner/$18-$28
Cookbook: *Magnolias Uptown/ Down South Southern Cuisine*

Elwood's Ham Chowder

1 tablespoon vegetable oil
¾ pound (or 1½ cups) country ham, coarsely ground or minced
1½ cups onion, medium diced
1 tablespoon garlic slices
6 cups collards (stemmed, cut, and washed)
2 teaspoons thyme (or to taste)
2 teaspoons parsley
Salt and black pepper, to taste

2 teaspoons Tabasco sauce (or to taste)
1 (14-ounce) can small diced or crushed tomatoes with juice
3½ cups chicken stock
1 cup beef stock (canned broth may be used)
3 cups red potatoes, diced into ¼-inch pieces

In a heavy pot, slowly render the ham with the vegetable oil obtaining as little color as possible. Add the onions and garlic. Continue cooking over low heat until the onions and garlic are soft (a little more oil may be needed if the ham does not have enough fat). Slowly add the collards and allow them to wilt; this process may take several additions as collards are bulky when raw, but they do wilt down like any green. Add remaining ingredients and slowly bring mixture to a simmer. Continue cooking for 20 to 30 minutes until the potatoes are cooked through and tender. Skim the chowder of any foam or oil that may appear during the cooking process. Check seasoning and serve hot.

Yield: 6-8 servings

Editors' Note: *"Rendering" refers to heating the ham (over low to moderate heat) until the fat melts away. The melted fat is then used for cooking the onions and garlic. When rendering ham, begin by placing ham in a heavy-bottomed pan with just a little oil. Slowly increase to a moderate heat to extract the fat without browning the meat. A country ham may be ordered by calling 1-800-392-2266.*

❧❧❧❧❧❧❧❧❧❧❧❧❧❧❧❧❧❧❧❧❧❧❧❧❧❧❧❧❧❧❧❧

Carpaccio of Fried Green Tomatoes

Tomato Chutney

1 cup onions, julienned
2 cups cider vinegar
2 cups sugar

3 cups Roma tomatoes,
  julienned with seeds removed
1 tablespoon red pepper flakes

Combine all ingredients. Set aside.

Tomatoes

1 egg, beaten
1 cup buttermilk
Tabasco sauce, to taste
12 green tomatoes, thinly sliced

1 cup seasoned flour
2 cups panko bread crumbs
3 cups oil for frying

Beat first 3 ingredients in a bowl. Dip tomato slices in flour; shake off. Place tomato slices in buttermilk mixture and coat with bread crumbs. Fry in hot oil until brown.

Tomato Salad

1 cup cherry tomatoes
1 cup yellow tear drops
1 cup Dixie Dew drops
½ cup red onion, julienned

½ cup yellow pepper,
  julienned
1 tablespoon garlic
½ cup olive oil

½ cup red wine vinegar
Salt and pepper, to taste
Goat cheese, crumbled
½ cup fresh basil, chopped

Combine all ingredients, saving some cheese and basil for garnish.

Assembly

Place tomato chutney in center of plate. Top with 3 fried tomato slices and a generous serving of tomato salad. Garnish with cheese and basil.

Yield: 4 servings

Editors' Notes: *This carpaccio (kahr-PAH-chee-oh) is a medley of delicious tomatoes. Yellow tear drops and Dixie Dew drops are regional variations of the cherry tomato (which may be used alone, in the salad, if the other ones are unavailable). For a "peppier" flavor, add extra Tabasco sauce; add extra red pepper flakes (in chutney) if you like a hot and spicy taste. Do not use a substitute for panko bread crumbs (available in Asian markets, some supermarkets, and online—see page 220) as they make all the difference in the crispy taste.*

"Magnolia's—perhaps the city's most celebrated restaurant."
—*Southern Living* magazine

"Magnolia's, a smart uptown space, specializes in updated Southern food."
—*The New York Times*

McCrady's

*McCrady's perfectly combines Charleston's love of history
with its hunger for new ideas*

Address: 2 Unity Alley
Charleston, SC 29401
(Historic District)
Telephone: (843) 577-0025

Web Site: www.mccradysrestaurant.com
Cuisine: Contemporary American
Executive Chef: Michael Kramer
Price Range: Dinner/$18-$29

Hearts of Palm Salad

Walnut Vinaigrette

¼ cup Dijon mustard
2 tablespoons honey
¾ cup red wine vinegar
¼ cup lemon juice

½ cup walnut oil
1 cup canola oil
1 teaspoon finely chopped rosemary
Salt and pepper, to taste

In a medium-sized mixing bowl, briskly whisk together first 4 ingredients. Continue whisking and slowly drizzle in oils until emulsified. Add remaining ingredients. Set aside.

Salad

½ pound mixed baby lettuces
Salt and pepper, to taste
¼ pound fresh hearts of palm, blanched
½ cup chèvre (goat cheese), crumbled

½ cup candied walnuts
¼ cup cucumber (seeded and sliced
into ¼-inch pieces), optional

Dress greens well; season with salt and pepper. Place greens on plate, top with hearts of palm, sprinkle with chèvre, candied walnuts, and cucumber.

Yield: 4 servings

Editors' Notes: *Walnut oil can usually be found in gourmet shops or ordered online (see page 220). It is expensive, but it can be kept in the refrigerator indefinitely. Candied walnuts are sometimes available in food specialty shops. However, you may make your own by using the "Candied Pecans" recipe on page 96 and substituting walnuts for the pecans.*

❦❦❦❦❦❦❦❦❦❦❦❦❦❦❦❦❦❦❦❦

Grilled Veal Tenderloin

Sauce

4 cups red wine
4 tablespoons sugar
2 tablespoons Madeira

Salt and pepper, to taste
2 tablespoons butter, softened

Place first 2 ingredients in a small saucepan over medium heat. Reduce to approximately 1 cup, or until mixture coats back of spoon. Stir in Madeira, over heat, for another minute. Then add remaining ingredients. Set aside and keep warm.

Mixed Vegetables

2 tablespoons butter
2 large portabello mushrooms,
  cut into 1-inch pieces
1 bunch asparagus tips, blanched

8 red potatoes, roasted
2 sweet potatoes, peeled, cut into
  1-inch cubes and roasted
Salt and pepper, to taste

Melt butter in a large saucepan. Add mushrooms and cook until soft, about 3 minutes. Add remaining vegetables; season with salt and pepper. Set aside and keep warm.

Veal

4 (6-ounce) veal steaks

Salt and pepper, to taste

Heat grill to medium-high heat. Season all sides of veal well with salt and pepper. Place on grill at "10 o'clock" position; after 3 minutes, turn to "2 o'clock" position to achieve a criss-cross pattern. Turn veal over and repeat. Set aside and keep warm. To serve, place vegetables on center of the plate with sauce around the vegetables. Center veal on top.

Yield: 4 servings

Editors' note: *The "10 o'clock" and "2 o'clock" positions refer to the arrangement of veal on grill for marking purposes (i.e., to develop criss-cross grill marks on the steaks). This wine sauce is also good served over veal medallions or scaloppine.*

Recipient of the prestigious Dirona Award (2004)

Named by Charleston's *Post and Courier* as "Restaurant of the Year" (2002)

Featured as one of *Esquire Magazine's* "Best New Restaurants of 1999."

─────────────────

*Built in 1778, McCrady's is housed within one of the oldest existing taverns
in the United States. During George Washington's southern tour in 1791,
a party was held for him in The Longroom.*

Poogan's Porch

Charleston's oldest award-winning restaurant

Address: 72 Queen Street
Charleston, SC 29402
(Historic District)
Telephone: (843) 577-2337
Web Site: www.poogansporch.com

Cuisine: Lowcountry cuisine
Executive Chef: Jay Jackson
Price Range: Brunch/$4.25-$8.95
Lunch/$5.95-$9.95
Dinner/$13.95-$23.95

Walnut Encrusted Stuffed Chicken

4 boneless, skinless chicken breasts
2 cloves fresh garlic, minced
1 cup yellow onion, diced
4 ounces smoked ham, diced
1 cup mushrooms, diced
1 stick unsalted butter
1 bunch fresh chives, chopped

2 tablespoons fresh parsley, chopped
1 cup dry white wine
1 cup heavy cream
1 cup flour
2 eggs, well-beaten
2 cups walnuts, crushed
2 cups canola oil

Using a meat mallet, pound chicken breasts to achieve uniform thickness; set aside. In a medium pan, sauté next 4 ingredients in butter. When onions become translucent, add next 4 ingredients and simmer, briefly, to reduce wine and further intensify flavors. Slowly incorporate flour and continue stirring until mixture thickens. Remove stuffing mixture from heat and set aside to cool. Place a heaping tablespoon of stuffing on each chicken breast; roll breast, while tucking in the ends, to form a pocket. Using a standard breading technique, dredge breasts into flour, egg wash (beaten eggs plus 1 tablespoon water), and the crushed walnuts. Heat oil in a cast iron pan to approximately 350°. Pan fry breasts on all sides to achieve a crisp, golden texture. Place in a 400° oven and continue cooking until done.

Yield: 4 servings

Editors' Notes: *The chicken breasts may be prepared, in advance, and refrigerated until time to cook them. We prefer frying the chicken in an electric frying pan where it is easier to regulate the temperature.*

~9~9~9~9~9~9~9~9~9~9~9~9~9~9~9~9~9~9~9~9~9~9~

Shrimp Bisque

1 pound jumbo-sized shrimp	1 bunch fresh thyme,
⅓ cup tomato paste	save some for garnishing
3 cups shrimp shells	1 tablespoon garlic, minced
¾ stick unsalted butter	1½ cup white wine
4 slices Applewood-smoked bacon	2 quarts heavy cream
½ cup white onion	Salt and white pepper, to taste

Peel, devein, and remove tails from shrimp; save shells for bisque. Slice shrimp in half, length-wise, and steam for 3 minutes (or boil for 2 minutes) until all shrimp are bright pink-colored. Rub tomato paste over shrimp shells; roast shells in oven at 325° for 15 to 20 minutes. Remove from oven and set aside. Place the butter, along with the bacon and onions, in a medium-sized sauce pan and render fat from the bacon. Remove the bacon and add the shrimp shells with thyme, garlic, and remaining butter. Cook, stirring constantly, until garlic begins browning. Add wine and reduce mixture by 90%. Add cream and bring to a boil; reduce to a simmer, being careful not to scorch mixture. Reduce mixture by one-fourth and strain. Top each serving of bisque with 4 shrimp (8 halves). Garnish with thyme and serve warm.

Yield: 6 servings

Editors' Notes: *The addition of the shrimp shells adds a nice color to the mixture. If desired, dice shrimp and stir directly into bisque (bihsk) instead of placing the whole shrimp on top. Our tester suggests adding a few drops of Texas Pete hot sauce to the bisque. Applewood-smoked bacon may be ordered by calling 1-800-392-2266.*

Stuffed Carolina Quail

1 cup spinach, wilted in butter	4 semi-boneless quail
4 ounces smoked Gouda cheese	2 tablespoons extra virgin olive oil
6 oven-roasted shallots	½ cup seasoned flour

Combine first 3 ingredients. Divide mixture into four portions and stuff into body cavity of quail. Brush each bird, liberally, with extra virgin olive oil and lightly dredge in flour. In a hot pan, sear quail on both sides to achieve a golden crust. Transfer to a 425° oven and roast approximately 8 to 10 minutes or until firm to touch.

Yield: 2 servings

Editors' Notes: *Quail can often be found in frozen meat section of most supermarkets.*

> "Once you've tasted the food at Poogan's Porch,
> you'll understand why magazines like
> *Bon Appetit, Gourmet,* and *Cuisine* have requested their recipes."
> —*TravelHost* magazine

Slightly North of Broad

Distinguished from the crowd by its decor and approach to food

Address: 192 East Bay Street
Charleston, SC 29401
(Historic District)
Telephone: (843) 723-3424
Web Site: www.slightlynorthofbroad.net

Cuisine: Maverick Lowcountry
Executive Chef: Frank Lee
Price Range: Lunch/$7-$12
Dinner/$10-$22

S.N.O.B.'s Award-Winning Maverick Grits

Grits

4 cups water
1 tablespoon butter
½ teaspoon salt

1-1½ cups stone ground grits
¼ cup cream

Bring first 3 ingredients to a boil. Stir in grits. Reduce heat to low and cook, stirring occasionally, until grits are thick and creamy (approximately 40 minutes). Remove from heat. Stir in cream and additional butter, if desired. Keep warm.

Topping

1 tablespoon butter
4 ounces country ham, julienned
4 ounces smoked pork sausage, cut in circles
  (may substitute andouille or other spicy sausage)
12 shrimp, peeled and deveined
8 sea scallops, fresh or "dry pack"

2 cloves fresh garlic, minced
Pinch of Cajun spice
¼ cup tablespoons green onion, diced
¼ cup fresh tomato, seeded and diced
1 tablespoon water
1 additional tablespoon butter

Sauté ham and sausage in 1 tablespoon butter. Add shrimp and scallops and sauté for 1 to 2 minutes. Add next 2 ingredients and sauté 30 seconds; stir in next 2 ingredients. Add remaining ingredients, scraping browned bits on bottom of pan (makes a delicious sauce for coating the shrimp, scallops, ham, and sausage). Spoon grits onto plates in equal portions. Place 2 scallops and 3 shrimp, per person, on grits and spoon equal parts of topping per plate.

Yield: 4 servings

Editors' Note: *We recommend using "dry pack" scallops, though harder to find, as they actually brown when sautéed. This recipe is a melding of two favorite Lowcountry dishes— Lowcountry Boil and Shrimp and Grits. Country ham and andouille may be ordered by calling 1-800-392-2266.*

৯৯৯৯৯৯৯৯৯৯৯৯৯৯৯৯৯৯৯৯৯৯৯৯৯৯৯৯

Deviled Crab Cakes

1¾ pounds crab claw meat	2 whole eggs	¼ tablespoon pepper
½ medium green bell pepper	½ cup half-and-half	2 tablespoons yellow mustard
½ medium red bell pepper	½ cup cracker meal	¾ teaspoon Tabasco
½ medium red onion	¼ tablespoon salt	2 tablespoons lemon juice

Pick claw meat clean and mix together all ingredients. Let sit refrigerated for 20 minutes, allowing time for cracker meal to absorb moisture. Form cakes and roll in cracker meal; deep fry or sauté in canola oil.

Yields: 14-16 medium crab cakes

Key Lime Tart with Passion Fruit Sauce
Crust

1½ sticks softened margarine	Pinch of salt	1 cup pecans, chopped
5 tablespoons 10-X sugar	2 teaspoons ice water	1 10-inch springform pan
2 cups all purpose flour	2 teaspoons vanilla	

Combine first 2 ingredients and blend well. Sift together flour and salt. Combine ice water with vanilla. Alternating, add first one-third of flour to sugar mixture. Then add one-third of water mixture. Continue adding, alternately, until all flour and water mixture are used. Stir in chopped pecans; dough will be crumbly. Chill in refrigerator for 15 minutes. Remove dough from refrigerator and roll between two sheets of wax paper to a thickness of ¼-inch. Lay crust into the pan and bake at 350° until light brown, approximately 20 minutes. When crust is light brown, remove from oven and pour filling into crust. Continue baking at 350° for 10 more minutes. Remove from oven to wire rack to cool. Chill before serving.

Filling

3 cups Eagle Brand Condensed milk	Zest (grated peel) of 2 limes
⅔ cup Nellie & Joe's Key lime juice	5 egg yolks, beaten together

Mix milk with juice and zest. Stir in egg yolks. Set aside until crust is ready

Passion Fruit Sauce

½ cup water	½ cup passion fruit purée	Pinch of ground ginger
2 tablespoons pineapple juice	(about 1 passion fruit)	1 tablespoon cornstarch
1 cup sugar	Pinch of salt	

Combine ¼ cup water with next 3 ingredients; bring to a rolling boil. Add last 3 ingredients and return to a boil. Dissolve cornstarch in remaining ⅛ cup water and add to boiling mixture. Cook and stir until thickened; strain and chill. Drizzle over tart.

Editors' Note: *Passion fruit, also known as granadilla or star fruit, is available in supermarkets on a seasonal basis. It is irreplaceable in this scrumptious fruit sauce!*

"Contemporary Southern cooking is the buzz phrase at a number of restaurants contributing to Charleston's increasingly sophisticated dining scene... standouts include Slightly North of Broad." —*USA Today,* May 1999

Dozens of sweetgrass basket stands, similar to the one shown above, are scattered along Highway 17-N between Charleston and McClellanville, SC. A dying art, these hand-woven baskets have played an integral part in Lowcountry communities for over 300 years and present one of the oldest forms of African art in the United States. They are made from sweetgrass, once abundant in the Charleston area; however, it is now more elusive, making the baskets even more valuable. The weavers pay gatherers to go to Georgia's barrier islands to collect the sweetgrass, where they must face snake bites, hornet stings, and other unpleasantries during the gathering process. The baskets are sewn with Palmetto, plentiful in the area, which they call "mater." Often purchased by museum and art collectors throughout the world, sweetgrass baskets range in cost from about $39 to over $300, depending upon the size and intricacy of design. The baskets shown above were created by one of our favorite Lowcountry basket weavers, Mazie Brown. A variety of sweetgrass baskets may be ordered from Mazie by calling 843-336-3454.

Other Lowcountry
Inns & Restaurants

Inn at Middleton Place

Located on the bluffs of the Ashley River and secluded among tall pines and live oaks

Address: 4300 Ashley River Road
Charleston, SC 29414
Telephone: (843) 556-0500
Reservations: 1-800-543-4774
E-mail: theinn@middletonplace.org

Web Site: www.middletonplace.org
Category: Country Inn
General Manager: George Buell
Rate: $189-$400 (seasonal)

Sausage Crêpes

Crêpes

1 cup whole milk
¼ cup + 1 tablespoon all-purpose flour
3 large eggs

2 tablespoons vegetable oil
  (plus additional for cooking crêpes)

Blend all ingredients together in a mixing bowl with a hand mixer. Set aside.

Sausage Filling

12 ounces sausage
½ cup of onion, chopped

½ cup green pepper, chopped
¼ Parmesan cheese, grated

In a frying pan, over medium heat, cook first 3 ingredients together. While sausage filling is cooking, start the crêpes in a separate frying pan. The frying pan, used for the crêpes, should be a small pan (the size the crêpe will be); a crêpe pan works best. Heat the frying (or crêpe pan) on medium-to-low heat. Once heated, add enough oil to coat bottom of pan. Once oil reaches medium heat, pour enough crêpe batter into the pan to barely cover bottom. As soon as batter starts bubbling, flip the crêpe; it should only take about 20 seconds to cook the other side. Repeat with the remainder of the batter. After you finish the crêpes, place them flat on a plate. Add the sausage mixture, with sausage drained and crumbled, to the center of each one and sprinkle with cheese. Fold sides of crêpe over and serve hot.

Yield: 4 servings

Spinach and Parmesan Dip

1 (8-ounce) block cream cheese, softened
1 (10-ounce) box frozen spinach,
   thawed and drained

¼ cup Parmesan cheese, grated
¼ cup onion, minced
1 teaspoon of garlic, minced

Mix all ingredients together until well-blended. Serve either warm or cold with your favorite crackers or chips.

Yield: 2 cups

The Inn's Shrimp and Grits

½ cup onion, chopped
½ cup red pepper, chopped
½ cup green pepper, chopped
1 cup all-purpose flour
1 cup shrimp, peeled and cleaned
Vegetable oil

1 teaspoon garlic, chopped
1 teaspoon cayenne pepper
Salt and pepper, to taste
Water, as needed
Sherry, to taste
2 cups of prepared grits

Prepare grits according to directions on packaging. While grits are cooking, sauté first 3 ingredients together until onions are transparent. Lightly toss the shrimp in flour; set aside. Heat a separate frying pan until hot and add enough oil to cover bottom of pan. When oil is hot, add next 3 ingredients. When all ingredients are hot, add onions and peppers from first pan. Once all ingredients are mixed together and hot, add the shrimp. When shrimp starts to get pink, add water (only enough to make the mixture have a darkened base). Simmer, until thickened, and add a splash of sherry. Pour the shrimp mixture over the grits and serve hot.

Yield: 2 servings

The Inn at Middleton Place is a recipient
of the American Institute of Architects highest award.

"Charleston's Middleton Inn is a stark 20th-century counterpoint to the adjacent Middleton Place, a carefully preserved 18th-century plantation. Determined to avoid the ersatz Colonial edifice you'd expect to see on the site, Charles Duell, a descendant of the plantation's original owner, commissioned the Southern architectural team of W. G. Clark and Charles Menefee to design a bold geometric structure. But the interiors make the case for antebellum charm: cypress paneling, hand-crafted furniture, and fireplaces in each one of the 54 rooms."

—Michael Z. Wise
Travel & Leisure magazine, November 2001

Litchfield Plantation

Tastefully secluded since 1750

Address: Kings River Road
Pawleys Island, SC 29585
Reservations: 1-800-869-1410
Telephone: (843) 237-9121
E-mail: vacation@litchfieldplantation.com

Web Site: www.litchfieldplantation.com
Category: Country Inn
General Manager: Karl Friedrich
Rates: $138-$620 (seasonal)

Chef Orobosa's Eggs Benedict with Sage Hollandaise Sauce

4 egg yolks
Dash white pepper
1 teaspoon lemon juice
1 tablespoon hot water
2 cups melted butter, divided

Salt and pepper
½-1 teaspoon fresh sage, chopped fine
4 English muffins, split
8 slices Canadian bacon, lightly browned
8 eggs, poached

In a pre-heated double boiler, combine egg yolks sprinkled with next 3 ingredients. Whisk over medium-high heat until slightly thickened. Remove pan from heat and whisk in 1 cup of butter. Add a pinch of salt and pepper; stir in sage. Whisk in remaining cup of butter. Keep sauce warm. Toast muffins. Place bacon on top of open-faced muffins (toasted side up) and place an egg on top of bacon. Top with sauce.

Yield: 4-8 servings

Editors' Notes: *An all-time favorite, sage adds a new and flavorful twist to the sauce. Be sure to use real butter, not margarine or a butter substitute.*

≈≈≈≈≈≈≈≈≈≈≈≈≈≈≈≈≈≈≈≈≈≈≈≈≈≈≈≈

Sweet Potato Bisque

3 tablespoons of vegetable oil
½ cup onion, diced
2½ ounces leeks, sliced length-wise
1 pound of sweet potatoes,
    peeled and sliced into 1-inch cubes

1 tablespoon curry powder
3 cups chicken broth
1 cup apple juice
Salt and pepper, to taste
Boiled egg, chopped for garnish

Sauté onions in oil until soft. Add leeks and cook for another 2 minutes. Add next 3 ingredients and cook until potatoes are tender. Blend mixture in a blender or a food processor until smooth. Return mixture to heat and add apple juice, salt and pepper. Stir thoroughly. Serve hot and garnish with chopped egg.

Yield: 6 servings

Editors' Notes: *Butternut squash may be substituted for sweet potatoes, if desired.*

Cowcountry Oyster Pie

48 oysters (about 1 pint)
6 cups Saltine cracker crumbs
2 tablespoons green onions, diced
2 tablespoons country ham, diced
2 cups mayonaise
2 cups half-and-half

2 tablespoons fresh lemon juice
2 teaspoons dry mustard
1 teaspoon salt and pepper mix
1 teaspoon Tabasco
½ teaspoon Worcestershire sauce
2 egg whites

Preheat oven to 350°. Drain oysters for minimum of 30 minutes in a strainer. Coarsely crush crackers, by hand, and reserve a small amount to sprinkle on top. Line each dish with enough cracker crumbs to cover the bottom. Top with oysters, using 8 oysters per serving; sprinkle with onions and ham. Combine remaining ingredients in a separate bowl until well-mixed. Top oysters with this mixture until they are just covered. Sprinkle remaining cracker crumbs over top of each individual pie. Refrigerate, for at least an hour, prior to baking. Bake pies for about 12 minutes or until set. Serve whole.

Yield: 6 individual servings (serve in individual containers)

Editors' Notes: *This recipe should be made in individual 1-inch deep ramekin dishes or shallow bowls (approximately 4 to 6-inches in diameter) and served as individual appetizers.*

Chosen as one of the "Top Ten Most Romantic Inns"
for 2000 by *American Historic Inns.*

Highest rated ("excellent") of the Grand Strand properties in the prestigious Zagat Survey, qualifying the Plantation as one the "Top 50 U.S. Inns and B&Bs".

*Litchfield Plantation is an extraordinary retreat
on the principal 600 acres of a 1750s coastal rice plantation.*

Price House Cottage

This National Register property lies in the heart of Summerville's Historic District.

Address: 224 Sumter Avenue
Summerville, SC 29483
Telephone: (843) 871-1877
E-mail: phcbb@aol.com

Web Site: www.pricehousecottage.com
Category: B&B
Owners/Innkeepers: Jennifer & David Price
Rate: $145 (year-round)

Pumpkin Belgian Waffles
with Vermont Maple Syrup Whipped Cream

(Adapted from *Morning Glories*, by Donna Leahy)

2 cups all-purpose flour
¼ cup sugar
4 teaspoons baking powder
1 teaspoon salt
1 teaspoon cinnamon
1 teaspoon ginger

¼ teaspoon cloves
1½ cups milk
1 cup pumpkin purée, canned
4 eggs, separated
1 cup butter, melted

Preheat waffle iron (Belgian or regular). In a large bowl, combine first 7 ingredients. Whisk together the next 2 ingredients plus egg yolks. Stir pumpkin mixture into the dry ingredients and add melted butter. Beat egg whites until stiff and fold into pumpkin mixture. Ladle batter onto waffle iron and cook until steam ceases to escape from the iron, producing a lightly browned waffle.

Flavored Whipping Cream

1 cup whipping cream

2 tablespoons pure maple syrup

Whip cream until peaks begin to appear. Add syrup. Continue whipping the cream until stiff peaks form. Serve waffles with pure maple syrup and a generous scoop of the flavored whipped cream.

Yield: 6

Artichoke Baked Eggs

(Adapted from *The New Basics Cookbook* by Rosso and Lukins)

1 medium tomato,
   sliced ¼-inch thick, peeled and seeded
2 tablespoons unsalted butter
8 ounces lean ham, cubed
2 tablespoons freshly grated
   Parmesan cheese
¼ teaspoon salt

4 artichoke hearts, thinly
   sliced lengthwise. Use canned,
   but not marinated, artichoke hearts
3 tablespoons sour cream
4 eggs, separated
Freshly ground pepper, to taste
Chopped fresh parsley to garnish

Preheat oven to 450° and place pot of water on stove to boil. Slice, peel, and seed tomato; place between paper towels to absorb moisture. Sauté ham in 1 tablespoon unsalted butter until slightly browned. Remove to paper towel to absorb any liquid. Place ½ cup of ham in each of the bottoms of two oval 9 x 5 x 2-inch ramekins. Place tomato slices over ham to cover in single thickness. Sprinkle with Parmesan cheese and salt. Place the artichoke slices evenly over cheese and cover with sour cream. Spread sour cream evenly and place two indentations on each preparation with back of a spoon that has been run under hot water. Place the egg yolks in the indentations. In a small bowl, break up the egg whites with a fork so that they will flow as a liquid; do not beat the whites. Pour egg whites into the ramekins, being careful to keep the egg whites from running over the edge of the ramekins. Place ½ tablespoon of unsalted butter on top of each ramekin. Place the ramekins in a shallow roasting pan (or Pyrex baking dish) for a water bath. Fill with boiling water to reach approximately ⅖ the way up the ramekins. Bake for 11 minutes. Remove from the water bath and place ramekins on individual plates. Sprinkle with freshly ground pepper and garnish with freshly chopped parsley. There will be a small amount of liquid on top of the ramekin at the end of cooking. This is melted butter and not uncooked egg.

Yield: 2 servings

Editors' Notes: *One of our recipe testers suggests chopping the tomato into ½–inch cubes, using a 5 x3 x2-inch ramekin, and baking for 16 minutes or until egg whites are opaque. For individuals who do not care for "runny" eggs, scrambling the eggs (and pouring over layers of ham, cheese, tomatoes, and artichokes) is recommended. This variation would need to be cooked for 30 to 40 minutes in a 325° oven.*

Featured on cover of *The INNside Scoop's* Winter 1999-2000 edition.

One of the earliest houses in Summerville, the main house was built as a summer retreat from Charleston's heat and humidity. The cottage, a former servant's quarters at the rear of the property, is a past recipient of the Summerville Preservation Society Restoration Award.

Carriage House Restaurant

Gourmet dining in elegant surroundings

Address: Kings River Road
Pawleys Island, SC 29585
Telephone: (843) 237-9322
Web site: www.litchfieldplantation.com

Cuisine: Continental Lowcountry
Executive Chef: Orobosa Uwagbai
Price Range: Dinner/$22-$29

Pecan Encrusted Red Snapper

½ cup pecans, chopped
1 tablespoon fresh basil,
    chopped and divided
1 tablespoon fresh thyme, divided
4 (6-ounce) filets of snapper
Cooking oil

1 cup shiitake mushrooms, sliced
½ cup shallots, chopped
3 tablespoons dry white wine
2 cups beef stock
2 cups heavy cream
Salt and pepper, to taste

Mix together first 3 ingredients. Rub mixture into the flesh side of the filets. Heat oil in sauté pan over medium heat. With pecan side down (skin side up), brown filets quickly in hot oil—no more than 10 to 20 seconds. Remove filets from pan and transfer to a baking dish with the pecan side up; reserve oil. Bake filets 5 to 10 minutes in a 350° oven. Cook mushrooms and shallots, with remaining basil and thyme, over medium heat in sauté pan about 5 minutes. Deglaze pan with white wine; add beef stock and reduce to one-half. Stir in remaining ingredients. Spread sauce, vertically, over one-half of the snapper (leaving the pecan crust on other half of fish exposed). Allow sauce to flow over onto the serving plate—just a little bit above and below the fish.

Yield: 4 servings

Editors' Note: *To better understand how sauce is supposed to be served on the snapper, visualize the fish as an oval; the sauce will form a perpendicular oval covering one side of the fish with a small amount flowing onto the plate (a little above and below the fish). Fresh red snapper may be ordered by calling 1-800-556-2783.*

Lemon Swirl Ice-Cream Pie

Lemon Curd

1 cup sugar
6 tablespoons (¾ stick) unsalted butter
⅓ cup fresh lemon juice

2 large eggs
2 large egg yolks
1 teaspoon lemon peel, grated

Combine sugar, butter (cut into small pieces), and fresh lemon juice in top of double boiler, over pot of simmering water. Stir until sugar dissolves and butter melts. Beat together remaining ingredients until well-blended. Gradually whisk warm butter mixture into egg mixture. Return mixture to double boiler and cook, stirring constantly (about 10 minutes), until curd is thick and leaves a "path" on back of spoon when finger is drawn across spoon; do not boil. Transfer lemon curd to bowl, whisking to smooth if necessary. Press plastic wrap directly onto surface of curd and chill until cold, at least one hour. Curd may be made up to 3 days ahead and kept refrigerated.

Crust and Filling

1¼ cups ground toasted almonds
   (about 5 ounces)
1 cup graham cracker crumbs
¼ cup plus 3 tablespoons unsalted butter,
   melted

2 teaspoons lemon peel, grated
½ teaspoon almond extract
½ gallon vanilla ice cream, softened slightly
1 (12-ounce) basket strawberries,
   sliced and sugared to taste (optional)

Preheat oven to 325°. Butter a 9-inch spring form pan (with 2¾–inch high sides). Mix first 5 ingredients in a medium bowl until mixture is evenly moist. Press crumbs over bottom and 1 inch up the sides of a prepared pan. After baking crust 8 minutes, cool pan on rack. Spread half of ice-cream in crust, then spoon half of lemon curd over ice-cream. Put remaining ice-cream over curd and top with remaining curd, adding by tablespoons. Use a small knife to swirl curd into ice-cream to form an attractive design. Freeze until just firm, about 1 hour. Wrap with plastic wrap and freeze overnight (may be prepared up to 2 days ahead and kept frozen). Let pie stand 10 minutes at room temperature before serving. Cut pie into wedges and serve topped with strawberries, if desired.

Yield: 6-8 servings

Editors' Note: *Simple and tasty, this is an excellent dessert to serve following a seafood meal.*

"You don't have to be a guest staying at this secluded country inn to enjoy dinner, but it helps the mood. The setting is fabulous . . . Their Carriage House Club Restaurant, set in a one-story, brick building near the main house, drips with posh . . . But I'm spellbound by the dramatic full-length windows, for they reveal a marvelous view of the moss-draped, tree-shaded outdoors."
—Mark G. Stith
Southern Living magazine, May 2003

Middleton Place

Dining with spectacular views of the gardens at world-famous Middleton Place

Address: 4300 Ashley River Road
Charleston, SC 29414
Telephone: (843) 556-6020
E-mail: restaurant@middletonplace.org
Web Site: www.middletonplace.org

Cuisine: Lowcountry plantation fare
Executive Chef: Tim Bedwell
Price Range: Lunch/$5.95-$12.95
Dinner/$15.95-$21.95
(Reservations required)

Middleton Place's Tomato Pie

9-inch deep-dish pie crust
10 Roma tomatoes, thickly sliced
½ cup fresh basil (cut with scissors)

6 tablespoons fresh chives, chopped
¾ cup mayonnaise
1½ cups white Cheddar cheese, shredded

Preheat oven to 400°. Place pie crust in a deep-dish pie plate, prick, and bake for 5 minutes (leave oven on). Layer the tomato slices, basil, and chives until crust is filled (there should be 2 to 3 layers of each). In a bowl, mix mayonnaise and cheese; spread mixture on top of last layer and sprinkle with additional cheese. Bake for about 35 minutes or until light brown. Let stand for 5 minutes before cutting.

Yield: 6 servings

Editors' Notes: *The addition of sliced onions (Vidalia, if available), included as one of the layers, complements this recipe nicely. As a variation, substitute yellow Cheddar or another cheese. Serve with a fresh green salad, and you have a complete meal.*

Restaurants
Charleston Area, South Carolina

~~~~~~

Corn Pudding

2 cups fresh yellow corn
2 whole eggs
3 cups heavy cream

¼ teaspoon nutmeg
Pinch of salt and white pepper

Place yellow corn in a greased casserole pan. Mix all other ingredients together. Pour mixture over corn and bake for 45 minutes at 350° or until golden brown.

Yield: 6-8 servings

Editors' Note: *Goes well with turkey and ham at Thanksgiving.*

Huguenot Torte

3 whole eggs
2 cups sugar
1 cup flour
½ teaspoon baking powder
½ teaspoon salt

4 Granny Smith apples, chopped
4 cups pecans chopped
½ teaspoon vanilla extract
Whipped cream, optional

Beat eggs until frothy and lemon-colored. Add remaining ingredients and mix well. Pour into a greased sheet pan and bake at 325° for 15 to 20 minutes.

Yield: 8-10 servings

Editors' Notes: *Granny Smith apples have freckled green skin and are slightly tart (we hope this isn't descriptive of Granny Smith, whoever she is!). Huguenot Torte (TOHRT) is yummy served with whipped cream and festive garnished with a sprig of mint.*

Middleton Place, a National Historic Landmark and carefully preserved 18th-century plantation, has survived the American Revolution, the Civil War, earthquakes, and hurricanes. It has been home to many generations of the Middleton family beginning with Henry Middleton, President of the First Continental Congress; his son Arthur, a signer of the Declaration of Independence; his grandson Henry, Governor of South Carolina and an American Minister to Russia; and his great-grandson William, a signer of the Ordinance of Secession. Today the plantation (including extensive gardens, the plantation stables, and the house museum) is owned and operated by Middleton Place Foundation.

Old Village Post House

Set in the heart of a charming, historic seaside community

Address: 101 Pitt Street
Mt. Pleasant, SC 29464
Telephone: (843) 388-8935
Web Site: www.oldvillageposthouse.com

Cuisine: Lowcountry Bistro
Executive Chef: John Scoff
Price Range: Lunch/$6.25-$9.95
Dinner/$8.00-$17.95
Sunday Brunch/$6.50-$10.95

Pork Tenderloin with Bourbon Bacon Sauce

1 pork tenderloin

½ cup Bourbon Bacon Sauce

Grill tenderloin to temperature desired (medium-rare to medium is recommended). See page 220 for grilling suggestions.

Bourbon Bacon Sauce

5 pieces of bacon, finely chopped
2 shallots, diced
1 teaspoon garlic, minced

1 cup bourbon
2 cups of brown stock
Salt and pepper, to taste

Cook bacon in a pot over medium heat for 2 to 3 minutes. Add next 2 ingredients and cook an additional 2 to 3 minutes. Stir in bourbon and reduce until it becomes syrup-like. Add stock and reduce by one-fourth. Season to taste and serve over sliced tenderloin.

Yield: 4 servings

Lowcountry Collards

8 pieces of bacon, chopped
1 large onion, chopped
1 tablespoon of minced garlic
¾ cup of cider vinegar
1 bunch of collards (picked, chopped, and cleaned)

½ cup Worcestershire sauce
1 tablespoon of Tabasco sauce
1 cup of water
½ cup of brown sugar
Salt and pepper, to taste

Cook first 3 ingredients, in a large pot over medium-high heat, for 4 to 5 minutes. Add next 6 ingredients and bring to a boil. Lower heat, cover, and cook on low until greens are tender (about one hour). Add salt and pepper.

Yield: 4 servings

Eggplant Napoleon with Herbed Goat Cheese

1 large eggplant (cut into ½-inch slices), breaded and fried

1 large zucchini (cut into 1½-inch slices), breaded and fried

Balsamic Reduction Sauce (recipe below)

1 tablespoon basil pesto (may be purchased already prepared)

1 cup Herbed Goat Cheese

1 tomato, peeled and cut into 1½-inch slices

1 red bell pepper, roasted and sliced

2 tablespoons fresh basil chiffonade

Extra virgin olive oil

Fry zucchini and eggplant in olive oil; drain and set aside. Prepare Balsamic Reduction Sauce and Herbed Goat Cheese (recipes below); set aside. Smear pesto (5-inch in diameter) onto center of plate. On top of pesto, stack the following ingredients in order indicated: 1 slice of fried eggplant, 1 tablespoon of Herbed Goat Cheese, 1 tomato slice, 1 tablespoon of Herbed Goat Cheese, 1 slice of zucchini, 1 tablespoon of Herbed Goat Cheese, and red pepper slices. Top with basil chiffonade. Drizzle olive oil and Balsamic Reduction Sauce (recipe below) on top.

Herbed Goat Cheese

1 cup of goat cheese, softened

¼ cup of soft butter

2 teaspoons tarragon, chopped

2 teaspoons chives, chopped

2 teaspoons parsley, chopped

2 teaspoons basil, chopped

1 tablespoon garlic, minced

2 teaspoons lemon juice

4 dashes of Tabasco

Salt and pepper, to taste

Combine all ingredients together and mix well.

Balsamic Reduction Sauce

2 cups of balsamic vinegar   ½ cup of sugar   2 tablespoons of honey

Combine ingredients and cook over medium-low heat until thick.

Yield: 4 servings

Editors' Notes: *Basil chiffonade is julienned basil (or basil cut into long, thin strips). Basil pesto can usually be found in most supermarkets with the pasta sauces. It may also be ordered online (see page 220).*

"It's quintessential Southern comfort from the front door to the backyard."
—Lee Jenkins, *Charleston City Paper* (3/10/2004)

Located not far from Shem Creek, where you'll find the area's local shrimping fleet, the Old Village Post House was built in 1888 as a grocery store and residence. Its name is a reference to the post houses of 18th century America, when innkeepers provided food, drink and lodging for postal riders and coaches traveling through sparsely populated areas.

Oscar's

Quite simply fine dining at its best

Address: 207 W. 5th Street North
Summerville, SC 29483
Telephone: (843) 871-3800

Cuisine: American Eclectic
Executive Chef: David Langenstein
Price Range: Dinner/$8-$24

Bananas Oscar with Candied Pecans

1 ripe banana,
    sliced lengthwise and halved
4 tablespoons light rum
4 tablespoons banana liqueur
4 tablespoons brown sugar

3 tablespoon butter
4 scoops vanilla ice-cream
4 tablespoons candied pecans
Whipped cream, optional
Chopped pecans, optional

Peel and slice banana; set aside. Combine rum and next 3 ingredients in a sauté pan over medium heat. Bring to a simmer and add banana; cook briefly on each side. Keep warm.

Candied Pecans

4 ounces melted butter   2 cups pecan pieces   1 cup brown sugar

Combine all ingredients, spread evenly on a baking sheet, and bake at 450° for 8 to 10 minutes (do not overcook). Remove from oven and cool.

Assembly: Place 2 scoops of ice-cream in bowl with candied pecans and toss to coat. Pour bananas and sauce over ice-cream. Garnish with whipped cream and more pecans, if desired.

Yield: 2 servings

Editors' Note: *Prepare candied pecans in advance and roll ice-cream scoops in cool pecans until covered. Place 2 scoops of pecan-covered ice-cream balls into individual banana split (or ice-cream) dishes and place in freezer until ready to use. Save extra candied pecans for making more ice-cream balls, topping green salads, or snacking.*

Deep Fried Oysters Stuffed with Brie

½ cup freshly grated horseradish
2 cups bread crumbs
½ tablespoon fresh basil
1 tablespoon freshly chopped parsley
½ cup milk
3 eggs, beaten
2 cups flour

Salt and pepper, to taste
Old Bay seasoning, to taste
18 large select oysters
6 ounces Brie
6 slices apple-smoked bacon
18 toothpicks
2 cups mesclun greens, for garnish

Heat oil in fryer to 350°. Mix horseradish and next 3 ingredients together until blended. Add milk to beaten eggs in a separate bowl. Season flour with salt, pepper, and Old Bay seasoning. Cut bacon strips into thirds. Cut a slit into side of each oyster; stuff with Brie, wrap with bacon, and skewer with a toothpick. Dredge stuffed oyster in flour, dip in egg mixture, and then coat with bread crumbs. Deep fry oysters until golden brown, removing toothpicks when done. Serve with Champagne Sauce and Onion Marmalade.

Yield: 6 servings

Editors' Notes: *Brie (BREE) is a popular French cheese that has a mellow, soft interior. If apple-smoked bacon is unavailable, substitute another smoked bacon or order apple-smoked bacon by calling 1-800-392-2266. Mesclun (MEHS-kluhn) greens, also known as salad mix, is a combination of small, tender salad greens.*

Champagne Sauce

3 ounces champagne
1 teaspoon shallots
1½ cups heavy cream

6 ounces butter
Parsley

Add champagne (sham-PAYN) and shallots to sauce pan; reduce by one-half. Add cream, reduce by one-half. Whip in butter. Garnish with parsley.

Onion Marmalade

1 jumbo onion (sliced)
¼ cup apple cider vinegar
2 tablespoons white sugar

2 tablespoons brown sugar
¼ cup dry sherry
Salt and pepper, to taste

Heat heavy sauté pan. Add onion and cook until brown. Add next 4 ingredients and cook until dry. Add salt and pepper.

Considered "a restaurant worth repeating" among locals since 1982.

The Rice Paddy

The Rice Paddy presents upscale Lowcountry cuisine in a historic waterfront location.

Telephone: (843) 546-2021
Address: 732 Front Street
Georgetown, SC 29442

Cuisine: Lowcountry
Executive Chef: Priestly Myers
Price Range: Lunch/$6.95-$13.95
Dinner/$19.95-$28.95

Shrimp and Corn Chowder

½ stick unsalted buter
½ pound small shrimp, peel and reserve shells
¼ cup onion, minced
1½ cups potatoes, peeled and diced
1 teaspoon salt

Pinch of cayenne pepper
3 cups fresh corn kernels
Milk (at least 1½ cups)
1 pint heavy cream

Melt butter in heavy saucepan. Add shrimp and shells; cook 5 minutes. Remove shells and discard. Set shrimp aside. Add onion to butter and cook 1 minute. Add next 3 ingredients and stir, constantly, until potatoes start looking translucent. Stir in corn and cook another 2 minutes. Add enough milk to cover the vegetables. Simmer until potatoes are tender, about 15 to 20 minutes. Stir in cream and shrimp. Adjust seasonings, as needed.

Yield: 4-6 servings

Editors' Notes: *For an even richer soup, our tester suggests using ¾ cup of milk and ¾ cup of half-and-half (fat-free works fine) for the 1½ cups of milk. She also stresses the importance of constantly stirring the mixture, after adding the potatoes, so the potatoes won't stick or brown (which does not have a pleasing appearance in a cream-based soup).*

Restaurants
Georgetown, South Carolina

ఞ-ఞ-ఞ-ఞ-ఞ-ఞ-ఞ-ఞ-ఞ-ఞ-ఞ-ఞ-ఞ-ఞ-ఞ-ఞ-ఞ-ఞ-ఞ

Greek Style Orzo

1 cup orzo
2 cups chicken stock (or broth)
¼ cup heavy cream
2 tablespoons olive oil

1½ teaspoons fresh dill weed, chopped
¼ cup feta cheese, crumbled
Freshly ground black pepper, to taste

Cook orzo in chicken stock. Test for proper al dente after about 7 or 8 minutes; continue cooking as needed. Drain and combine with remaining ingredients. Serve immediately.

Yield: 4 servings

Editors' Notes: *Orzo (OHR-zoh), Italian for "barley," is a tiny rice-appearing pasta available at most supermarkets. It is often used in soups. "Al dente" is an Italian phrase used to describe the cooking of pasta (or other food) just to the point where there is a slight resistance when it is bitten into, but not overcooked or soft. Feta is a classic Greek cheese which has a rich, tangy flavor and is easily crumbled.*

Mustard Coated Grouper with Herbed Cream Sauce

4 (6-8 ounce) grouper filets
Salt and pepper, to taste
Dijon mustard
4 teaspoons mustard seed
All-purpose flour

4 cups olive oil or clarified butter
2 tablespoons white wine
½ cup fish or chicken stock
1 cup heavy cream
1 tablespoon fresh herbs, chopped

Season filets with salt and pepper. Spread each with a thin coat of mustard. Press 1 teaspoon of mustard seed onto each filet and dredge in flour. Heat oil in heavy skillet. Place fish in pan and brown evenly on both sides. Transfer fish to oven-proof dish and bake at 350° about 10 minutes. Meanwhile, discard excess oil from skillet and return to burner. Deglaze pan with next 3 ingredients and reduce until slightly thickened. Stir in herbs and check seasoning. Serve over grouper.

Yield: 4 servings

Editors' Notes: *Basil, thyme, and parsley work well for the herbs. Use less if dried herbs are used. Fresh grouper may be ordered from MaineLobsterDirect.com or by calling 1-800-556-2783.*

> "A cookery that has flair and flavor, with a finesse and consistency
> that keep the most discriminating palates of Georgetown
> returning again and again."
> —*Frommer's The Carolinas and Georgia*, 6th Edition

Seewee Restaurant

A general store turned into a restaurant serving homemade specialties

Address: 4808 Highway 17N
Awendaw, SC 29429
(north of Charleston)
Telephone: (843) 928-3609

Web Site: www.thefoodscoop.com/
seewee.html
Cuisine: Southern-style cooking & seafood
Price Range: Lunch/$5.95-$10.95
Dinner/$8.95-$19.95

Mary's Okra and Tomato Soup

1 meaty ham bone
4 cups ripe red tomatoes, cored and chopped

4 cups fresh okra, cut cross-wise
Salt and pepper, to taste

Place ham bone in 4 cups of boiling water. Lower heat and continue cooking until meat falls off bone. Add tomatoes (or purée) and cook for about an hour. Add okra last, season with salt and pepper, and cook on low heat until tender (about thirty minutes).

Yield: 6-8 servings

Contributor's Note: Four cups of tomato purée or 4 cups of canned tomatoes (undrained) may be substituted for fresh tomatoes. Two (6-ounce) packages of frozen okra may be substituted for fresh okra. For a good vegetable soup, add desired amount of fresh or frozen green lima beans and corn. Add beans with tomatoes and add corn with okra. Cook an additional hour.

Editors' Notes: *Instead of using a ham bone, brown 1 pound of ground chuck (or Italian-style chopped-up sausage) in a Dutch oven, breaking up with a metal spatula. Add 4 cups of water, tomatoes, and okra; season to taste. Before serving, sprinkle soup with grated Parmesan or Cheddar cheese. Extra good with additional vegetables (petite lima beans and shoepeg white corn) added. A dollop of sour cream, served on top, is also a tasty addition.*

Lowcountry Boil

3 pounds small white potatoes
Salt and pepper, to taste
Old Bay seasoning, to taste
1 lemon, sliced
3 garlic cloves

3 pounds Hillshire Sausage,
    cut into 1-inch slices
5 pounds corn-on-the-cob,
    fresh or frozen
5 pounds shrimp, shells on
3 dozen small clams (in shell)

Put potatoes and seasonings in pot with enough water to cover; simmer until almost done. Add sausage and corn; cook until done. Add clams and shrimp; cook until pink. Serve hot.

Yield: 15 servings

Editors' Note: *Along the South Carolina/Georgia coast, a Lowcountry Boil is more than a popular meal, it is an event steeped in Lowcountry tradition. The classic coastal dish, sometimes referred to as Frogmore Stew, offers diners a variety of culinary choices in one big pot. It is served in a casual outdoor setting.*

Sweet Potato Casserole

4 large sweet potatoes,
    cooked and peeled
4 eggs
1 cup brown sugar
1 stick butter, softened

1 tablespoon vanilla
1 cup evaporated milk
1 tablespoon apple pie spice
1 cup pineapple, crushed and drained
1 cup marshmallows, small or large

Mix first 8 ingredients well and pour into a greased 8x10-inch casserole dish. Top with marshmallows and bake at 350° for 30 minutes or until set.

Yield: 6-8 servings

Editors' Notes: *Flaked coconut and/or chopped pecans also make nice additions to this classic Southern dish.*

"You'll love the food at this little gem of a restaurant!"
—*Southern Living* magazine, 2003

Recommended as one of the "top choices" for Lowcountry cuisine by travel writer Lynn Seldon, *New York Post*.

Listed as one of South Carolina's Secrets in
100 Secrets of the Carolina Coast,
by Randall H. Duckett and Maryellen K. Duckett

Woodlands Dining Room

Woodland's Dining Room, the only AAA Five Diamond award-winning dining room in South Carolina, enjoys a stellar reputation from food critics around the world.

Address: 125 Parsons Road
Summerville, SC 29483
Telephone: (843) 875-2600
Web Site: www.woodlandsinn.com/
dining.cfm
Cuisine: New American

Executive Chef: Ken Vedrinski
Price Range: $59 (A la carte menu)
$120 ("Tasting" menu)
$120 (Chef's Table in
the kitchen)

Butternut Squash Soup

3 strips smoked bacon
1 large sweet onion, chopped
3 stalks celery, peeled and chopped
1 large butternut squash, peeled, seeded,
diced and cubed into 1-inch cubes
4 cups chicken stock (may use canned)

1 leek (white part only), chopped
1 cup crème fraîche (krehm FRESH)
or whipping cream (see page 220)
Salt and white pepper, to taste
2 tablespoons of organic honey
Chives and pancetta (or smoked duck)

Sauté first 3 ingredients, then add next 3 ingredients. Simmer until squash is soft; add next 4 ingredients and blend together. Pass through a strainer. Garnish with chives and pancetta or smoked duck.

Yield: 4-6 servings

Editors' Notes: *For ease in peeling squash, pierce it with a fork and then cook it in a microwave about 5 minutes (or until tender) as you would cook a baking potato. Peeled and cubed butternut squash is now available in the produce section of many grocery stores. Save the pulp of the squash, after straining, and place it in a casserole dish topped with bread crumbs. Bake at 350° for 30 minutes for a delicious side dish. A leek has a white stalk with a bulbous end, and it is related to both the onion and the garlic. According to legend, Nero thought a large consumption of leeks would improve his singing voice; he devoured them. Pancetta (pan-CHEH-tuh) is a salty, Italian bacon which can be ordered by calling Nueske's at 1-800-392-2266.*

Butter-Poached Maine Lobster

Lobster

2 (1¼ pounds) live Maine lobsters
¼ cup white wine

1 large shallot, minced
¼ cup unsalted butter, cold

In a large stock pot, bring 1 gallon of water to a boil. Submerge live lobsters in water for 3 minutes; remove and submerge in ice-water to stop cooking process. Remove lobster claws and tails from shells (meat will not be fully cooked). In a small saucepan, bring white wine and half the minced shallot to a simmer. Reduce by one-half and whisk in butter. When butter emulsifies, add lobster meat and poach over medium-low heat (about 2 minutes).

Corn, Squash, and Mushrooms

2 fresh ears Silver Queen corn
(may substitute yellow corn)
¼ cup unsalted butter, cold
¼ cup fresh tarragon, finely chopped
Salt and white pepper, to taste

1 large sunshine Kobash
(or butternut) squash,
peeled and finely diced
½ cup chicken stock
½ pound fresh chanterelle mushrooms

Remove corn kernels from 1 cob. Run the second cob over a box grater to remove corn milk, then pass the milk through a fine sieve. In a sauté pan, sauté corn kernels with remaining minced shallot. Add corn milk and cook until creamy. Whisk in butter and add tarragon, salt, and white pepper to taste. Using a large sauté pan, sauté squash over low heat, until soft; add chicken stock and simmer 10 minutes. Heat olive oil in medium sauté pan until oil begins to smoke. Add mushrooms and sauté until lightly caramelized. Add salt and white pepper to taste. On each serving plate, place the squash so the corn can be spooned on top of it. Place lobster next to the squash-corn mixture and top with the mushrooms.

Yield: 4 servings

Editors' Notes: *Live Maine lobster may be ordered by calling MaineLobsterDirect.com at 1-800-556-2783.*

"Woodlands Resort & Inn was recently named, by the readers of *Condé Nast Traveler,* as their second favorite small hotel in North America."
— *Condé Nast Traveler*, November 2000

"… The most atmospheric, full-service place to stay in the region."
— *Departures*, November/December 2000

*A white-pillared Classical Revival building,
originally constructed in 1906, Woodlands stands upon 42 landscaped acres.*

"The most beautiful city in North America" —*Le Monde*

One of the "Top 12 Trendy Hot Spots in the World" —*New York Times*

One of "America's Top 10 U. S. Cities to Visit" —*Conde Nast Traveler*

One of "Top 200 places in the Country" —*Forbes Magazine*

One of "Top 10 Southeast Cities for Family Vacations" —*Family Fun Magazine*

"The stretch of coast from Savannah southward is...the most beautiful place in the world." —Margaret Mitchell, author of *Gone With the Wind*

Welcome to Savannah, the sultry and mysterious "Belle" of the Southeastern coast. Savannah captivates the suitors that come to call with her natural beauty, eccentric charm and traditional Southern Hospitality—because Savannah is genteel, gracious and captivating. Savannah is the beautifully preserved hidden treasure of the Low Country. Come unlock the history, romance and beauty that lies within. Explore every nook and cranny because you are her guest and Savannah loves sharing her treasures with you.

Web Site for Savannah, GA
www.savannahvisit.com

Savannah

"Soul of the South"

Picturesque Johnson Square is a magical place to savor Savannah

Ballastone Inn

Savannah's first and premiere Bed and Breakfast Inn

Address: 14 E. Oglethorpe Ave.
Savannah, GA 31401
(Historic District)
Reservations: 1-800-822-4553
Telephone: (912) 236-1484

Web Site: www.ballastone.com
Category: Historic Inn
Owners/Innkeepers:
Jim & Jennifer Sallandi
Rates: $195-$475 (seasonal)

Melon Breakfast Soup

1 ripe honey dew
1 ripe cantaloupe
¼ cup orange juice
2 ripe bananas

2 tablespoons lemon juice
½ cup whipped cream or plain yogurt
2 tablespoons fresh or dry dill
Sliced strawberries or a fresh mint sprig

In a food processor, purée melons 2 cups at a time, adding a little orange juice to assist in purée process. Purée melons until smooth and lump free. Pour into a large bowl. Next, purée bananas, adding lemon juice to prevent browning. Add puréed bananas to melon mixture. Then add the dill and whipped cream (or plain yogurt) to melon and banana mixture. Gently whip together and chill two hours or overnight. Garnish with sliced strawberries or a fresh mint sprig.

Yield: 6 servings

Editors' Notes: *If purchasing pre-cut melon chunks, use about 2 cups of honey dew and 2 cups of cantaloupe. We prefer this recipe prepared without the bananas and with whipped cream. Save the cantaloupe halves and ladle soup into them for a novel and impressive presentation. This is an ideal breakfast or luncheon soup to serve during the warmer months. Other easy and delicious fruit soups (or a refreshing fruit "smoothie") may be created by replacing the melon with 2 cups of your favorite fruit (either fresh or frozen/thawed); our favorite fruit choices include cantaloupe, peaches, strawberries, raspberries, or frozen orange juice concentrate. Add ½ cup whipped cream (or low-fat half-and-half) and approximately 2 tablespoons sugar (or Splenda). Blend in a blender until smooth, adding more or less cream/half-and-half depending on desired thickness (less for soups and more for smoothies). Serve chilled. Any of these variations may be flavored, to taste, with a white wine.*

అఅఅఅఅఅఅఅఅఅఅఅఅఅఅఅఅఅఅఅఅఅఅఅఅఅఅఅ

Sweet Rolls

½ cup water
½ cup milk
3 tablespoons butter
1 teaspoon salt
2 tablespoons sugar
4-5 cups all-purpose flour

¼ cup warm water
½ teaspoon sugar
1 tablespoon yeast
1 egg
1 cup butter or margarine, room temperature

½ cup light brown sugar
1 tablespoon cinnamon
1 cup pecans, optional
½ cup raisins, optional

Combine first 5 ingredients in a saucepan. Heat mixture until butter is melted. Set aside to cool. Pour 4 cups of flour into a large bowl or mixer bowl; make a well in center and set aside. In a small mixing bowl, combine next 3 ingredients and allow mixture to rise (about 5 minutes). After first mixture has cooled, add egg. Combine two mixtures. Stir and pour into flour well. Using dough hook of a mixer, mix until smooth and elastic. Remove dough from bowl. If dough is very sticky, add more flour until dough is soft and manageable. Knead dough by hand for an additional 3 to 5 minutes or until dough is smooth. Put dough into a well greased bowl and cover with plastic. Allow to double in size (35 minutes to 1 hour). While dough is rising, whip together next 3 ingredients. Set aside. Once dough has doubled in size, beat down and divide into two equal pieces. Roll out one piece at a time and spread with butter mixture. Once dough is completely covered, sprinkle with nuts and/or raisins. Begin rolling dough from top to bottom, pulling the dough as it is being rolled. Once the dough is completely rolled, cut each log into 2-inch round pieces and place into greased pans. Repeat with remaining dough. Cover each pan with plastic and allow dough to double in size (about 30 minutes). Once doubled, unwrap and bake in a 350° oven 25 to 30 minutes or until golden brown. Allow to cool slightly, and then pour or drizzle icing over top of rolls.

Yield: 12 rolls

Icing

1 (1-pound) box powdered (10-X) sugar   ¼ cup half-and-half (or milk)

Mix together until smooth. Add more milk, if needed.

Editors' Note: *Our friend who tested this recipe, one of the best home-bakers we know, reports: "It is the best sweet roll recipe I've ever used." Instead of using the dough hooks of a mixer, she kneaded the dough (by hand) for 9 minutes. She recommends putting all the rolls into a 9 x 13-inch pan, sprayed with a non-stick spray, for the second rise and baking time.*

"Best In the State" —*Zagat Survey*, 2001

"It is worth the effort to obtain such accommodations
if you really want to walk in Savannah's spirit." —*The New York Times*

"Romantic is doubtless an over-worked adjective, but it is now quite appropriate when referring to this stylishly-appointed jewel, which possesses a thoroughly gracious and beguiling sense of historic continuity."
—Andrew Harper's *Hideaway Report, June 2004*

Eliza Thompson House

Southern hospitality and romantic elegance for discriminating travelers

Address: 5 West Jones Street
Savannah, GA 31401
(Historic District)
Reservations: 1-800-348-9378
Telephone: (912) 236-3620

Web Site: www.elizathompsonhouse.com
Category: Historic Inn
Innkeeper: Jean Bearden
Rates: $169-$269 (seasonal)

Baked Brie with Almonds

1 (9-inch) refrigerated pie crust
1 small round Brie

4-5 tablespoons peach preserves
Sliced almonds, put a few aside for topping

Preheat oven to 350°. Slice Brie in half (through the middle) and place one-half in center of the crust (see note below). Spread a small amount of preserves on top of Brie and then place the second half of Brie on top. Spread another layer of preserves on top of second half of Brie and sprinkle with sliced almonds. Fold the pie crust around the Brie, pinching edges together; top with additional almonds. Bake for 20 minutes or until crust is golden brown (if cheese starts oozing out of pastry, go ahead and remove from oven). Serve with Ritz crackers, plain bagel chips, or toast rounds.

Yield: 8-10 servings

Editors' Notes: *This dish is always a favorite! A wedge of Brie may be used, but it is easier to encase a round of Brie in the pastry. It is easier to work with the pastry when a one-quarter wedge of the pie crust is cut out and the remaining pie shell is pieced back together (this makes a smaller pastry circle which is easier to cover the Brie with). Our testers used a Pillsbury refrigerated pie crust with good results and agree that this recipe is much better when served fresh out-of-the-oven than when sitting at room temperature a few hours. However, it may be prepared in advance and baked about 25 to 30 minutes before serving time. To provide a glossy crust, mix an egg yolk with a little water and brush on top of pastry prior to baking. Raspberry preserves works well with this recipe as a substitute for the peach preserves.*

❦❦❦❦❦❦❦❦❦❦❦❦❦❦❦❦❦❦❦❦❦❦❦❦

Salsa Egg Casserole

½ cup mild salsa
½–1 cup shredded Cheddar cheese
4 eggs

1 tablespoon chopped green chilies,
  optional
¾ cup milk

Preheat oven to 350°. Grease a 1 quart casserole dish and spread salsa on bottom of dish. Sprinkle Cheddar cheese evenly over the salsa. Mix together the next 3 ingredients and pour mixture over cheese. Bake at 350° for 30 to 40 minutes or until eggs are firm. Serve with additional salsa, on the side, if desired.

Yield: 3-4 servings

Editors' Notes: *This casserole is also good topped with crumbled pre-cooked bacon; just add before baking. Instead of using a casserole dish, this recipe may be prepared in a 9-inch pie dish and then served in wedges. When prepared in this way, it appears similar to a crustless quiche. Either way it is a good and easy-to-prepare recipe which may be assembled in advance and refrigerated until time to bake.*

Miss Virginia's Peach and Pecan Dip

1 (8-ounce) block cream cheese
½ cup peach preserves

1 cup chopped pecans
Crackers or bread rounds

Bring the cream cheese to room temperature and blend in a small food processor (or with a hand beater) until smooth. Stir in peach preserves and mix well. Fold in chopped pecans, reserving a teaspoonful to sprinkle on top. Refrigerate for at least 2 hours before serving. Serve chilled or at room temperature with your favorite crackers or toasted bread rounds.

Yield: 10-12 servings

Editors' Notes: *Another flavor of preserves, such as apricot or strawberry, may be substituted for the peach. This dip also makes a nice topping for small open-faced sandwiches on a party tray. For a tasty variation, substitute a chutney for preserves.*

The Eliza Thompson House, a Federal style three-story mansion is one of the oldest bed and breakfast inns in Savannah. Built for Eliza Thompson in 1847, the landmark recalls a prosperous time in Savannah when elegant parties in fine homes were popular.

The Foley House Inn

A unique combination of Southern hospitality and European charm

Address: 14 W. Hull Street
Savannah, GA 31401
(Historic District)
Reservations: 1-800-647-3708
Telephone: (912) 232-6622

Web Site: www.foleyinn.com
Category: Historic Inn
Owners/Innkeepers:
Beryl & Donald Zerwer
Rates: $200-$345 (seasonal)

Tomato and Basil Spread

¾ cup mayonnaise
½ cup sour cream
¼ teaspoon salt
⅛ teaspoon white pepper

½ tablespoon Accent
3 Roma tomatoes, unpeeled and sliced
½ cup fresh basil, finely chopped
White or wheat bread rounds

Mix together first 5 ingredients. Stir in tomatoes and basil. Keep refrigerated until ready to use. Spread on top of bread rounds.

Editors' Notes: *Roma tomatoes are medium-sized and oblong-shaped. This makes an attractive and delicious spread for open-faced sandwiches.*

༺༻༺༻༺༻༺༻༺༻༺༻༺༻༺༻༺༻༺༻༺༻༺༻༺༻༺༻

Cheese Blintzes with Cherries

Batter

1 cup milk	4 eggs	Pinch salt
1 cup flour	¼ cup sugar	Butter-flavored
1 tablespoon sour cream	1 teaspoon vanilla	cooking spray

Combine first 3 ingredients, blending well. Mix in 1 egg at a time, using a hand-beater, until batter is smooth. Stir in next 3 ingredients. Heat a crêpe (KRAYP) or 6-inch frying pan over high heat until very hot, but not smoking. Spray bottom of pan with cooking spray or wipe with a piece of slightly buttered waxed paper; return to lowered heat. Cover bottom of pan with thin layer of batter, turning in all directions until batter covers entire bottom of pan. Pour out any excess (crêpes should be ultra-thin). Cook until golden on one side, approximately 1 minute, and then turn and cook until golden on other side. When cooked, remove crêpe and stack on a platter. Repeat until all batter is used, re-greasing pan between crêpes. Makes 6-8 crêpes, depending on size of pan.

Filling

1 cup cottage cheese	1 egg yolk	½ teaspoon vanilla
4 ounces cream cheese	3 teaspoons sugar	

Mix all ingredients for the filling and set aside.

Coulis

½ cup cherries, pitted	¼ cup sugar	1 tablespoon cornstarch,
½ cup water	½ teaspoon lemon juice	dissolved in water

Boil fruit and water for 3 minutes. Over medium heat, stirring constantly, add sugar and lemon juice. Bring mixture back to a boil and slowly stir in the dissolved cornstarch mixture. Boil coulis (kool-LEE) 1 minute to thicken.

Assembly

Fill each crêpe with approximately 3 tablespoons of filling. Fold outsides to center and roll blintze (BLIHNTS) until completely closed. Place rolled blintzes in a pan and sauté about 2 minutes, turning once. When ready to serve, place blintzes in a 350° oven for about 20 minutes. Ladle coulis over blintzes after transferring to serving platter or individual plates.

Yield: 6 servings

Editors' Notes: *If possible, prepare crêpes in advance. The crêpes may be frozen stacked; they may be filled before freezing or after defrosting. Preparing crêpes in advance is a tremendous time-saver and highly recommended. Raspberries or blueberries, substituted for the cherries, also work well in this recipe.*

Named by *Discovering Traveler*
as a Top "Romantic Hideaway of 1999"

Rated one of ten "Most Romantic Inns" in the country
by *Vacation* Magazine.

The Gastonian

*The only Relais & Chateaux property in Georgia, The Gastonian
is known all over the world for its legendary hospitality and historic elegance.*

Address: 220 E. Gaston Street
Savannah, GA 31401
(Historic District)
Reservations: 1-800-322-6603
Telephone: (912) 232-2869

Web Site: www.gastonian.com
Category: Historic Inn
Owner/Innkeeper: Anne Landers
Rates: $250-$425 (seasonal)

Lemon Ricotta Cheese Pancakes

1 cup all-purpose flour
3 tablespoons sugar
4 teaspoons baking powder
½ teaspoon salt

6 teaspoons lemon juice
2 cups part skim milk ricotta cheese
6 eggs, separated
¼ cup corn oil

Combine first 4 ingredients in bowl of an electric mixer. Beat in next 2 ingredients until smooth. Beat egg whites until stiff peaks form; set aside. Beat eggs yolks and oil into flour mixture. Fold eggs whites into batter after all ingredients are combined. Stir until smooth. Heat a lightly greased griddle (or skillet) over medium-high heat. Ladle batter onto griddle to form 3-inch cakes. Cook until small bubbles form and the edges begin browning, 2 to 3 minutes. Turn cakes and continue cooking 1 to 2 minutes longer, until just cooked through. Repeat procedure until all batter is used.

Yield: 12 pancakes

Editors' Notes: *Light and delicious, these pancakes are ideal to serve on a spring morning. We think the addition of 2 teaspoons of lemon zest enhances the wonderful flavor even more. Garnish with powdered sugar and serve with syrup, if desired.*

Vidalia Onion Bites

1 cup mayonnaise
1 cup Parmesan cheese
1 Vidalia onion, finely chopped

Sliced bread, crust removed
(white or wheat works best)

Mix all ingredients and spread onto bread. Cut into bite-size pieces and bake at 375° for approximately 10 minutes or until light brown.

Yield: About 3 dozen servings

Editors' Note: *An easy and delicious hors d'oeuvre using Georgia's famous Vidalia onions. If Vidalia onions are unavailable, use another sweet onion.*

Almond Skillet Cake

¾ cup butter or margarine
1-1½ cups sugar
2 eggs
1-1½ cups all-purpose flour, sifted

Pinch of salt
1 teaspoon almond flavoring
½ cup sliced almonds
Sugar to taste

Melt butter; add to sugar, in a large mixing bowl, and mix well. Beat in eggs, one at a time. Add next 3 ingredients, mixing well. Line a cast iron skillet with aluminum foil (foil should be hanging over sides of skillet). Pour batter into skillet, cover with almonds, and sprinkle with sugar. Bake for 40 minutes at 350°. Remove from skillet when cool, but do not slice until the next day.

Yield: 6-8 servings

Editors' Note: *This recipe has become one of our favorites!*

Featured in February 2002 edition of *Architectural Digest.*

"...one of the best inns in the United States." —Andrew Harper's *Hideaway Report*

"...the Grand Dame of Savannah inns." —*Great Country Inns*

"...The most famous of Savannah inns and justifiably so."
—*The New York Times*

"...one of the 12 most romantic inns on the East Coast." —*The Discerning Traveler*

Hamilton Turner Inn

Savannah's "Grand Victorian Lady"

Address: 330 Abercorn Street
Savannah, GA 31401
(Historic District)
Reservations: 1-888-448-8849
Telephone: (912) 233-1833

E-mail: info@hamilton-turnerinn.com
Web Site: www.hamilton-turnerinn.com
Category: Historic Inn
Owners/Innkeepers: Jane & Rob Sales
Rates: $175-$295 (seasonal)

Benjamin's Baked Pancake

3 eggs
1 cup flour
1 teaspoon cinnamon
1 teaspoon nutmeg

2 tablespoons sugar
1 teaspoon vanilla
1½ cups milk
3 tablespoons butter

Preheat oven to 375 to 400°. Combine first 7 ingredients. Mix well. Melt butter until bubbly (but not brown) and pour into a deep-dish pie pan or a square casserole dish. Quickly pour all batter into pan and put into preheated oven. Bake for 20 to 30 minutes or until golden brown and firm. The sides will be high and dry; center will be shallow and soft. Slip pancake onto plate and fill center with fruit and/or sour cream, jam, or sprinkle with 10-X sugar and a squeeze of lemon.

Yield: 4 servings

Editors' Notes: *This is a versatile dish which lends itself to a variety of delicious variations. We especially like the dish sprinkled with 10-X sugar, topped with a dollop of sour cream, and finished off with strawberries sprinkled with more 10-X sugar. It is also excellent sprinkled with 10-X sugar and lemon juice. If uncertain which filling to use, serve it plain and provide an assortment of toppings so each person may make their own selection.*

Anna's Mango Chutney Spread

1 (8-ounce) block cream cheese,
   room temperature
½ stick butter, softened
1-2 teaspoons curry powder (or to taste)

¼ cup green onions or chives,
   finely chopped
1 jar mango chutney, use as needed

Line small loaf pan (or use an 8-ounce ramekin) with plastic wrap, allowing enough extra wrap to cover the dish when filled. Blend together first 3 ingredients and stir in onions or chives. Chill overnight (or for several hours) so shape holds when unmolded. Just before serving, remove from pan (or ramekin) and remove plastic wrap. Top with enough chutney to cover and serve with crackers and/or fresh vegetables.

Yield: 10-15 servings

Editors' Note: *Our tester suggests garnishing the top of this spread with toasted pecans or another type of nut and using green onions for extra crunch. Real butter and regular (not fat-free) cream cheese seem to work best. Other types of chutneys may also be used in this recipe. Add curry powder, gradually, to suit your personal taste; some prefer much more than others.*

Ozella's Famous Shortbread

2 sticks real butter, softened
¾ cup sugar

2 cups self-rising flour
Powdered 10-X sugar

Cream butter and sugar, in a mixing bowl of a stand-up mixer, on medium-low speed until fluffy. Add flour and mix thoroughly. Stop once, scrape sides, and mix again. Roll or spread batter out (about one-half inch thick) onto a greased or parchment-lined cookie sheet. Bake in 325° oven for 30 minutes or until lightly browned. Sprinkle with powdered sugar and cut into small squares.

Yield: Approximately 30 pieces of shortbread

Editors' Notes: *This 3-ingredient recipe seems too easy to be so good. Margarine or a "light" butter will not work in this recipe. Real butter is needed to produce the rich, buttery flavor that makes it so tasty. Also, be sure not to substitute regular flour for self-rising flour. Wonderful served with afternoon tea. Keep shortbread stored in an airtight container and extra batter on-hand in freezer.*

*Built in 1873 for a wealthy jeweler,
the Hamilton-Turner House represents one of the finest examples
of the Second French Empire styles of architecture in the United States.*

Kehoe House

A stately Renaissance Revival mansion overlooking Columbia Square

Address: 123 Habersham Street
Savannah, GA 31401
(Historic District)
Reservations: 1-800-820-1020
Telephone: (912) 232-1020

Web Site: www.kehoehouse.com
Category: Historic Inn
Owner: The Kessler Collection
Innkeeper: David Moore
Rates: $199-$429 (seasonal)

Mini Crab Cakes Kehoe with Caper Remoulade

1 egg
½ cup mayonnaise, more if needed
1 teaspoon Dijon mustard
2 tablespoons parsley, chopped
1 tablespoon cilantro, chopped
¼ teaspoon black pepper, freshly ground

Juice of 1 lemon
Dash Worcestershire sauce
1 pound backfin lump crabmeat
½ cup bread crumbs
Vegetable oil

Preheat oven to 350°. Combine first 8 ingredients and place in refrigerator until ready to add crab. Pick through crab for shells, then fold into mixture. Stir in bread crumbs, and shape mixture into 1 x 1-inch rounds. Over medium heat, add a small amount of oil to sauté pan. Add crab cakes in batches, turning for a golden color on both sides. Transfer cakes to paper towels to absorb extra oil. Repeat, wiping out pan as needed. Bake crab cakes on sheet pans 6 to 8 minutes. Transfer to chafing dish or warm in small batches.

Yield: 36 mini crab cakes

Caper Remoulade

½ cup mayonnaise
1 tablespoon Dijon mustard
2 tablespoons capers
2 tablespoons scallions, chopped

1 tablespoon cilantro, chopped
1 tablespoon cornichons, chopped (optional)
1 tablespoon fresh lemon or lime juice
1 dash Tabasco

Combine all ingredients and serve in a side dish.

Cherry Scones

4 cups all-purpose flour
½ cup sugar
4 teaspoons baking powder
½ teaspoon salt
1½ sticks chilled unsalted butter, diced

3 eggs
1 cup heavy cream
1 tablespoon vanilla
1 cup dried cherries, diced
  (may substitute another fruit, if desired)

Preheat oven to 375° and line baking sheets with parchment paper. Sift first 4 ingredients into a large bowl. With latex or vinyl gloves, work butter into flour mixture with fingertips. Beat 2 eggs and add to mixure, then whisk in cream. Stir in vanilla and cherries. Mix until combined and then knead briefly. Roll out dough, onto a floured surface, into a square ¾-inch block. Cut 2 x 2-inch squares; cut each square in half to form triangles. Place scones onto a baking sheet, arranging slightly apart. Brush tops with remaining beaten egg and bake 16 to 18 minutes. Transfer to wire rack and cool.

Yield: 18 scones

Bananas Foster French Toast

2 eggs
1 cup heavy cream
¼ teaspoon vanilla
⅛ cup brown sugar
1 tablespoon cinnamon

3 tablespoons butter, more if needed
4-5 slices brioche or challah bread,
  ¾-inch thick slices
2 ripe bananas sliced lengthwise, then in half
1½ tablespoons powdered sugar

Heat non-stick skillet on a medium setting. Beat eggs and whisk in cream and vanilla; set aside. Mix brown sugar and cinnamon; set aside. Place butter in skillet and melt (to coat skillet surface). Dip bread into egg mixture, sprinkle with cinnamon sugar mixture on both sides. Then cook bread on each side until golden brown and set aside (can keep warm in oven on low heat). Repeat adding butter to skillet for each batch. Next, melt more butter in the skillet and add the bananas with remaining cinnamon sugar. Be careful not to overcook. After bananas are caramelized, then top the French toast with the bananas. Dust with powdered sugar and serve with warm maple syrup.

Yield: 4 servings

Featured as one of Savannah's "best" in the June 2004 edition of Andrew Harper's *Hideaway Report*

"An eclectic mix of styles makes this distinctive brick house one of Savannah's finest mansions and an outstanding inn in a city known for its historic guest houses." — *Georgia Journal*, 1997

The Presidents Quarters

An inn of distinction harboring Savannah history—a place in time where diplomats, generals, and governors planned and influenced Savannah's history.

Address: 225 E. President Street
Savannah, Georgia 31401
(Historic District)
Reservations: 1-800-233-1776
Telephone: (912) 233-1600

Web Site: www.presidentsquarters.com
Category: Historic Inn
Innkeeper: Patricia Beblowski
Rates: $109-$250 (seasonal)

Apple Krispin' Bread

1 egg
½ cup corn oil
½ cup milk
1 cup sugar
1 teaspoon vanilla

2½ cups sifted white flour
1 teaspoon baking soda
½ teaspoon baking powder
¼ teaspoon salt
2 cups diced Granny Smith apples

Topping

1 cup brown sugar
2 tablespoons flour
1 teaspoon cinnamon

⅓ cup chopped nuts
(walnuts, hazelnuts, or pecans)

Preheat oven to 350°. Beat together first 5 ingredients. Add next five ingredients and mix, lightly, until lumpy. Mix topping in separate bowl. Pour mixture into a prepared loaf pan (buttered, oiled, or sprayed with baking spray) and crumble 2 to 3 tablespoons of topping over dough. Bake for 45 minutes or until top is firm (check the middle, with a toothpick, for doneness). To moisten bread, freeze overnight before eating.

Yield: 15-20 servings

∽∾∽∾∽∾∽∾∽∾∽∾∽∾∽∾∽∾∽∾∽∾∽∾∽∾

Crabby Mushroom Caps

4-ounces cream cheese
½ pound crab meat
1 tablespoon mayonnaise
Pinch of dill

Dash of liquid smoke
1 pound fresh mushrooms
Melted butter
Parsley or chives

Soften cream cheese; mix in next four ingredients. Remove stems from mushroom caps and, if needed, wipe caps with damp paper towel (never wash fresh mushrooms). Brush caps with a light coating of melted butter. Fill caps with crab mixture. Bake for 15 minutes at 375°. Garnish with parsley or chives.

Yield: Fills approximately 24 mushroom caps

Editors' Note: *This mixture is also excellent served chilled as a spread on crackers.*

Artichoke Dip

4 ounces cream cheese
1 (14-ounce) can artichokes,
   drained and coarsely chopped
1 tablespoon mayonnaise (real or low-fat)

½ cup fresh Parmesan cheese, grated
1 teaspoon lemon or lime juice
1 pinch of seasoning salt
Paprika, for garnish

Soften cream cheese in microwave about 40 seconds; stir in next 5 ingredients and place into a greased casserole dish. Bake at 350° about 15 to 20 minutes or until top is golden brown. Sprinkle top with paprika. Serve hot with crackers.

Yield: 8-10 servings

Editors' Note: *Our testers recommend serving this dip with a mild-flavored cracker, such as Ritz crackers or Wheat Thins, in order to taste the artichokes better.*

"Gracious living indeed! And the staff is genuinely friendly and interested."
—Terry Houston, *The London Herald*

Located on Oglethorpe Square, these twin Federal style townhouses were built in 1855 under the auspices of the Estate of W. W. Gordon (grandfather of Juliette Gordon Lowe). It is across the street from The Owens-Thomas House, famous for its Regency architecture and the balcony from which Marquis de Lafayette once presented a speech during a visit to Savannah.

The Stephen Williams House

A stellar example of a 19th century Federal-style house

Address: 128 W. Liberty Street
Savannah, GA 31401
(Historic District)
Telephone: (912) 495-0032

Web Site: www.thestephenwilliamshouse.com
Category: B&B
Owner/Innkeeper: Albert Wall
Rates: $165-$325 (year-round)

Stephen Williams House Breakfast Casserole

1 pound bulk sausage
4 slices white bread
1 medium onion, finely minced
1 (8-ounce) can mushrooms, drained
1 cup Cheddar or Swiss cheese
6 eggs

2 cups milk
1 teaspoon Worcestershire sauce
1 dash Tabasco sauce
¾ teaspoon salt
½ teaspoon pepper
¼ cup fresh Parmesan cheese, grated

Preheat oven to 350°. Brown sausage; chop finely and drain. Break up bread and put into buttered 13 x 9 x 2-inch baking dish. Sauté onion. Spoon sausage evenly over bread, onion over sausage, and mushrooms over onion. Sprinkle with Cheddar or Swiss cheese. Beat together next six ingredients and pour over mixture in baking dish. Just before baking, sprinkle with Parmesan cheese. Bake 35 to 40 minutes.

Yield: 6-8 servings

Editors' Notes: *Can be prepared the night before and refrigerated. Serving in individual ramekins makes a nice presentation. Canned (grated) Parmesan cheese may be substituted if fresh Parmesan is unavailable. Garnish with fresh rosemary.*

❧❧❧❧❧❧❧❧❧❧❧❧❧❧❧❧❧❧❧❧❧❧❧❧❧❧❧❧❧❧

Madeira Wine Jelly

4 cups Madeira wine
6 cups sugar

6 ounces liquid Certo
Paraffin

Mix first two ingredients in top of a large double boiler (or a heavy pot). Place over boiling water and stir until sugar dissolves; remove from heat and stir in Certo. Skim foam, if there is any. Pour mixture into hot, sterilized 8-ounce jelly jars and cover with ⅛–inch hot paraffin.

Yield: 8-10 half pints

Editors' Notes: *Madeira (muh-DEER-uh) wine is a Portuguese wine which can be very sweet or quite dry. Certo is an ingredient which aids in gelling process of jelly; Ball fruit jell liquid pectin may be substituted, if desired. If you have a canner, which seals the jelly, paraffin is not necessary. After pouring mixture into jars, center the heated jar lids on jars and screw band down evenly and firmly. Process filled jars in a water bath canner for 10 to 15 minutes. This jelly is a lovely color and delicious served with croissants.*

Imperial Crab Spread

¼ cup Hellmann's mayonnaise
2 teaspoons lemon juice
1 tablespoon small capers
½ teaspoon Worcestershire sauce

Dash of Tabasco sauce
1 pound fresh lump crabmeat
Bremner wafers or Carr's crackers

Mix first five ingredients in a medium bowl; gently toss in crabmeat. Taste before serving; the flavor may be enhanced by adding a little more lemon juice. Serve cold with wafers or crackers.

Yield: 12 servings

Recipient of the 2003 Preservtion Award
from the Historic Savannah Foundation

━━━━━━━━━━━━━━━━━━━━━━━━━━━━

"However you choose to experience all that Savannah has to offer, The Stephen Williams House is not to be missed...it is an absolute treasure."
—*The Magazine of Naples*, February 2004

"The Stephen Williams House represents Savannah's most intimate inn and truly conveys the impression that you are an honored guest in a pririvate home. Much of the furniture throughout the manor would grace a museum..."—Andrew Harper's *Hideaway Report*, June 2004

17 Hundred 90

Captures the authentic flavor of Georgia's first and most romantic city

Address: 307 E. President Street
Savannah, GA 31401
(Historic District)
Telephone: (912) 236-7122
Web Site: www.17hundred90.com

Cuisine: American Regional
Executive Chef: Brian Benthal
Price Range: Lunch/$6.95-$10.95
Dinner/$15.95-$26.95

Veal Medallions with Lemon Caper Butter

8 veal medallions, cut ¾-inch
  thick from center loin
1-2 tablespoons of olive oil
Seasoned flour
¼ cup white wine (not a sweet wine)
½ lemon (or more, if preferred), juiced

1 small can artichoke
  hearts, drained
1-2 tablespoons of capers
Salt and pepper, to taste
1 stick unsalted butter,
  cut into small pieces

Cover veal with plastic wrap and pound, with a meat mallet, to less than ¼-inch thick. Pre-heat oven to 180°. Heat a sauté pan and add olive oil after pan is hot, but not smoking. Dredge veal lightly in flour, shaking off excess. Add medallions to sauté pan in batches, being careful not to crowd the pan. Cook until golden brown on both sides, about 1 to 2 minutes on each side. Add more olive oil, as needed. When done, place meat on an oven-proof platter and keep warm. After all medallions are cooked, deglaze pan with wine and lemon juice; cook until reduced. Add remaining ingredients. Whisk butter into sauce and continue whisking until butter is incorporated and sauce is creamy. Spoon sauce over veal medallions and serve.

Yield: 4 servings

Editors Notes: *Capers are found with the condiments in a super market. The lemon caper butter is the crowning glory of this wonderful veal dish. Chicken cutlets may be substituted for veal, if desired.*

ഏഏഏഏഏഏഏഏഏഏഏഏഏഏഏഏഏഏഏഏഏഏഏ

Roasted Rack of Lamb

2 racks of lamb, Frenched
Salt and pepper, to taste

1 teaspoon olive oil
½ cup red wine

Preheat oven to 425°. Salt and pepper racks and set aside. Add oil to skillet and add lamb when oil is hot (almost smoking). Sear, meat-side down, about 2 minutes to brown. Turn over, when meat freely loosens, and sear same amount of time on other side. Attempt to brown all sides, including ends. When lamb is well-seared, take out and let cool. Pour off excess fat and deglaze pan for sauce by adding wine and scraping all browned bits off bottom of pan. Set aside.

Mustard Coating

1½ tablespoons Dijon mustard
1½ tablespoons grain mustard
2 cloves fresh garlic, chopped

2 teaspoons fresh rosemary
1 teaspoon Lawry's seasoning salt
¼ teaspoon freshly ground pepper

Combine all ingredients. Using a pastry brush, apply coating over entire surface of meat (except the bones).

Bread Crumbs

½ cup seasoned bread crumbs   ½ teaspoon garlic powder   ½ teaspoon dry mustard

Mix together all ingredients and roll coated lamb into seasoned bread crumbs. Pan spray or coat with oil an oven-proof pan and put lamb in pan, rack side down. Place in preheated oven. While lamb is cooking, finish preparing sauce (below). Using a meat thermometer, cook lamb to desired temperature or 130° for rare (about 15 to 20 minutes). Take out of oven and let sit for 5 to 10 minutes. Internal temperature will continue to increase 5 to 10 degrees. Cut between the ribs and divide lamb into 4 servings.

Sauce

1½ cup beef stock   Kitchen Bouquet, optional

Add stock to skillet where deglazing has been done. Simmer liquid down to about one-third to thicken sauce, leaving approximately 1 cup of sauce. Season to taste with salt and pepper; add a little Kitchen Bouquet to darken, if desired. Serve over sliced lamb.

Yield: 4 servings

Editor's Note: *Fresh rack of lamb may be purchased from Nueske's by calling 1-800-392-2266. Add 1 teaspoon butter to sauce, melt, and stir in before serving. Delicious served with roasted rosemary-scented potatoes and baby peas sautéed with shallots.*

Georgia Trend magazine singled out 17 Hundred 90
as a favorite spot for "financiers, business people, and professionals."

17 Hundred 90 has been a gourmet tradition in Savannah
for over a century and has been acclaimed as
"the most elegant restaurant in Savannah" by *Gourmet Magazine*.

45 Bistro

Reflective of Savannah's class and style

Address: The Marshall House
123 E. Broughton St.
(Historic District)
Telephone: (912) 234-3111
Web Site: www.marshallhouse.com/dining.shtml

Cuisine: Eclectic
Executive Chef: Ryan Behneman
Price Range: Dinner/$15-$28

Broccolini and Stilton Cream Soup

3 tablespoons butter
1 small onion, chopped
⅔ cup celery, chopped
3 cups Broccolini, chopped
4 tablespoons dry white wine

3 cups chicken broth (low salt)
1½ cups heavy cream
1 cup Stilton cheese, crumbled or diced
Tabasco sauce, to taste (optional)
Salt and white pepper, to taste

Parboil Broccolini (or pre-cook about 5 minutes in the microwave in 1 cup of water) and set aside. Melt butter in a sauce pan and add onion and celery; sweat about 5 minutes. Add Broccolini and cook until tender. Add wine. After wine cooks down a bit, add broth and bring to a boil. Add roux (see page 220) to thicken (or omit for a thinner soup). Purée in a food processor. Return mixture to pot and bring back to a boil. Add cream and cheese (adding more for a stronger flavor or less for a milder taste). Adjust seasoning.

Yield: 5-6 servings

Editors' Notes: *Broccolini is a trademarked name for the vegetable produced when broccoli and Chinese kale is crossed. Unlike broccoli, the slender stalks are topped with a bouquet of tiny buds resembling a miniature broccoli head. If unavailable, substitute broccoli florets (about 2 heads of broccoli for this recipe). If Stilton cheese cannot be found, substitute a domestic blue cheese or Gorgonzola. To cut down on the calories, we substituted low-fat half-and-half for the cream, and it worked fine. For an even heartier soup, stir in about ½ cup of cooked Arborio or plain rice before serving.*

Restaurants
Savannah, Georgia

ჼჄჼჄჼჄჼჄჼჄჼჄჼჄჼჄჼჄჼჄჼჄჼჄ

Filet of Salmon Gratinéed with Asiago Cheese

Small can of hearts of palm
Small can artichoke hearts, quartered
Olive oil
Salt and pepper, to taste

3 pounds filet of salmon
1½ cups white wine
1½ cups Asiago cheese, grated
Paprika for garnishing

Preheat oven to 350°. Cut hearts of palm into ½-inch pieces and sauté with artichokes in olive oil; salt and pepper to taste. Keep warm. Place salmon in pan, cover with wine, and top with cheese. Cook for 9 to 11 minutes until fish is firm, basting occasionally. When ready, cheese should be melted and slightly brown. Place salmon on plate and top with artichokes and hearts of palm. Garnish with paprika.

Yield 6 servings

Editors' Notes: *Asiago (ah-SYAH-goh) is an Italian cheese with a rich, nutty flavor—it is succulent melted on top of the salmon. This dish is also good served over ratatouille (ra-tuh-TOO-ee), as it is served at 45 Bistro. Trout may be substituted for salmon (either fresh trout or Maine salmon may be ordered from www.MaineLobsterDirect.com or by calling 1-888-556-2783).*

Prince Edward Island Mussels
with a Citrus Lemon Grass Coconut Milk

1 pound live mussels
Zest (grated peel) and juice of 1 lime
Zest (grated peel) and juice of 1 lemon
2 tablespoons lemon grass, chopped

2 tablespoons peeled, chopped ginger
3 ounces coconut milk
½ cup white wine

Wash shells of mussels and scrub down in cold water. Put aside. Combine remaining ingredients and pour into a sauté pan immediately after adding mussels to hot sauté pan. Cover pan with lid. Cook on high heat for 3 to 4 minutes until mussels open up. Throw away any mussels that do not open. Pour liquid from sauté pan over mussels to serve.

Yield 2 servings

Editors' Notes: *If mussels (or clams) do not open up, they are not alive and must be discarded. Lemon grass can usually be found fresh in produce department or chopped in frozen section of grocery store. Use only the brown root part of lemon grass, not the green part. Peel fresh ginger with a teaspoon; chop and freeze, in advance, to have ready at time of preparation. Coconut milk is found in canned goods area of grocery stores. Clams may be substituted for mussels, but they may need to be cooked longer. Lemon grass is an important herb in Thai and Vietnamese cooking. Use the white base (up to where leaves start) for flavoring this recipe and discard before serving. If unavailable, use a little extra lemon zest.*

"Everything is a winner at 45 Bistro."
—*Savannah Morning News* (April 5, 2002)

Belford's

Casual fine dining in City Market

Address: 315 W. St. Julian St.
Savannah, GA 31401
(City Market)
Telephone: (912) 233-2626
Web Site: www.belfordssavannah.com

E-mail: info@belfordssavannah.com
Cuisine: American regional
Executive Chef: George Denmark
Price Range: Breakfast/$4.95-$12.95
Lunch/$6.95-$12.95
Dinner/$16.95-$24.95

Grouper Anglais

Vegetable cooking spray
1 cup panko bread crumbs
½ teaspoon dried thyme
½ teaspoon dried marjoram
1 pound grouper filets
Salt and pepper, to taste

1 tablespoon clarified butter
½ medium onion, diced
1 cup diced peppers
  (green, red, and/or yellow)
1 cup Chardonnay or other white wine
½ cup cooked crabmeat

Preheat oven to 350°. Spray a baking sheet with vegetable cooking spray and set aside. In a shallow bowl or plate, mix the first 3 ingredients. Lightly season the filets with salt and pepper; dredge in bread crumb mixture, shaking off any excess. Place filets on baking sheet. Bake until cooked through, about 10 to 12 minutes. While filets bake, heat the clarified butter in a large non-stick pan over medium heat. Add onion and peppers and sauté until tender, about 7 minutes. Add wine and simmer for 2 to 3 minutes more, stirring occasionally. Stir in crabmeat and heat through. Serve filets topped with the wine and crabmeat sauce.

Yield: 2 servings

Editors' Notes: *Clarified butter, also referred to as drawn butter, is an unsalted butter that has been slowly melted and the milk solids skimmed out. Panko bread crumbs are larger, coarser crumbs often used in Japanese cooking and provide a delicious crunchy crust. They are available in the Oriental section of many grocery stores or in Asian markets. Grouper may be substituted with sea bass, tilapia, or catfish filets (any of which may be purchased by calling 1-800-556-2783).*

Parmesan Tomato Stack

¼ cup extra-virgin olive oil
¾ cup balsamic vinegar
½ cup Parmesan cheese, shredded
1 cup mozzarella cheese, shredded
½ cup panko bread crumbs

1 tablespoon dried oregano
1 tablespoon dried basil
Vegetable oil cooking spray
6 large, ripe tomatoes (unpeeled and sliced about ½-inch thick)

Preheat oven to 450°. Combine oil and vinegar; set aside. Combine cheeses, bread crumbs, and herbs. Lightly coat a baking sheet with vegetable cooking spray. Arrange tomato slices on the baking sheet, leaving at least ½-inch between them. Generously sprinkle bread crumb mixture on each tomato slice. Place another slice of tomato on top of each and top with more bread crumb mixture. Bake 3 to 5 minutes or until bread crumb mixture is lightly browned. Remove from oven and drizzle each tomato stack with the oil and vinegar dressing. Serve immediately.

Yield: 6 servings

Belford's Bread Pudding

1 egg
2 cups milk
¼ cup white sugar
¼ cup packed brown sugar
1 stick butter, melted
1 teaspoon nutmeg

1 tablespoon vanilla
1 teaspoon cinnamon
3 cups cubed bread
1 cup golden raisins
½ cup pecans or walnuts, optional

Preheat oven to 350°. Lightly grease an 8 or 9-inch square baking dish and set aside. Lightly beat egg in a large bowl. Add next 7 ingredients and stir to combine. Add cubed bread, stirring to coat well. Allow bread to soak for at least 10 minutes, stirring once or twice, to ensure it absorbs liquid mixture. Stir in raisins and nuts (if using) and spread mixture into greased baking dish. Bake until firm (a knife inserted in middle should come out clean) about 40 to 45 minutes. Cool, slightly, before serving.

Yield: 6 servings

Editors' Note: *We like this dish topped with warm caramel sauce (buy in ice-cream section of grocery store), a dollop of whipped cream, and a sprinkling of extra nuts.*

"The Grouper Anglais was stuffed with a tasty flavorful blue crabmeat ... Every bite was a sheer joy." —*Creative Loafing*, January 13, 2001

Winner of "Best Menu Item" at the inaugural Taste of Savannah (January 2001) for the Crab Cakes.

The Boar's Head

Casual fine dining, in an old cotton warehouse, overlooking the Savannah River

Address: 1 North Lincoln Street
Savannah, GA 31401
(Waterfront)
Telephone: (912) 651-9660
Web Site: http://savannahmenu.com/
boarshead

Cuisine: New American Cuisine
with a Southern Flair
Executive Chef: Philip Branan
Price Range: Lunch/$8-$15
Dinner/$15-$25

Philip Branan's Black-Eyed Pea Soup

¾ pound dried black-eyed peas
¼ pound bacon, diced
1 cup white onion, chopped
1 cup celery, chopped
1 cup carrot, chopped
2 cloves garlic, minced
¾ cup tomatoes, diced, with juice
1 cup fresh collards, rinsed,
stems removed, diced

1½ quarts rich chicken stock
1 smoked ham hock
½ teaspoon kosher salt
¼ teaspoon dried oregano
⅛ teaspoon dried thyme
⅛ teaspoon ground white pepper
½ cup cooked ham, diced
1½ teaspoon chopped fresh cilantro
1 ounce sherry

Soak peas overnight in cold water. Melt down bacon's fat, over medium heat, in a large, heavy-bottom soup pot. Add next 3 ingredients and cover. Cook until onions are soft, about 10 minutes. Add garlic and cook about 10 seconds. Drain peas and add to the pot, along with tomato and collards. Cover with stock and add ham hock; season with next 4 ingredients. Bring to a boil. Reduce heat to low and simmer, covered, for about 1½ hours. Remove ham hock and dice any meat left on bone. Return ham hock to pot, along with diced ham and cilantro. Finish with sherry and adjust seasonings, if necessary.

Yield: 8 cups

Editors' Note: *Ideal to serve on New Year's Day with hot, buttered cornbread.*

❦❦❦❦❦❦❦❦❦❦❦❦❦❦❦❦❦❦❦❦❦❦❦❦❦❦

Boar's Head Grill and Tavern Savannah Trifle

Vanilla Custard Sauce

1 cup sugar	8 egg yolks
1 quart heavy cream	1 tablespoon vanilla
Dash of salt	1 tablespoon Grand Marnier

Combine first 3 ingredients in a heavy-bottom pot. Scald. Place yolks in a stainless steel bowl and whip until lemon-colored. Once cream is scalded, slowly pour half of cream mixture into yolks, whipping slowly. Next, temper (gradually add) yolk mixture back into remaining cream mixture—slowly whipping, all the while. This tempering process prevents yolks from scrambling. Put mixture back over low heat; cook, stirring with a wooden spoon, until custard has thickened and sticks to back of spoon. Remove from heat and add last 2 ingredients. Cool completely before assembling.

Assembly

1 (20-ounce) sponge cake, torn into pieces	Whipped cream
1½ ounces of Grande Marnier	Sliced almonds, toasted

Ladle 1½ cups sauce into bottom of an 8-inch crystal bowl. Top with a layer of cake, sprinkle Grand Marnier over cake, and repeat process (sauce/Grand Marnier/cake) for two more layers. Top cake on third layer with Grand Marnier, custard, whipped cream, and toasted almonds. Fruit, such as sliced strawberries, may be added for a festive touch. Refrigerate until time to serve.

Yield: 8-10 servings

Editors' Notes: *Grand Marnier (GRAN mahr-NYAY) is a rich, cognac-based, orange-flavored liqueur. Trifles are a specialty dessert of the Lowcountry, and this one is superb.*

In *Romantic Days and Nights in Savannah* (2001),
Georgia Byrd cites The Boar's Head as Savannah's
"Most Romantic Restaurant"

"Great black-eyed pea and ham soup--
everything is made from scratch, the old-fashioned way!"
—*Savannah Magazine*, June 1999

The first restaurant on Savannah's famous River Street

Bodi's Sophisticated Palate and Homemade Desserts

A delightful find on Savannah's Southside

Address: 238 Eisenhower Drive
Savannah, GA 31406
Telephone: (912) 355-6160
Web Site: www.eatinginsavannah.com/
bodis.html
Cuisine: Specialty items and Desserts

Proprietor: Richard Halperin
Price Range: Breakfast/$3.95-$7.95
Lunch/$5.95-$8.95
Note: Also sells gourmet food products
and cooking aids

Shrimp Salad with Honeydew

¾ honeydew melon
  (halved, seeded, and cubed)
1½ pounds medium-sized shrimp
  (cooked, peeled, deveined, tail removed)
1 cup mayonnaise
2 tablespoons tomato paste

1 tablespoon lemon rind, grated
1 teaspoon superfine sugar
Salt, to taste
White pepper, to taste
Lettuce leaves
Watercress sprig, optional

Mix melon with shrimp. In a separate bowl, combine next 6 ingredients. Add melon and shrimp to sauce mixture and stir until well-blended. Chill. Serve on lettuce leaves and garnish with watercress spring, if desired.

Yield: 4 servings

Editors' note: *A refreshing twist to shrimp salad, an all-time Lowcountry favorite. If using larger shrimp, cut in half. If purchasing pre-cut melon, use about 1½ cups.*

Richard's Oatmeal Cookies

1½ cups sifted flour
1 teaspoon salt
1 teaspoon baking soda
1 cup butter
1 cup packed brown sugar
1 cup sugar

2 eggs
1 teaspoon vanilla extract
3 cups rolled oats
1 cup chopped pecans
1 cup raisins, optional

Sift together the first 3 ingredients. Cream butter and sugars in a mixing bowl until light and fluffy. Beat in eggs. Add sifted dry ingredients and mix well; stir in vanilla. Blend in remaining ingredients. Drop by teaspoonfuls onto greased cookie sheets and bake at 350° for 10 to 15 minutes, or until lightly browned.

Yield: 3 dozen medium-sized cookies

Editors' note: *Make a double batch and keep the extra dough in the freezer for next time. This is a cookie that your family will want you to fix again.*

Two-Version Praline Cheesecake

Graham Cracker Crust

1 cup graham cracker crumbs
¼ cup finely chopped pecans

¼ cup butter, melted

Combine all ingredients in a bowl and mix well. Press over the bottom of a 9-inch springform pan. Chill.

Filling

3 (8-ounce) blocks cream cheese
1¼ cups packed brown sugar
3 eggs

2 teaspoons vanilla extract
1 cup whipping cream

Soften cream cheese and beat in a mixing bowl until light and fluffy. Gradually beat in 1 cup of sugar. Beat in the eggs 1 at a time, mixing well after each addition. Stir in remaining ingredients and pour into prepared crust. Sprinkle top with remaining one-fourth cup brown sugar. Bake at 450° for 10 minutes and then reduce temperature to 275°. Bake 1 hour. Cool on a wire rack. Remove side of the pan and place onto a serving plate.

Yield: 10-12 servings

Featured in the *Savannah Morning News*
May 30, 1999

Driftaway Cafe

Fun dining in a relaxed atmosphere

Address: 7400-D Skidaway Road
Savannah, GA 31406
Telephone: (912) 303-0999
Web Site: www.driftawaycafe.com

Cuisine: Casual coastal cuisine
Price Range: Lunch/$6-$12
Dinner/$14-$25

Herb River Crab Dip

1¾ tablespoons chopped shallots
(approximately 1 small shallot)
⅓ cup white wine
1¾ tablespoons Texas Pete hot sauce

2 (8-ounce) blocks cream cheese,
cut into cubes and softened
5 to 6 ounces crab meat
(claw meat works fine)
⅔ teaspoon Florida Bay Spice

Sauté shallots in white wine and hot sauce. Bring to a boil and reduce to a simmer for three minutes. Add cream cheese and whisk constantly until smooth and no longer lumpy. Remove from heat and gently fold in crabmeat. Place in storage container and refrigerate. Serve chilled with crackers, tortilla chips, or toast rounds.

Yield: 8-10 servings

Editors' Notes: *Lots of supermarkets now sell refrigerated crab meat in their seafood departments. However, if fresh crab meat is not available, substitute canned or frozen. If using packaged crab meat, be sure to drain it before incorporating it into dip. This dip also works well as an omelette filling (see page 153 for an omelet recipe that can be used).*

๛๛๛๛๛๛๛๛๛๛๛๛๛๛๛๛๛๛๛๛๛๛๛๛๛

Crispy Scored Flounder with Apricot Shallot Glaze

1 small whole flounder,
    (headed, gutted, and scaled)
All-purpose flour, seasoned
Cooking oil

¼ cup Apricot Shallot Glaze
Parsley, chopped
Red pepper, finely diced
Lemon wedge, seeded

Score flounder, diagonally, by slicing the flounder to the bone in a criss-cross pattern on both sides. Liberally coat each side of flounder with flour and gently drop into hot fryer oil. Cook until the fish is a nice golden brown and floating in the hot oil; remove and drain. Serve on a large oval plate topped with ¼ cup of Apricot Shallot Glaze. Garnish with a pinch of chopped parsley, red pepper, and a lemon wedge.

Yield: 1 serving

Editors' Notes: *Flounder can usually be purchased "H & G" (headed and gutted) from most seafood retailers; it may also be ordered online from MaineLobsterDirect.com or by calling 1-800-556-2783. Flounder filets, scored very slightly, may also be used. Other fish alternatives would be grouper, catfish, or tilapia.*

Apricot Shallot Glaze

2½ tablespoons peanut oil
1 clove garlic, peeled and chopped
½ cup shallots, chopped
2½ tablespoons soy sauce
1 cup red wine vinegar

½ teaspoon red chili flakes
½ teaspoon Tabasco sauce
¾ cup Smucker's apricot preserves
¾ cup water
4 tablespoons cilantro, finely chopped

In a heavy-bottom saucepan, sauté garlic and shallots in peanut oil for about five minutes or until softened. Add next 4 ingredients, while stirring constantly. Add preserves and water; stir over medium heat until thickened to sauce consistency, taking caution not to let bottom scorch or burn (approximately 15 to 20 minutes). The sauce is the right consistency when it coats the back of a spoon. Remove from heat, cool slightly, and stir in cilantro.

Yield: 2½ cups

Editors' Notes: *The glaze makes about 6 generous servings (which equals to about 2 ounces or 4 tablespoons for each serving of fish). For another flavor, substitute orange, pineapple, or peach preserves for the apricot preserves. This glaze is also delicious served with chicken fingers, grouper fingers, or coconut-crusted shrimp.*

Voted "Savannah's Best Outdoor Dining"
—*The Connect Readers' Guide,* 2004

Johnny Harris Restaurant

Serving the "Best Barbeque" since 1924

Address: 1651 E. Victory Drive
Savannah, GA 31404
Telephone: (912) 354-7810
Web Site: www.johnnyharris.com

Cuisine: American Southern
Executive Chef: Jamie Carver
Price Range: Lunch/$4.95-$9.50
Dinner/$9.95-$23.85

Seafood Pasta Fantasia

¼ cup olive oil
6 clams, cleaned and washed
¼ cup yellow squash, sliced
¼ cup red onion, diced
¼ cup sun-dried tomatoes (packed in oil)
¼ cup red pepper, sliced
¼ cup broccoli, blanched
Salt and pepper, to taste

2 garlic cloves, minced
6 scallops, eye removed
½ cup shrimp, tail removed
½ cup dry white wine
2 cups pasta, cooked and drained
½ cup cheese, grated
   (Romano or Parmesan)
Parsley

In a lare skillet, heat the olive oil and add clams. Cover and allow clams to steam until opened. Add next 7 ingredients and sauté about 3 minutes. Add remaining seafood and cook until shrimp is a light pink. Deglaze skillet with white wine. Stir in cooked pasta and allow to simmer in sauce about 3 minutes. Serve in a hot dish topped with cheese and garnished with parsley.

Yield: 2 servings

Editors' Notes: *Angel hair pasta is recommended for this dish. Additional seafood (such as mussels, fresh fish, or salmon) may be added to or substituted for seafood in recipe, if desired.*

Restaurants
Savannah, Georgia

Sweet Mustard Chicken

3 tablespoons fine, dry bread crumbs
2 tablespoons brown sugar
1 teaspoon dried tarragon
1 teaspoon kosher salt
½ teaspoon black pepper

2½ pounds chicken breasts
  (skinned and boneless)
4 tablespoons olive oil
2 tablespoons Dijon mustard
Lemon wedges, seeded

Preheat oven to 500°. Mix together the first 5 ingredients and set aside. Using a meat mallet, pound out the breasts until about ¼-inch thick. Rub the olive oil over the entire chicken breast; place in a baking pan lined with aluminum foil. Next, rub the mustard on top of the chicken. Sprinkle chicken breasts with the crumb mixture and bake about 18 minutes. Serve hot and garnished with the lemon wedges.

Yield: 5-6 servings

Editors' Notes: *This dish is excellent served with rice.*

Strawberries à la Carver

1 cup heavy cream
4 tablespoons 10-X sugar
1 pint vanilla ice-cream
Juice of 1 orange, strained
2 ounces of Grand Marnier

10 ounces dark rum
1 quart strawberries
  (washed, stemmed, chilled)
Sprig of fresh mint, optional

Whip cream until stiff and add sugar. Blend in next 4 ingredients. Fill champagne glasses with strawberries and top with ice-cream mixture. Garnish with fresh mint, if desired.

Yield: 8 servings

Editors' Notes: *Grand Marnier (GRAN mahr-NYAY) is a rich, cognac-based liqueur which contributes to the flavor of this delightful summer dessert.*

Johnny Harris BBQ sauce chosen "favorite sauce" in nation-wide contest. — *Bon Appetit* (1996)

"To enter the door at Johnny Harris Restaurant is to step back to a time when eating out was a special treat."
—Richard Allen, *Savannah Morning News* (1997)

The Lady and Sons

Good home cooking in an atmosphere of true Southern hospitality

Address: 102 W. Congress St.
Savannah, GA 31401
(Historic District)
Telephone: (912) 233-2600
Web Site: www.ladyandsons.com
Cuisine: Southern

Proprietor: Paula H. Deen
Price Range: Lunch/$5.99-$14.99
Dinner/$14.99-$21.99
Cookbook: *The Lady & Sons*
Savannah Country Cookbook
(+ 2 more)

Bubba's Beer Biscuits

2 cups Bisquick
¼ cup sugar

½ can beer (6 ounces)
1 tablespoons butter, melted

Preheat oven to 400°. Mix ingredients well, adjusting the sugar according to how sweet a biscuit you prefer. Spoon into well-greased muffin tins. Bake for 15 to 20 minutes. Serve with Molasses Pecan Butter (page 39).

Yield: 10 medium-sized biscuits

Editors' Notes: *These look more like rolls than bisquits, and the beer gives them a pleasing yeasty flavor.*

Squash Casserole

2 cups cooked, mashed yellow squash
2 cups Ritz cracker crumbs
1 cup evaporated milk
1 cup shredded cheese,
such as Cheddar or Swiss
1 cup onion, chopped

2 eggs, lightly beaten
1 teaspoon salt
1 teaspoon pepper
Pinch of sugar
6 tablespoons butter

Place squash in a large bowl. Add next 4 ingredients and stir well. Stir in remaining ingredients and pour into a greased 1-quart casserole. Bake at 350° for 40 minutes.

Yield: 4 servings

Baked Spaghetti

Sauce

1 cup canned diced tomatoes	2 tablespoons chopped fresh parsley
1 cup tomato sauce	¾ teaspoon Italian seasoning
½ cup water	¾ teaspoon The Lady's seasoned salt
¼ cup diced onions	¾ teaspoon The Lady's house seasoning
¼ cup diced green pepper	¾ teaspoon sugar
1 clove garlic, chopped	1 small bay leaf

Combine all ingredients in a stockpot and bring to a boil. Reduce heat and simmer, covered, for 1 hour.

Beef and Pasta

¾ pound ground beef	½ cup Cheddar cheese, grated
1 pound uncooked angel hair pasta	½ cup Monterey Jack cheese, grated

Crumble ground beef in a saucepan and cook until no pink remains; drain off fat. Add the browned beef to stockpot and simmer for another 20 minutes. While sauce simmers, cook pasta according to package directions. Cover bottom of a 13x9 x2-inch pan with sauce, a layer of pasta, and one-half of the cheese. Repeat layers, ending with the sauce. Bake at 350° for 30 minutes. Top with remaining cheese and return to oven. Continue cooking until cheese is melted and bubbly. Cut into squares before serving.

Yield: 4-5 servings

Editors' Note: *Lawry's seasoned salt may be substituted for The Lady's seasoned salt. The Lady's house seasoning may be made by stirring together 1 cup salt, ¼ cup black pepper, and ¼ cup garlic powder. Keep seasoning in a shaker.*

Ranked the "#1 International Meal in America for 1999"
by Jerry Shriver, *USA Today.*

Featured on cover of *Savannah Magazine* (Sept.-Oct. 1999)

Paula Deen has appeared as a guest on

QVC	*Ready, Set, Cook*
Good Morning, America	*The Food Network*

Since November 2002, Paula Deen has hosted "Paula's Home Cooking" on *The Food Network*. It is the only show on the network led by a "down-home" Southern cook.

The Pirate's House

Boasting 15 unique dining rooms, each with its own charm

Address: 20 E. Broad Street
Savannah, GA 31401
(Historic District)
Telephone: (912)233-5757
Web Site: www.thepirateshouse.com

Cuisine: American Southern cuisine
Executive Chef: Derek Benoit
Price Range: Lunch/$7-$12
Dinner/$16-$28

Baked Daufuskie Oysters

1 tablespoon unsalted butter	24 medium-sized Daufuskie oysters
2 cloves garlic, minced	Kosher salt
1 sprig fresh rosemary	Seasoned bread crumbs
1 sprig fresh thyme	½ cup Parmesan cheese, shredded
1 quart heavy cream	½ cup Monterey Jack cheese, shredded
Salt and pepper, to taste	Parsley flakes, optional

Melt butter in a sauce pot and sauté next 3 ingredients for 3 minutes; stir in cream. Bring mixture to a boil, then reduce heat so cream does not boil over (which it will do quickly if not watched). Simmer about 20 minutes, stirring every few minutes or until sauce has reduced by half. After seasoning with salt and pepper, strain sauce to remove herb stems or large pieces; let sauce cool to room temperature. Shuck, wash, and drain the oysters (but leave them on half shell). Place oysters on a bed of course salt (Kosher salt) in a shallow baking pan; this salt provides a stable base for oysters. Top each oyster (on half shell) with 1 to 2 tablespoons of sauce, a thin layer of bread crumbs, and a thin layer of the two cheeses. Place in a pre-heated 425° oven for about 10 minutes or until cheese is bubbling and just starting to brown. Remove, sprinkle with chopped parsley, if desired, and serve immediately.

Yield: 4-5 servings

Editors' Notes: *Daufuskie (DAWH fusky) oysters are high quality oysters found on Daufuskie Island, a barrier island located between Hilton Head Island, SC and Tybee Island, GA estimated to be between 80,000 to 120,000 years old. Any high-quality oyster may be used (our food tester used oysters from Rhode Island with excellent results).*

Boursin Cheese Mashed Potatoes

3 large baking potatoes,
    peeled and diced into 1-inch cubes
2 cups heavy cream

1 stick unsalted butter, melted
4-ounces Boursin cheese
Salt and white pepper, to taste

Cook potatoes in boiling water or a microwave until tender. Drain potatoes and place in a food processor with remaining ingredients. Mix until thoroughly blended. Serve warm.

Yield: 4-6 servings

Editors' Notes: *Boursin (boor-SAHN) is a white, smooth cheese with a buttery texture. Other favorite cheeses may be substituted for the Boursin, if desired.*

Key Lime Pie

1 (4-ounce) can Borden's condensed milk
Zest (grated peel) of 1 small lime
5 medium egg yolks
¾ cup lime juice (about 4 limes)

1 teaspoon sugar
Graham cracker pie crust mix
1 cup whipped cream

Preheat oven to 350°. Place condensed milk in a mixing bowl; add lime zest and egg yolks. Whip mixture with a wire whisk until completely smooth. Fold in lime juice, sweetened with sugar, using a rubber spatula. Set aside for 10 minutes. Prepare graham cracker pie crust, following instructions on package. Line a 9-inch pie plate with crumbs and toast in oven for 3 minutes. Pour pie filling into pie shell and return to oven for another 3 minutes. Refrigerate overnight before serving. Serve topped with whipped cream (or a frozen dairy topping) and garnish, if desired, with a twist of fresh lime.

Yield: 6 servings

Editors' Notes: *Substitute lemon zest (for lime zest) and lemon juice (for lime juice) for a delicious lemon pie. Top with whipped cream or a classic, browned meringue topping.*

The Pirate's House is located on one of the most historic spots in Georgia. It is here that Trustees Garden, the first experimental garden in America, was located. This historic tavern is listed as a house museum by The American Museum Society.

Soho South Cafe

Where food is an art

Address: 12 W. Liberty Street
Savannah, GA 31401
Telephone: (912) 233-1633
Web Site: www.sohosouthcafe.com

Cuisine: American comfort and European flair
Proprietress/Chef: Bonnie Retsas
Price Range: Lunch/$6.25-$9.75
Dinner/$9.50-$20.95
Sunday brunch/$3.95-$10.95

Crab and Asparagus Quiche

1 (10-inch deep-dish) pie shell
3 whole eggs
2 egg yolks
1 cup heavy cream
1 cup sour cream
1½ cups Gruyère cheese
1 whole shallot, minced,
    then sautéed in 1 teaspoon
    butter until soft (let cool)
¼ cup Boursin cheese
1 tablespoon minced dill

1 tablespoon tarragon, minced
1 teaspoon salt
¼ teaspoon white pepper
⅛ teaspoon cayenne
¼ teaspoon nutmeg
1 bunch fresh asparagus, trimmed
    and blanched for 3 minutes in
    boiling, salted water (cool and
    slice cross-wise)
½ pound jumbo lump crabmeat,
    picked over

Line pie shell on bottom and up the sides of a a deep-dish pie pan. Bake in 350° oven about 10 minutes or until crust is pale golden brown. Whisk together first 16 ingredients. Mix in asparagus and crab. Bake at 325° for 60 to 75 minutes, or until filling is set and no longer jiggles.

Yield: Serves 6-8

Editors' Notes: *Boursin (boor-SAHN) is a smooth, white cheese with a buttery texture.*

Restaurants
Savannah, Georgia

Créme Brulee

1 quart heavy cream	12 egg yolks
½ cup sugar	1 teaspoon pure vanilla extract
Pinch salt	Additional sugar for topping

Place six (8-ounce) ramekins in a roasting pan and preheat oven to 300°. Heat first 3 ingredients together and bring to a simmer, stirring occasionally. While whisking the egg yolks, slowly ladle the hot cream into the yolks (while constantly whisking mixture). Stir in vanilla and ladle custard into ramekins. Pour enough water into roasting pan to reach half-way up sides of the ramekins. Bake for 35 to 40 minutes until center of custard jiggles like gelatin and is no longer a liquid. Remove ramekins from pan and chill completely. When ready to serve, sprinkle tops of individual custards with enough sugar to cover; caramelize using a hand-held torch or by placing under the broiler for a few minutes (be careful not to overcook as it will appear burnt and taste bitter). The sugar topping should be amber-colored and crisp.

Yield: 6 servings

Almond Cream French Toast
Filling

½ cup sugar	2 egg yolks
½ cup butter, softened	1 tablespoon flour
¾ cup almonds, finely ground	¾ teaspoon vanilla extract
2 whole eggs	⅛ teaspoon almond extract

Beat first 2 ingredients together in mixer. Add remaining ingredients and beat until fluffy.

Batter and Toast

2 eggs	6 large, baked croissants
½ cup whole milk	(sliced horizontally)
1 tablespoon pear brandy	Almonds, sliced
(may substitue amaretto or spiced rum)	Granulated sugar

Whisk together first 3 ingredients; set aside. Spray a 9 x 13-inch pan with non-stick pan spray. Dip bottoms of 6 croissants into batter and line-up in pan; spread half the filling over the croissant bottoms. Next, dip the tops of the 3 croissants into batter. Place on top of the filling, covering the first layer of croissants. Sprinkle with almonds. Repeat the layering process once more. Sprinkle sugar, liberally, over top layer. Bake in a 325° oven about 45 minutes. Cut into six generous servings and serve warm with maple syrup.

Yield: 6 servings

Selected as "1 of Top 500 Restaurants" in US by 2001 Chef's Guide to American Restaurants.

Toucan Cafe

A festive atmosphere with a little Caribbean, a little Greek Isles, a lot of whimsy

Address: 531 Stephenson Avenue
Savannah, GA 31406
Telephone: (912) 352-2233
Web Site: www.toucancafe.com

Cuisine: Eclectic
Executive Chef: Jim Leclair
Price Range: Lunch/$6-$10
Dinner/$10-$20

Eggplant Torte

1 medium to large eggplant
1 tablespoon salt
½ cup flour
Pinch thyme, basil, salt, and pepper
2 eggs
Cooking oil

8 ounces spinach, wilted
¼ cup creamy feta
1 tomato, sliced
1-1½ cups tomato basil sauce
Sliced provolone cheese
1 cup roasted orzo pasta

Peel and slice eggplant. Season with salt and let stand for 10 minutes; pat dry. Add seasonings to flour. Dip eggplant into flour and then into egg. Cook in lightly oiled pan (hot, but not smoking) until eggplant is lightly browned on both sides. Top each slice with spinach, creamy feta, and a stack of 3 tomato slices. Top with tomato sauce and cheese. Cook in 400° oven until cheese melts and center is warm (10 to 15 minutes). Serve over roasted orzo pasta.

Creamy Feta

12 ounces fresh feta cheese, crumbled
4-6 ounces heavy cream

Black pepper, to taste

In food processor, blend feta (FEHT-uh) with next 2 ingredients until smooth.

Roasted Orzo Pasta

Place dried orzo (found in pasta section of grocery store) in 400° oven 8 to 10 minutes until browned. Cook in boiling, salted water until tender. Strain and serve with the eggplant.

Yield: 4-6

Tilapia With Smoked Corn & Crawfish Relish

Crawfish Relish

1 pound smoked crawfish, deveined and peeled

2 cups whole kernel corn, smoked

3-4 ounces hearts of palm, coarsely chopped

½ red pepper, finely diced

2 tablespoons cracked pepper

¾ cup green onions, finely chopped

1½ tablespoons pesto

2 tablespoons red wine vinegar

1 tablespoon olive oil extra virgin)

Salt and freshly ground pepper, to taste

Mix all ingredients together and chill in non-aluminum bowl until ready to serve.

Editors' Notes: *Small to medium-sized shrimp (shelled and deveined) may be substituted for crawfish (CRAY-fish). The amount of meat needed for this recipe is approximately 1½ cups.; save shells for making stock. A dash of liquid smoke may be used for flavoring corn.*

Red Pepper Sauce

4 tablespoons onion, coarsely chopped

2¼ teaspoons garlic

3 green peppercorns

2 roasted red peppers or 1(12-ounce) jar, drained

Sweat onions and garlic in a small amount of oil until onion is translucent and tender; mix with peppercorns and peppers in a blender. After blending well, add following ingredients:

1½ teaspoons fresh basil

¾ teaspoon fresh oregano

¼ teaspoon thyme

¼ teaspoon turmeric, optional

¼ cup chicken stock

Salt and pepper, to taste

Heat sauce to boil in same saucepan used to sweat onion and garlic. Reduce to a slow simmer and slightly reduce. If using dried herbs, instead of fresh, reduce amount by one-third.

Tilapia and Orzo

Salt and pepper

4 (6-8 ounces) tilapia filets

Olive oil

½ pound orzo pasta

Salt and pepper tilapia. Sauté in oil in pan pre-heated over medium heat (avoid over-crowding). Turn once after 3 to 5 minutes; continue sautéing until done, adding additional oil as needed. Cook orzo by package directions.

Assembly

To serve, ladle Red Pepper Sauce into plate. Place a portion of orzo pasta in center of plate and top with tilapia. Garnish tilapia with Crawfish Relish that is cool, but not icy cold.

Yield: 4-6 servings

Editors' Notes: *A tablespoon of cream, added to pepper sauce just before serving, smooths out the flavors nicely. If relish and pasta are left over, mix together for a tasty luncheon salad.*

Featured in *Savannah Magazine,* July/August 1999.

Mrs. Wilkes' Boarding House

Old-time family style dining

Address: 107 W. Jones Street
Savannah, GA 31401
(Historic District)
Telephone: (912) 232-5997
Web Site: www.mrswilkes.com

Cuisine: Home-style, Southern cooking
Proprietors: Marcia & Ronnie Thompson
Price Range: Lunch/$12
Cookbook: *Mrs. Wilkes' Boardinghouse Cook Book* (+ 1 more)

Country Fried Steak

1½ pounds cubed steak
Worcestershire sauce
Salt and pepper, to taste
Pinch of garlic powder
Flour for dredging

¼ cup vegetable oil
½ cup minced onion
2 cups hot water
3 tablespoons flour

Place steak in a casserole dish and generously sprinkle with Worcestershire sauce. Cover and marinate overnight. Remove from marinade and generously sprinkle with salt, pepper, and garlic powder. Dip steak in flour and shake. Heat oil and quickly fry steak until brown, but do not cook inside too much. This is done by cooking both sides on high heat, turning quickly, and then reducing heat to low to finish cooking. Boil onion in another pot with one-fourth cup of water for about 5 minutes. When finished cooking steaks, remove from pan; leave about 3 tablespoons browned crumbs (not burned) and drippings from steak in skillet. Add onion and 3 tablespoons flour. Stir until slightly browned. Slowly pour in the remaining hot water as it thickens. Season with salt and pepper to taste. The gravy may be served over rice or steaks.

Yield: 3-4 servings

Restaurants
Savannah, Georgia

Fried Okra

1½ pounds fresh okra
Salt and pepper

Flour
Corn oil (or other cooking oil)

Cut okra crosswise into ¾-inch slices. Season with salt and pepper. Toss okra in flour and shake off excess. Heat about ½ inch of oil in a skillet. Fry okra over medium heat. Stir and turn until light brown and tender. Remove with a spatula and drain on paper towels.

Yield: 4 servings

Savannah Red Rice

4 strips bacon,
   fried to a crisp and crumbled
2 medium onions, diced
2 medium green peppers, diced
2 cups cooked rice

6-8 tomatoes
   (peeled, chopped, and cooked)
1 cup tomato sauce or catsup
½ teaspoon Tabasco sauce
Salt and pepper, to taste
2 tablespoons grated Parmesan cheese

Preheat oven to 325°. Sauté onions and peppers in bacon drippings; remove from pan and combine with next 5 ingredients. Salt and pepper, to taste, and mix well. Pour into a greased casserole dish and sprinkle with cheese. Bake for 30 minutes or until rice is dry enough to separate and fluff with a fork.

Yield: 4-6 servings

Editors' Notes: *Fresh tomatoes may be substituted with 1 (16-ounce) can tomatoes. The addition of 1 pound of cooked shrimp, ground beef, sausage, or ham will transform this Lowcountry classic into a delicious one-dish meal. Red rice is also good topped with grated Cheddar cheese. Garnish with parsley.*

Winner of the 2000 James Beard

"At age ninety-four she (Mrs. Wilkes: 1907-2002) is the queen of all the surveys, the grande doyenne of Southern dining." —John T. Edge, 2000

Featured in *The Atlanta Journal, The Belgian Weekly Gazette, Bon Appetit, Esquire, The Boston Globe, The New York Times, Pittsburg Post-Gazette, Redbook, Savannah Morning News, Sky, Southern Living, Time, Town and Country,* and profiled on David Brinkley's evening news program.

Cumberland Island, GA
www.cumberlandisland.com

"This 3 by 18-mile Eden has been a favorite retreat of island collectors world-wide..." —*Travel & Leisure Magazine*

Hilton Head Island, SC
www.hiltonheadisland.org

"Hilton Head's 12 miles of beachfront are considered among the world's most beautiful, perhaps because they're fringed by forests of live oaks, palmettos, and tall pine trees. Settled by planters in the 1770s, this low-key coastal community truly feels separate from the rest of the world."
—Susan Breslow Sardon
www.About.com (Honeymoons/Romantic Getaways)

Little St. Simons Island, GA
www.gacoast.com

"In either direction, as far as you can see, the beach stretches gloriously empty of man and his amenities." —*Atlanta Magazine*

Sapelo Island, GA
www.sapeloisland.org

"Sapelo is a pearl in a string of sea islands protecting Georgia's lowcountry coastline on the Atlantic Ocean. It is a special place where the few remaining residents trace their heritage to Afican slaves who toiled there in the18th and 19th centuries, a heritage still evident in the tiny coastal community of Hog Hammock."
—Susan E. Laird, *Water's Edge* (January 2000)

St. Simons Island, GA
www.gacoast.com

"As you drive beneath the canopies created by moss-draped oak trees lining the roads of St. Simons Island, you feel stress flee your body. The pressures of the city and the crush of the working world simply can't survive in this sort of environment." —*Chuck Mavis, Lodging.com / Travelbase*

Tybee Island, GA
www.tybeeisland.com

This laid-back, small barrier island is the ideal place for sunbathing or swimming and surfing in the waves of the Atlantic Ocean. Tybee Island has remained a beach-lovers paradise with plenty of character since the close of the Civil War.

—WorldWeb.com

The Lowcountry's Barrier Islands

*A landmark on St. Simon's Island, the lighthouse replaces
the island's first lighthouse, destroyed by retreating Confederate troops in 1862.*

Greyfield Inn

Located on America's largest wilderness island and a designated national seashore

Address: P. O. Box 900 (mainland office)
Fernandina Beach, FL 32035
Telephone: 1-888-243-9250
E-mail: seashore@greyfieldinn.com

Web Site: www.greyfieldinn.com
Category: Historic Inn
Innkeepers: The Ferguson Family
Rates: $395-$575 (seasonal)

Apple, Sage, & Sausage Breakfast Gravy

3 ounces butter
3 ounces flour
½ apple, diced
2 cups whole milk

2 sprigs fresh thyme
2 leaves of fresh sage
1¼ pounds ground sausage
Biscuits

Make a roux (see page 220) with butter and flour. Set aside. In a medium sauce pan, sweat the apple about 5 minutes; add next 3 ingredients. Bring to a boil and thicken with the roux. Simmer for 15 to 20 minutes. Meanwhile, brown the sausage in another medium saucepan. Once browned, drain excess fat. Strain the milk mixture into the sauce pan with the browned sausage. Return to a simmer and adjust seasoning. Serve over split hot biscuits.

Yield: 4 servings

Editors' Notes: *To "sweat" the apple, cook it in a small amount of butter over low heat with a piece of foil (or parchment paper) placed directly on top of it. Then cover the pot tightly, The apple will soften, without browning, while cooking in its own juices. This classic recipe is definitely worth the trouble, and it is always a hit.*

Potato Pancakes

4 large Idaho potatoes, peeled
1 cup heavy cream
1 egg, beaten
1 tablespoon garlic, minced

2 tablespoons fresh chives, finely diced
1 tablespoon fresh oregano, finely diced
Salt and pepper, to taste
Vegetable oil

Shred potatoes into large shreds; use a box grater and shred directly into bowl, keeping potato juice. Stir in next 6 ingredients. To make cakes a uniform size, hand-pack mixture into a ramekin (or use a scoop). Heat vegetable oil in bottom of skillet until sizzling. Add cakes and cook over medium high heat until brown on each side. Drain on paper towels.

Editors' Notes: *Delicious topped with crème fraîche (see page 220) flavored with freshly chopped chives and a dash of lemon juice.*

Spinach and Artichoke Dip

1 can (8-ounces) artichoke hearts, drained
1 tablespoon garlic, minced
2 tablespoons dry sherry
Dash of salt and pepper
Dash Tabasco

Dash nutmeg
2 tablespoons butter
1 (8-ounce) block cream cheese
½ pound chèvre (goat cheese)
Large handful of fresh spinach

Combine first 7 ingredients in a small pot and simmer for 5 minutes. Mix the cheeses together thoroughly. Add the artichoke mixture to the cheese mixture and blend well. Rough chop (or tear into small to medium pieces) spinach and combine with artichoke and cheese mixture; heat in a double boiler (or in the microwave) until warm. Serve with crackers (such as Triscuit thin crisps) or pita (PEE-tah) bread.

Yield: 2 cups

"On this island, at this magnificent Georgia Coast Inn, time seems to have stood still...It all evokes a sense of serenity and oneness with nature that is restorative...The Greyfield Inn has become a favorite of notables, especially those seeking time off from being noted...One has the impression of staying in someone's fabulous home, without any of the obligations..." —*Town & Country* magazine

"Seventeen miles of powdery sands and shimmering ocean offer solitary walking and shelling...Greyfield is a Gatbyesque inn...On a private compound overlooking the marsh where wild horses graze and huge, old live oaks spread limbs to the ground, Greyfield presents Cumberland on a silver platter."

—*National Geographic Guide to America's Hidden Corners*

Greyfield Inn

Candlelight dinners at The Greyfield Inn are draped in casual elegance

Address: P. O. Box 900
    Fernandina Beach, FL 32035
    (mainland office address)
Telephone: 904-261-6408
E-mail: seashore@greyfieldinn.com

Web Site: www.greyfieldinn.com
Cuisine: Lowcountry/Southern fusion
Executive Chef: Ian Kitch
Price Range: Dinner/$75
    (includes boat ride to island)

Zabaglione
(zah-bahl-YOH-nay)

4 large egg yolks
½ cup granulated sugar
½ cup champagne
1 cup whipping cream

1 tablespoon amaretto or brandy, to taste
4-5 cups fruit (such as berries,
    peaches, or nectarines)
⅓ cup almond macaroons, crushed

Fill a large bowl halfway full with iced water; set aside. Next, fill a large metal pot with 2 to 3 inches of water and bring to a boil over high heat. Place the first 2 ingredients in a large bowl and sit bowl on top of the metal pot with water. Whisk yolks, vigorously, to avoid them from scrambling. Continue whisking until yolks begin thickening and lighten in color. Stir in champagne and continue whisking until mixture is thick enough so that a trail is left as whisk passes through the mixture (may take 5 to 10 minutes, depending on the heat of the water). Remove from heat and continue whisking custard another minute or so. Set the custard bowl in the ice water bath (set aside earlier), to cool. Whip cream to stiff peaks and stir in liqueur. With a rubber spatula, fold the whipped cream into the custard. Refrigerate at least 4 hours, but no more than 24 hours. To serve, arrange the fruit in 6 parfait glasses or dessert bowls. Spoon the Zabaglione over the fruit and garnish with the macaroon crumbs.

Yield: 6 servings

Editors' Notes: *Thc bowl, containing the custard to be whisked, should sit on top of the pot with the boiling water in order for the custard to be steamed and not scrambled. However, our tester used a double-boiler (for the custard) and reported that it worked fine for her. She served the Zabaglione over peaches. This dish (sometimes called Zabione) is somewhat labor-intensive, but the results make it worth the effort.*

Spicy Black-eyed Peas

1 cup dried black-eyed peas, washed
8 cups water
2 tablespoons cilantro, coarsely chopped
¼ cup extra virgin olive oil

2 teaspoons ground coriander
2 teaspoons ground cumin
¼ cup red wine vinegar
Salt and pepper, to taste

Place peas and water in a saucepan and boil until peas are tender. Drain and cool. Purée 1 cup of the peas with next 5 ingredients and adjust seasoning with salt and pepper to taste. Fold the puréed peas into the remaining whole peas. Adjust seasoning.

Yield: 4 servings

Editors' Notes: *Serve Spicy Black-eyed Peas and Pineapple Salsa with grilled Cobia, Salmon, Haddock Swordfish, Mahi Mahi, Red Snapper, Sea Bass, Tilapia, Cod (or any other firm flesh fish that won't fall apart on a grill or in a skillet). It is served with Cobia at Greyfield Inn.*

Pineapple Salsa

½ cup Myers or any dark rum
¼ cup light brown sugar, lightly packed
½ red onion, finely diced
1 red pepper, finely diced
3 ounces pineapple juice

1 tablespoon ground coriander
2 teaspoons pickled ginger, finely chopped
1 tablespoon cilantro leaves,
  roughly chopped
1 pineapple, peeled and sliced

Combine first 8 ingredients in a sauce pan and reduce by half over medium heat. Place pineapple slices in a single layer in a shallow roasting pan or an oven-proof dish (a 9 x 13-inch pan works well). Pour mixture over pineapple slices and roast in a 350° oven for 30 minutes. Remove from oven and cool. Dice pineapple into medium pieces and place in the refrigerator. Chill at least 4 hours before serving.

Yield: 4 servings

Editors' Notes: *This salsa may be made a day in advance and, if kept refrigerated, will remain good for several days or more. Pineapple Salsa also goes well with chicken or pork. It may be prepared using canned unsweetened pineapple slices. Use 1½ (20-ounce size) cans, drain and reserve juice to use in recipe. Use caution when reducing rum; it can easily flare-up over an open flame.*

"It is one of Cumberland's easy contradictions that we enjoyed cosmopolitan conversation and food...in a place where, outside the window, a family of wild turkeys strutted by in the twilight...When we opted for a day at the beach...we emerged onto what is surely one of the East Coast's most gorgeous beaches."
—*Gourmet* magazine

Main Street Inn

A exquisite blend of old-time Southern charm and modern luxuries

Address: 2200 Main Street
Hilton Head Island, SC 29926
Reservations: 1-800-471-3001
Telephone: (843) 681-3001
E-mail: info@mainstreetinn.com

Web Site: www.mainstreetinn.com
Category: Small luxury inn
General Manager: Diana Devers
Rates: $159-$249 (seasonal)

Banana Bread

2 cups dark brown sugar
2 sticks butter, softened
3 eggs
2 teaspoons vanilla
3 bananas, mashed

2 teaspoons lemon juice
¼ teaspoon salt
1 teaspoon baking powder
2 teaspoons cinnamon
1 cup all-purpose flour

Preheat oven to 350°. Mix sugar and butter in a mixer (of food processor) until creamy; add next 4 ingredients and blend well. In a separate bowl, combine remaining ingredients. Stir flour mixture into egg mixture (adding a small amount of milk, while mixing, if extra liquid is needed). Pour batter into greased loaf pan and bake for 1 hour or until an inserted toothpick comes out clean. Let bread cool for 10 minutes before removing from pan; cool completely before slicing. Good served room temperature or chilled.

Yield: 1 loaf

Editors' Notes: *This bread is also good with the addition of 1 cup chopped pecans or walnuts. To make a tasty Peach Bread, substitute 2 medium peaches (peeled and diced or puréed) for the bananas. The following topping is good on either the Banana or the Peach bread.*

Cinammon Pecan Topping

1 cup chopped pecans
2 teaspoons ground cinnamon
4 tablespoons melted butter

⅔ cup brown sugar, packed
½ cup all-purpose flour

Combine all ingredients until mixture is crumbly. Place on top of batter before baking.

≈≈≈≈≈≈≈≈≈≈≈≈≈≈≈≈≈≈≈≈≈≈≈≈≈≈

Arbin's Spinach Omelet

2 eggs
Milk, about ⅛ cup
Salt and pepper, to taste
¼ cup fresh spinach, chopped

2 tablespoons green onion, chopped
1 tablespoon red pepper, finely chopped
Butter, enough to stir-fry vegetables
  and cook omelet

Whisk eggs and milk together; add seasoning and set aside. Stir-fry next 3 ingredients in butter. Pour egg mixture into a skillet (or an omelet pan) and top with the spinach mixture. When the bottom of omelet is firm and set, complete the procedure by folding the omelet over.

Yield: 1 omelet

Editors' Notes: *Omelet pans are inexpensive and make the preparation of an omelet much easier. When using an omelet pan, you simply pour half the mixture into each side of the hinged-pan. When the egg begins bubbling, place the filling on one side and close the omelet pan. Within a minute or so, the omelet is ready. It is one of the simplest breakfast dishes to prepare. Microwave omelet pans are also available and come with directions on omelet preparation. The fillings one may use for an omelet are endless and include: black olives, tomatoes, green peppers, onions, asparagus, mushrooms, ham, and/or bacon. Frozen spinach may be used, but thaw and drain well before adding to omelet. We personally feel any omelet is better with the addition of cheese (about ½ cup for the recipe above); just one type of cheese (such as Cheddar) may be used or a combination of several types (feta, chèvre, Swiss, Monterey Jack, Parmesan) may be added. For seafood lovers, a delicious crab filling for this omelet can be found on page 132.*

More like one customarily finds at a country inn or resort, breakfast at The Main Street Inn is made-to-order and included in the room's rate. However, upon request, omelets (such as the one appearing above) are available for a small additional charge.

From breakfasting on a private balcony
to enjoying aroma therapy and hydrotherapy massages
in a courtyard scented by blossoming trees,
this luxurious inn is fashioned after a European boutique hotel.
—*Country Inns*

"Unlike the expected oceanfront condos and resorts,
this intimate, luxury hotel is a fresh idea
that will definitely test your resolve to tour the island.
—Dana Adkins Campbell, *Southern Living* magazine

Old Fort Pub

Regarded as the island's most romantic dining spot

Address: 65 Skull Creek Drive
Hilton Head Island, SC 29926
Telephone: 843-681-2386
E-mail: manager@oldfortpub.com
Web Site: www.celebrationusa.com

Cuisine: American Cuisine
with French Influences
Executive Chef: Eric Sayers
Price Range: Dinner/$19-$30
Sunday brunch/$13-$18

Lobster Ravioli

1¼ pounds lobster, cooked and meat removed
1 egg
3 tablespoons mayonnaise
2 tablespoons parsley, chopped
4 tablespoons peppers, diced

½ cup fresh bread crumbs
2 tablespoons oil
1 tablespoon old bay
Ravioli sheet (see Editors' Notes)
1 egg yolk

Chop lobster meat into small pieces. Mix together next 7 ingredients. Brush ravioli sheet with egg yolk, spoon mixture onto ravioli sheet and fold into a rectangle. Seal edges. Drop into boiling water and cook for 2 minutes. Remove and place in a bowl. Serve topped with Tarragon Alfredo Sauce.

Tarragon Alfredo Sauce

1 teaspoon garlic, chopped
2 teaspoons shallot, chopped
2 tablespoons white wine
¾ cup heavy cream

¼ cup Parmesan cheese
2 teaspoons tarragon, chopped
Salt and pepper, to taste

Sauté garlic and shallot in a sauce pan for a few minutes until aroma releases; deglaze with white wine. Add heavy cream and bring to a boil. Add cheese, which will thicken the sauce while reducing it to a sauce consistency. Stir in tarragon, after sauce thickens, and season with salt and pepper.

Editors' Notes: *Use won ton or dumpling wrappers (available at most supermarkets in the refrigerated or produce section) for making individual ravioli. Just place mixture in center of circle (or square) and cook as described in recipe. Pasta sheets are often available where fresh pasta is cut and sold. Fresh Maine lobster may be ordered by calling 1-800-556-2783; however, shrimp also works well in this dish.*

Summer Roma Tomatoes with Baby Mozzarrella

1 cup dark balsamic vinegar
1 tablespoon honey
1 ounce fresh basil stems, chopped
3 ounce vegetable oil
4 Roma tomatoes, remove eye and slice

1 head of iceberg lettuce, cut into four wedges
16 slices bocconcini mozzarella cheese
  (sometimes called "Baby" mozzarella)
16 pepadews (pickled peppers)
1 red onion, sliced

Place vinegar in a saucepan and bring to a boil; reduce by three-fourth and add honey. Return mixture to a boil and remove from heat. Let cool. Place next 2 ingredients in a small pot and heat to 120°. Remove from heat and cool. Strain out basil stems and discard. Arrange sliced tomatoes around plate, placing lettuce in the center. Place the mozzarella inside pepadews and place on plate. Drizzle reduction and oil over salad. Garnish with red onion.

Yield: 4 servings

Editors' Notes: *If baby mozzarella is not available, use some sort of fresh (not vacuum-packed) mozzarella cut into bite-size pieces.*

Grilled Veal Chops with Mediterranean Salad

4 (12-ounce) veal chops   1 pound fingerling potatoes, roasted

Season and grill veal chops to desired temperature. Put aside and keep warm.

Sauce

8 ounces veal demi-glace   2 tablespoons black truffle, shaved

Mix shaved truffle into demi-glace and heat. If veal demi-glace cannot be found, a brown gravy may be substituted and flavored with red wine and chopped shallots.

Mediterranean Salad

1 tablespoon olive oil
16 kalamata olives, pitted
4 ounces feta cheese

½ ounce fresh basil, finely sliced
4 marinated baby artichokes
16 grape tomatoes

After heating oil in a sauce pan, add remaining ingredients and warm through. Heat sauce and place on plates. Add roasted potatoes (shown above) and divide the salad four ways. Place a serving of salad on each veal chop and top with sauce.

Yield: 4 servings

Editors' Notes: *Small white or red-skin potatoes may be substituted for fingerling potatoes (just quarter before roasting in olive oil). If truffles are unavailable, add a dash of black truffle oil to the vegetables. If desired, a wild mushroom (such as porcini, morel, or shiitake) may be used as a substitute for truffles, which are difficult to find. For ordering truffles online, see page 220.*

"A great place to cap off a week-end getaway on the island. It's a romantic and quaint restaurant offering some of the best food on the island." —*Pagewise, Inc.*

Lodge on Little St. Simons Island

The ultimate island escape

Address: P.O. Box 21078
    Little St. Simons Island, GA 31522
Reservations: 1-888-733-5774
Telephone: 912-638-7472
E-mail: LSSI@mindspring.com

Web Site: www.littlestsimonsisland.com
Category: B&B
General Manager: Joel Meyer
Rates: $450-$675 (seasonal/all-inclusive)

Tasso Gravy

2 tablespoons butter
¼ cup tasso, sliced
3 tablespoons all-purpose flour

2 cups chicken stock
Salt and white pepper, to taste

Melt butter over low heat. Add tasso and sauté for 1 minute or two, browning slightly. Add flour and stir until well-combined. Continue cooking over low heat for another 2 to 3 minutes, stirring frequently to prevent from scorching. Increase heat to medium and, gradually, add 1 cup of the chicken stock (stirring or whisking, vigorously, until the broth begins thickening and is smooth). Reduce heat and simmer for 15 minutes. Stir frequently while continuing to simmer mixture another 5 minutes. Season to taste with salt and white pepper.

Yield: 4-6 servings

Chef's Notes: *This gravy is excellent served over stone-ground grits, biscuits, grilled or fried green tomatoes, rice, or pasta. To create a Lowcountry classic, add picked, deveined shrimp to the gravy and simmer until shrimp are cooked (about 2 minutes). Thin the gravy with stock or water, if needed. Spoon the mixture over stone-ground grits and sprinkle with parsley. For a nuance of taste and color, add strips of a roasted red or yellow pepper.*

Editors' Notes: *Tasso (TAH-soh) may be difficult to find in some parts of the country ; however it may be ordered by calling 1-800-392-2266. For a simple substitute, try combining about 3 tablespoons of a smoky sausage with 3 tablespoons of Canadian Bacon, both diced small; add a dash or two of Tabasco. Andouille (ahn-DOO-ee) sausage also works well as a substitute, if available. Chicken broth may be substituted for chicken stock; reserve 4 tablespoons to add if thinning is needed.*

ᵍᵒᵍᵒᵍᵒᵍᵒᵍᵒᵍᵒᵍᵒᵍᵒᵍᵒᵍᵒᵍᵒᵍᵒᵍᵒᵍᵒᵍᵒᵍᵒ

Pasta Salad with Sun-dried Tomatoes

½ pound bow tie pasta, cooked and drained
1 (14-ounce) can artichoke hearts,
   drained and chopped
½ cup black olives, pitted and chopped

½ cup sun-dried tomatoes, chopped
   (sometimes available julienned)
¼ cup red onion, diced
2 tablespoons Parmesan cheese

Mix all ingredients together and then toss well with dressing. Chill and serve.

Dressing

2 tablespoons Balsamic vinegar
1 tablespoon basil
1 tablespoon thyme

1 tablespoon mustard
Salt and pepper, to taste
1 cup olive oil

Mix all ingredients together, in a food processor or a blender, except for the oil. Slowly add the oil while the processor (or blender) is running; continue processing until well-blended.

Yield: 6 servings

Coconut Pound Cake

1 pound butter, softened
2 cups sugar
2 cups all-purpose flour, divided

6 eggs
8 ounces sweet coconut, flaked
2 teaspoons coconut extract

Cream first 2 ingredients; add 1 cup of flour and beat until smooth. Add eggs, one at a time, incorporating each one into batter. Mix in remaining cup of flour and remaining ingredients. Pour into a greased and floured tube or Bundt pan. Bake at 350° for one hour until golden and a tester comes out clean.

Coconut Glaze

1 cup sugar   ½ cup water   1 tablespoon coconut extract

Combine all ingredients and simmer together for 10 minutes. Pour or brush over warm cake.

Yield: 1 cake

The Lodge on Little St. Simons Island was voted by readers of *Condé Nast* as the "Best Small Hotel in North America."

═══════════════════════════════

"There are only a few places in the world where one can find natural beauty, tranquility, and gourmet dining in a private island setting. We're lucky. We have one of those places right here in Georgia."

— *Northeast Georgia Living*, Fall 2003

The Wallow

An unique cultural experience in historic Hog Hammock community

Address: P. O. Box 34
Sapelo Island, GA 31327
Telephone: 912-485-2206
E–mail: bluemoonbrunswick@mindspring.com

Web Site: www.thewallow.com
Category: B&B
Innkeeper: Cornelia & Julius Bailey
Rates: $55-$65 (year-round)

Cowcountry Pralines

2 cups light brown sugar
1 cup evaporated milk

1 cup pecan halves
½ teaspoon pure vanilla

Mix sugar and milk in a large saucepan. Stir until sugar is melted; boil (approximately 5 minutes) until mixture reaches soft boil stage (at which point mixture should be bubbly and caramel-colored). Remove from heat and stir in remaining ingredients. Stir with a wooden spoon for another 2 to 3 minutes, then let mixture stand in pot for 20 to 25 minutes (stirring occasionally until it cools enough to drop onto waxed paper without running). Drop by large spoonfuls onto waxed paper, pressing each mound of mixture out to flatten (for traditional pralines) or leave in small mounds. Let cool. If large, "flattened" pralines are made, wrap each one separately in plastic wrap.

Yield: 12 medium-size pralines (about 24 small "mounds")

Editors' Note: *Pralines (PRAY-leens), a famous Southern confection, are always a treat. Cornelia refers to this recipe as her "Mama's Choice." The secret to making successful pralines is cooking the sugar mixture the right amount of time before it removing from the heat. Cornelia says she relies on the "old-fashioned" cold-water method, "like her Mama" did, rather than trusting a candy thermometer's accuracy. To do this, simply drop a small amount of the syrup into a container of very cold water (or directly onto a piece of waxed paper). When the syrup falls into the bottom of the container, it should form a "soft ball" (between 234° to 240° according to a candy thermometer) that flattens, on its own, when removed. Our tester, an avid candy-maker, says she did not use a candy thermometer, but boiled the candy for 5 minutes and let it sit for the time instructed. She says,"This is a really good recipe and one I will use at Chrimas time." After wrapping each praline in saran wrap, briefly place the wrapped candy in the microwave on high (only a few seconds) to shrink and seal the wrap.*

Geechee Pumpkin and Grits

8 cups boiling water	4 slices smoked bacon
¾ teaspoon salt	1 cup canned pumpkin
2 cups grits, washed	1 tablespoon sugar

Place water and salt into a sauce pan and bring to a boil. Add grits and cook according to package directions. Cover and simmer about 10 minutes. Set aside. Fry bacon in a frying pan until crisp; drain. Stir bacon, pumpkin, and sugar into grits until thoroughly blended and slightly sweet (add more sugar, if desired).

Yield: 8 servings

Editors' Notes: *Do not use instant grits when making this recipe.*

Hot Milk Cake

3 cups all-purpose flour	3 cups sugar
3 teaspoons baking powder	1 cup plus 2 tablespoons hot milk
1 teaspoon salt	2 tablespoons butter
6 eggs, beaten	2 teaspoons pure vanilla

Preheat oven to 350°. Sift together first 3 ingredients into a bowl. Stir in eggs and mix well. Blend in remaining regredients using a mixer. Pour into a greased and floured Bundt pan and bake for 1 hour or until an inserted wooden toothpick comes out clean.

Yield: 1 cake

Editors' Notes: *The milk should be hot, but not boiling. Vanilla flavoring may be substituted with almond or any other flavoring desired. Good served with fresh, sliced strawberries and whipped cream.*

Featured in *Coastal Living*, May/June 2004

"...a charming inn whose simple rooms are furnished with vintage Georgian antiques."
—Chris Dixon, *The New York Times* (November 14, 2003)

"The Wallow is a pleasant and comfortable six bedroom inn owned and operated by Cornelia and Julius Bailey, who live next door."
—Terry Evans, *The Georgia Magazine* (2004)

Beach Bed & Breakfast

Overlooking the Atlantic Ocean, Beach Bed & Breakfast
offers stellar accommodations accented with style and comfort.

Address: 907 Beachview Drive
St. Simons Island, GA 31522
Telephone: (912) 634-2800
E-mail: reserve@
beachbedandbreakfast.com

Website: www.beachbedandbreakfast.com
Category: B&B
Owner/Innkeeper: Joe McDonough
Rates: $220-$495 (seasonal)

Beach Bed and Breakfast Casserole

¾ cup seasoned Italian bread crumbs
1 pound sausage
½ cup mushrooms, sliced
4 eggs
1 cup whole milk

½ teaspoon mayonnaise
½ Vidalia onion, grated
½ teaspoon mustard
Salt and pepper, to taste
½ cup Cheddar cheese, shredded

Cover bottom of a greased Pyrex dish with bread crumbs. Sauté sausage; crumble and drain. Layer sausage and mushrooms over bread crumbs. Beat eggs and blend in next 3 ingredients. Stir in remaining ingredients and refrigerate overnight. Before baking, top with cheese. Bake in a 350° oven for at 35 to 45 minutes.

Yield: 6-8 servings

Editors' Note: *If Italian bread crumbs are unavailable, use regular breadcrumbs seasoned with Italian seasoning.*

Strawberry Tea Scones with Cream

3 cups of self-rising flour
½ cup sugar
1 stick butter, cut into pieces

¾ cup buttermilk
1 cup fresh strawberries, chopped

Mix flour and sugar; cut butter into mixture with a pastry blender or fork. Make a well in center of flour. Add strawberries to buttermilk (until milk rises to 1 cup), then stir into flour mixture. Save any extra strawberries for topping. Knead flour mixture on a floured surface. Once kneaded, roll dough out to about a ⅜-inch thickness and turn to flour both sides. Use a small cookie or biscuit cutter to cut out biscuit-sized scones. Bake at 400° for 10 minutes. Cool on a rack.

Glazing

1 cup 10-X powdered sugar

2 tablespooons milk

Add powdered sugar to milk and mix until pasty. With a pastry brush, "paint" on glazing while scones are still warm

Heavy Whipping Cream

1 pint heavy whipping cream   ¼ cup sugar   1 teaspoon vanilla

Whip cream until stiff, adding sugar and vanilla. Serve with scones.

Yield: 2 dozen medium-sized scones

Editors' Note: *These incomparable tea scones (better than any we recall ever having in England or Scotland) are one of the afternoon delights served at "Lucille's Tea by the Sea" (located on main floor of Beach Bed and Breakfast) each Wednesday and Friday afternoon. Reservations may be made by calling 912-634-2800.*

Featured in *Private Pilot* (July 2003)

Featured in *The Georgia Trend* magazine (October 2002)

Featured on cover of *The INNside Scoop* B&B newsletter (July 2003)

JMac's

Casual dining at its finest on St. Simons Island

Address: 407 Mallory Street
St. Simons Island, GA 31522
Telephone: (912) 634-0403
Web Site: www.jmacsislandrestaurant.com

Cuisine: American accented
by "flavors of the world"
Chef: Archie Prince
Price Range: Dinner/$9-$28

Garlic and Maple Roasted Pork Chops

2 cloves garlic, minced
1 small bunch of parsley, chopped
1 small sprig of fresh rosemary
⅓ cup maple syrup

4 tablespoons vegetable oil
4 (12-ounce) double-cut pork chops
Salt and pepper, to taste

Blend first 3 ingredients, one-half of syrup, and 2 tablespoons of oil in food processor until a smooth paste forms. Preheat oven to 375°. Season pork chops with a pinch of salt and freshly cracked pepper. Brush mixture on both sides of chops. Heat remaining oil in skillet over medium heat. When oil is hot, sauté both sides of chops; place in oven. Brush chops with remaining maple syrup every 5 to 7 minutes until done. After 20 to 25 minutes, remove from oven and place on a serving plate covered with foil for 10 minutes before serving.

Yield: Serves 4

Editors' Notes: *A butcher can custom-cut chops for you upon request. Basically, double-cut pork chops are just extra-thick pork chops. Serve chops with Black-eyed Pea and Butternut Squash Hash (page 163) or your favorite side dish.*

Black-eyed Pea and Butternut Squash Hash

1 large butternut squash	1 small onion (diced)
Salt and pepper, to taste	2 cups fresh or frozen black-eyed peas
2 tablespoons vegetable oil	(boiled until tender)
2 tablespoons butter	1 cup cooked greens (your favorite)

After cleaning, peeling, and dicing squash, boil for 5 to 7 minutes in salted water until tender. Strain and cool. Place oil and butter in skillet or sauté pan. Add onions and cook over medium high heat until translucent. Add butternut squash and cook approximately 5 minutes, stirring often. Add peas and chopped greens and cook about 5 more minutes until heated throughout and tender. Season with salt and pepper to taste. Place in serving bowl or casserole dish. Keep warm until main course is ready.

Yields: 4 servings

Editors' Notes: *See page 102 for an easy way to peel and prepare butternut squash. For extra flavor, cook greens and peas together with a ham hock or Goya's ham seasoning. Be sure to squeeze excess water from the greens; this will prevent them from being runny or soupy. Other vegetables may also be added, as desired. Corn and boiled (or roasted) peanuts are excellent additions.*

Best Ever Choco-Chip Macaroons

2 cups sugar	4 cups shredded coconut
¼ cup water	1 cup chocolate chips
6 egg whites	

Cook sugar and water to 245° (use a candy thermometer for accuracy). Whip egg whites to stiff peaks, then slowly pour hot sugar into egg whites; whip ten minutes until cool. Fold in coconut and chocolate chips. Using a tablespoon, drop mixture onto greased cookie sheet. Cook at 375° for 8 to 10 minutes until a light golden brown.

Yields: 2 dozen

Editors' Note: *This is a light and delicious sweet which we sometimes prepare as a sample at our book signings.*

"For dinner, make reservations at the charming JMac's. After dinner, stroll down to the pier for a view of the St. Simons Lighthouse."
--Southern Living, September 2000

17 Street Inn

A unique B&B at the beach

Address: 12 17th Street
Tybee Island, GA 31328
Reservations: 1-888-999-0607
Telephone: (912) 786-0607
E-mail: hmr1@aol.com

Web Site: www.tybeeinn.com
Category: B&B
Proprietors: Helen Miltiades
Jim Morris
Rates: $90-$165 (seasonal)

Banana Nut Bread

1½ cups of mashed bananas (3 large)
¾ cup of vegetable oil
2 eggs
2 cups all-purpose flour

½ cup chopped pecans, optional
1 teaspoon baking powder
½ teaspoon salt
¾ cup sugar

Pre-heat oven to 325°. Mix first 3 ingredients in a large bowl with a wooden spoon. Stir in remaining ingredients. Pour into a greased loaf pan (9 x 5 x 3 or 8½ x 4½ x 2½). Bake until a wooden pick, inserted in center of bread, comes out clean—approximately 60 to 70 minutes. Cool 10 minutes before removing from pan. Let bread cool completely before slicing.

Yield: 1 loaf

Editors' Note: *When baking bread for gift-giving, delight the recipient with a batch of "Flower Pot Bread." Prepare unpainted, red clay flower pots by scrubbing each one thoroughly in hot, soapy water. Rinse well under hot running water and dry overnight. Once dry, oil the inside and rim of the pots with as much vegetable oil as the pot will absorb. Set the pots on a piece of heavy-duty aluminum foil in a cold oven. Heat oven to 400° and then turn off heat; leave pots in the oven to cool. Once the pots are completely cooled, oil them again. Repeat the same "oven process" once more, and the pots will be ready to fill. Be sure to grease them well before each use, especially around the rim. The bread dough seals the hole in the bottom of the pot, and so there is no leakage to worry about. If desired, the pots may be lined with parchment paper before filling. Baking time will vary with recipe and size of pots used. Bake (at temperature recipe calls for) until loaves sound hollow when tapped lightly on top. After baking, let loaves stand in pots about 5 minutes before loosening and turning out onto racks to finish cooling. The 3-inch pots make individual loaves, and 5-inch pots make nice medium-sized loaves. The number you can make is, of course, determined by the specific recipe being used.*

Canadian Bacon Quiche

4 slices Canadian bacon
½ cup chopped onion
2 tablespoons all-purpose flour
1 cup Cheddar cheese, grated

1 tablespoon parsley flakes
2 eggs
1 (12-ounce) can evaporated milk
1 frozen pie shell, thawed

Pan fry bacon and chop into small pieces. Mix bacon with next 4 ingredients in a bowl. Mix eggs and milk in another bowl. Place dry mixture into uncooked pie shell and pour liquid mixture on top. Bake quiche (KEESH) at 350° for 30 to 45 minutes or until firm.

Yield: 6-8 servings

Editors' Notes: *Regular bacon may be substituted for Canadian bacon. For a special treat, try using Nueske's Applewood smoked Canadian bacon (may be ordered by calling 1-800-392-2266). The addition of chopped spinach is also good.*

Cheesy Breakfast Casserole

1 (12-ounce) can Pillsbury crescent rolls
1 pound sausage, mild or medium hot
2 cups Monterey Jack cheese

2 cups sharp Cheddar cheese
6 eggs

Spray a 9 x 13-inch pan with baking spray and line pan with crescent rolls. Bake at 375 ° for 7 minutes. Fry or broil sausage. After draining, arrange in pan over baked crescent rolls. Place one cup Monterey jack cheese and 1 cup of Cheddar cheese over sausage. Beat eggs and pour over sausage (should be enough to fill in around sausage and cheese). Top with remaining cheese and bake 35 to 40 minutes.

Yield: 8-10 servings

Highly recommended by *The INNside Scoop* B&B newsletter.
—February 2003

Georges of Tybee

Where excellence prevails in food, service, and atmosphere

Address: 105 E. Highway 80 (1 mile, on left, past Lazaretto Creek Bridge)
Tybee Island, GA 31328
Telephone: (912) 786-9730

Web Site: www.georgesoftybee.com
Cuisine: New World Continental
Executive Chef: Robert Wood
Price Range: Dinner/$16~$24

Three Onion Bisque

3 medium shallots
1 large Vidalia (or sweet) onion
1 large Spanish onion
1 sprig rosemary
3 sprigs thyme
1 sprig sage
1 bay leaf

Olive or canola oil
3 tablespoons chopped garlic
⅓ cup Arborio rice, uncooked
¾ cup Madeira wine
3 cups chicken stock
2 cups heavy cream
Salt and white pepper, to taste

Peel onions; cut off ends, cut in half crosswise, and rub lightly with oil. Salt and pepper onions; roast at 400° for about 30 minutes or until golden brown. Set aside. Prepare a bouquet garni by wrapping herbs and bay leaf in cheese cloth and tying it with a butcher's string. Preheat a large pot over medium heat. Add enough oil to cover bottom of pot; add roasted onions and garlic. Sauté for 3 minutes, stirring a couple of times. Add rice and the bouquet garni and continue sautéeing for 2 more minutes. Deglaze pan by adding the Madeira and stirring along bottom of pot. Reduce mixture by one-half, then add chicken stock. Simmer for 30 minutes. Add cream and simmer for another 15 to 20 minutes. Remove bouquet garni and squeeze liquid back into the soup. Purée soup in a blender in 4 or 5 batches, then place in a clean pot. Return bisque (bihsk) to stove over low heat, seasoning with salt and white pepper. If you prefer a thicker soup, reduce on low heat until desired consistency.

Yield: 4-6 servings

Editors' Notes: *Arborio (ar-BOH-ree-oh) rice is an Italian grain shorter and fatter than other short-grain rice (do not substitute regular rice) and often used for risotto. This soup is definitely worth the effort! It has become a Christmas Eve traditional dish at our house.*

❦❦❦❦❦❦❦❦❦❦❦❦❦❦❦❦❦❦❦❦❦❦❦❦❦❦❦❦❦❦

Skillet Seared Yellowfin Tuna
Rice Cakes

3 jalapeños, seeded and minced
½ cup of cilantro, chopped
2 eggs
2 teaspoons salt

½ cup flour
1 teaspoon baking powder
3 cups cooked Jasmine rice

Combine first 4 ingredients in a bowl. Add next 2 ingredients to make a thick paste, then fold in rice with a spatula. Form batter into one-half inch thick cakes and set aside.

Orange Sauce

3 cups orange juice (without pulp)
2 tablespoons shallots, thinly sliced
1 teaspoon hot chili paste
½ cup heavy whipping cream

1 teaspoon wasabi paste
   (more or less, to taste)
½ cup mayonnaise
1 tablespoon water

Place first 2 ingredients in a stainless steel pan or pot and reduce to 1 cup. Over medium heat, add next 2 ingredients. Reduce to 1 cup; set aside and keep warm. In another bowl, combine last 3 ingredients and set aside for drizzling over tuna and rice cakes.

Sesame Seed Wilted Spinach and Yellowfin Tuna

Salt and pepper, to taste
6 (6-ounce) portions yellowfin tuna,
   cut into steaks
2 tablespoons olive oil

1 tablespoon butter
1 tablespoon sesame seeds
½ pound fresh spinach
¼ cup white wine

Preheat oven to 350°. In a medium hot pan, sear rice cakes until crispy on both sides. Finish cooking them in oven for about 10 minutes. Meanwhile, heat a cast iron or non-stick pan on high. Salt and pepper both sides of tuna steaks and sear them in olive oil, until desired doneness (rare to medium-rare is best). In another hot pan, toast sesame seeds in butter. Add spinach and wine; cook until wilted. Season with salt and pepper. Ladle about 1½ ounces of orange sauce onto each person's plate. Place spinach on top of sauce in middle. Set a rice cake on top of spinach. Cut tuna in half; place each half of tuna on each side of rice cake.

Yield: 6 servings

"The warmly lit interior, with its appealing bar,
is perfect for a romantic evening." —*Fodor's Travel Guide* (2001)

━━━━━━━━━━

Featured in *Southern Living* magazine (April 2000)

Recipient of the prestigious "Silver Spoon Award" by *Georgia Trends* (2002)

Little St. Simons Island, a barrier island off the Georgia coast
(Photo courtesy of The Lodge at Little St. Simons Island, GA)

Other Recipes

Original artwork by Amy Moreno

Lowcountry Oyster Roast

One of the Lowcountry's most popular forms of entertainment, an oyster roast provides an opportunity for savoring roasted oysters, scenic views of sea and marsh, Spanish moss dangling from ancient Live Oaks, and a sense-of-place richly woven with tradition.

Plantation-style Roasted Oysters

1 bushel of fresh oysters

Pick up oysters the day you plan to serve them. Keep oysters cool, but do not store on ice. If oysters have not already been cleaned when purchased, wash them down with garden hose to remove as much mud as possible. Do not wash too much, or the (desired) salty flavor may be washed away.

Yield: 1 bushel of oysters serves 4-5 people

Editors' Notes: *Oysters are in season during the "r" months of September through April. Some guests will consider the oysters an appetizer, and others will eat them as the main course. Allow for this when planning your menu. Also, be sure to have plenty of food available for guests who are not oyster-eaters. The attire for an oyster roast is casual.*

Food Ideas for Main Course

Okra & Tomato Soup (page 100)   Red Rice (page 145)   Beer Biscuits (page 136)
Smoked Ham, sliced   Potato Salad (page 171)   Lemon Squares (page 39)
Barbecue Beef and/or chicken   Cole Slaw (page 171)   Praline cookies (page 171)

Condiments for Oysters
Melted butter
Lemon wedges
Ritz or saltine crackers
Cocktail sauce and/or catsup
(serve in oyster shells)

Drinks
Iced-tea
Soft drinks
Beer
Wine

Et Cetera
Oyster knives
Roll of paper towel or napkins
Containers for disposing oyster shells
Gloves—1 size fits all
(for holding oysters while opening them)

Cole Slaw

4 cups cabbage, shredded	⅓ cup sugar
½ cup mayonnaise, more or less as needed	1 cup pickle relish, drained
	1 medium carrot, grated

Mix all ingredients together until well-blended. Refrigerate before serving.

Yield: 4-6 servings

Home-style Potato Salad

1½ cups cubed, cooked potatoes	¾ teaspoon salt
¼ cup diced celery	⅛ teaspoon pepper
½ cup chopped pickles	⅛ teaspoon mustard
¼ cup chopped pimento	⅛ tablespoon vinegar or lemon juice
1 tablespoon minced onion, optional	¼ cup bell pepper, chopped
2 hard boiled eggs (chopped), optional	⅛ cup mayonnaise

Place all ingredients into a mixing bowl, except mayonnaise. Stir mayonnaise in lightly with a wooden spoon, mixing well. Add more pepper, if desired, and chill. Garnish with paprika.

Yields: 6 servings

Praline cookies

½ cup soft butter or margarine	1½ cups all-purpose flour
2 cups dark brown sugar	1 teaspoon vanilla extract
1 egg, beaten	1-1½ cups pecans, coarsely chopped

Pre-heat oven to 375°. Mix together first 3 ingredients until creamy; stir in remaining ingredients. Drop dough onto a greased cookie sheet, using about 1 tablespoon for each cookie. Bake 8 minutes or until done. Cookie dough may be frozen, but bring to room temperature before baking.

Yields: 3 dozen cookies

Editors' Note: *The recipes on this page were contributed by Mrs. Wilkes' Boarding House (see pages 144-145) and ones the restaurant is often asked to prepare for Lowcountry oyster roasts held in the Savannah area. An order form for Mrs. Wilkes cookbook, "Mrs. Wilkes' Famous Recipes," is available at: www.mrswilkes.com/cookbook.htm.*

Very primitive, very easy, so very wonderful...

"I use empty oyster shells to hold cocktail sauce, and I always make a big pot of chili (for non-oyster eaters) which we keep warm on the oyster roast chimney. There is an old wash tub filled with Cokes, beer, and a bottle of wine sitting out. Lee dumps the oysters onto the sheet metal, over the hot fire, and covers them with a crocker sack that has been soaking in a bucket of water. The oysters steam to the desired doneness. Some people like them really cooked, but most people just want them warmed through. When the oysters are done, Lee shovels them onto our big picnic table, and everyone digs in."

—Jackie Morrison, Laurel Hill Plantation

Maxine Pinson's
Potpourri of Ice-cream Recipes

Basic Vanilla Ice-Cream

2 (14-ounce) cans sweetened condensed milk
1 quart half-and-half

1 tablespoon, plus 1 teaspoon,
   vanilla extract

Combine all ingredients, mixing well. Pour ice-cream mixture into freezer can of a 1 gallon hand-turned or electric freezer. Freeze according to manufacturer's instructions.

Yield: 2½ quarts

Variations

Black Forest Ice-Cream: Stir 1 (5.5-ounce) can chocolate syrup and 1 (16 ½-ounce) can pitted Bing Cherries, drained and halved, into ice-cream mixture just before freezing.

Black Walnut Ice-Cream: Substitute 1½ teaspoons black walnut extract for vanilla. Add 2 cups of coarsely chopped black walnuts to ice-cream mixture before or during freezing.

Butter Pecan Ice-Cream: Add 1 tablespoon butter flavoring and 2 cups coarsely chopped toasted pecans to ice-cream mixture just before freezing.

Cherry Pecan Ice-Cream: Substitute 1 teaspoon almond extract for vanilla, and add ⅓ cup maraschino cherry juice to ice-cream mixture; freeze ice-cream as directed. Stir ¾ cup quartered maraschino cherries and ¾ cup chopped pecans into ice-cream after freezing.

Chocolate Malt Ice-Cream: Stir 2 cups chocolate malt balls, chopped coarsely in blender, into ice-cream mixture just before freezing.

Cinnamon Ice-Cream: Stir in 2 tablespoons ground cinnamon (more or less, according to personal taste) into ice-cream mixture just before freezing. When served, garnish with a cinnamon stick.

Coffee Ice-Cream: Combine ¾ cup hot water and 1 tablespoon instant coffee granules, stirring until granules dissolve. Let cool slightly. Stir coffee mixture into ice-cream mixture just before freezing.

Lemonade Ice-Cream: Add 1 (6-ounce) can frozen lemonade concentrate (yellow or pink), thawed and undiluted, to ice-cream mixture before freezing.

Maple Walnut Ice-Cream: Stir 1½ cups real maple syrup into ice-cream mixture before freezing. Pour in ¾ cup chopped walnuts during freezing process or stir in after freezing, while ice-cream is still soft.

Mint Chocolate Chip Ice-Cream: Stir ½ cup green crème de menthe and 1(6-ounce) package semi-sweet chocolate mini-morsels into ice-cream mixture before freezing.

Mocha Ice-Cream: Combine 1 cup hot water and 1 tablespoon instant coffee granules, stirring until granules dissolve. Let mixture cool slightly. Stir coffee mixture and 1 (5.5-ounce) can chocolate syrup into ice-cream mixture just before freezing.

Oreo Ice-Cream: Break up 15 Oreo cookies into small pieces. Stir into ice-cream mixture just before freezing.

Peach or Strawberry Ice-Cream: Pour 3-4 cups of fresh (or frozen) peaches/strawberries, sprinkled with sugar to taste, into ice-cream mixture in a blender. Blend before freezing.

Peanut Butter Ice-Cream: Stir ¾ cup chunky peanut butter into ice-cream mixture just before freezing. Serve ice-cream with chocolate syrup, if desired.

Peppermint Candy Ice-Cream: Substitute 2 teaspoons peppermint extract for vanilla. Add 2 cups hard pepppermint candies to ice-cream mixture before blending in a blender. For a crunchier taste, stir in an additional cup of crushed peppermints (or 1 cup of mini-chocolate chips) while ice-cream is still soft enough for stirring.

Strawberry-Banana-Nut Ice-Cream: Stir 3 bananas, mashed; 1 pint strawberries, coarsely chopped; add ¾ cup chopped pecans into ice-cream mixture just before freezing.

Toffee Ice-Cream: Stir 1 (6-ounce) package Heath bar bits into ice-cream mixture just before freezing.

Editors' Notes: *To get the full benefit (especially the rich taste and creamy texture) of these recipes, do not use fat-free condensed milk or fat-free half-and-half. Reduced fat substitutes will work, but the taste and consistency are compromised (more with some flavors then others). These ice-cream recipes may be used for "make-your-own-sundae" parties where guests can make their own creations from an assortment of ice-creams and toppings. They may also be used to make ice-cream pies, parfaits, or to fill meringue shells.*

"Our Foods staff has taken the liberty of naming Maxine Pinson of Savannah the queen of ice-cream. We first planned to test her basic recipe and six variations. But we enjoyed all those so much that we picked three more flavors to test--then chose six more. We think you'll get carried away with this recipe, too." —*Southern Living* magazine, August 1988

Photo courtesy of Middleton Place—Charleston, SC

The Middleton Oak, located upon the magnificent grounds of Middleton Place outside Charleston, served as an Indian Trail tree long before Columbus discovered America. Overlooking the Ashley River, the Middleton Oak's enduring grace and beauty captures the essence of The Lowcountry and the captivating mystique that is uniquely hers.

INNformation
for
INNgoers

How I Got Hooked on B&Bs

Bill in front of Mrs. Hudspith's B&B in Edinburgh, Scotland.
The old photograph is faded, but the memories remain vivid.

I experienced my first B&B (bed and breakfast inn) during a trip to Ireland in 1971. My husband, Bill, and I were only there one night, but that was all it took for me to become a B&B aficionado forever. Now, over thirty years later, my enthusiasm for B&Bs continues.

During the summer of 1971, while Bill was an exchange student at Exeter University Law School in England, we had opportunities to visit Ireland, France, Italy, Scotland, Spain, Germany, Belgium, Holland, and Switzerland. Relying upon *Europe on Five Dollars A Day,* a travel guide published by Arthur Frommer for budget-conscious travelers, I developed our itinerary and made reservations at B&Bs in each country.

Of all the B&Bs we experienced, our most memorable was a small B&B in Edinburgh, Scotland. It was located on the street where *The Prime of Miss Jean Brodie,* by Muriel Spark, was filmed. Each morning, from our seat at the breakfast table, we watched a horse-drawn milk wagon making deliveries to homes along the cobble-stoned street in suburban Edinburgh.

The innkeeper, Mrs. Hudspith, was a wonderful Scottish lady who kept a fire blazing in the dining room and a table covered with freshly baked goodies. A pot of tea, warmed by a knitted teapot "cozy," stayed full. If it had not been for her kitchen guard dog, Bruce, I would have been tempted to sneak into her kitchen, after hours, for more of her homemade treats. Perhaps, that is why big-eyed Bruce was stationed in that particular spot—and he *never* left. I tried being nice to the mongrel, but he just glared and growled at me. I soon realized there was no use in trying to make a truce with Bruce. I thought it really annoying that this inhospitable Scot had to share the same name of my favorite cousin and our Scottish forebear, king Robert the Bruce. It was sitting around Mrs. Hudspith's communal table, next to a warming fire after a day of touring in drizzly weather, that I became forever enamored with B&Bs. I love meeting new people and sharing stories. There is no better place for doing this than B&Bs.

How could I ever forget Mr. and Mrs. Willy from Vancouver, an octogenarian couple we met over breakfast at Mrs. Hudspith's? We stayed in touch for years. When our first child was born, Mrs. Willy crocheted a little pink cap and sent it to her. Each Christmas Bill and I received alluring Canadian calendars from the Willys, always accompanied by an invitation to visit them. I hoped we might be able to one day, but we never were. Our chance meeting was a "one moment in time" experience through which I feel my life was enriched.

Since that memorable trip in 1971, I have stayed at a variety of highly acclaimed resorts and world-class hotels, within the States and abroad. However, none of my fancy hotel experiences—from The Waldorf-Astoria in New York City to Rome, Italy's Hotel Excelsior—has provided me with the same cherished memories as those I have from favorite B&Bs. There is a major difference between simply *staying* somewhere and *experiencing* a place in its totality. I prefer the experiential, and I doubt my love for the wonderful world of B&Bs will wane.

Definitions and Distinctions

Homestay, Host-Home

This type of establishment is an owner-occupied private home where the business of paying guests is secondary to its use as a private residence. The hosts are primarily interested in meeting new people and making some additional monies while continuing their present employment or retirement. Frequently located in residential areas, zoning or other government restrictions may prevent the use of signs, public advertising, etc. Usually between 1-3 rooms, these homes are often a member of, and usually inspected by a reservation service organization (RSO) but are rarely required to be licensed or inspected by local applicable governmental agencies. Breakfast is the only meal served. In some instances, it may be an unhosted apartment where breakfast is self-serve.

Bed and Breakfast

Formerly a single family dwelling usually in the 4-5-room range, this owner-occupied establishment has an equally mixed use as home and lodging with lodging superseding home more often than not. It is located in a legally zoned area and meets all the tax, fire, building and health requirements for this size and use of property. This establishment advertises publicly and can legally post a sign. Like the homestay or host home, because of its size, these B&Bs usually cannot support a family unit, so the B&B is often one partner's job and the other has outside income. Often the property is purchased specifically to be a B&B, but many are converted family homes. Reservations may be made directly with the property.

Bed and Breakfast Inn
(sometimes just called a Breakfast Inn)

Generally small, owner-operated businesses providing the primary financial support of the owner. Usually the owner lives on premises. The building's primary usage is for business. Inns advertise, have business licenses, produce their own brochures, comply with government ordinances, pay all appropriate taxes and post signs. Breakfast is the only meal served and only to overnight guests. The inn may host events such as weddings, small business meetings, etc. Room numbers range from 4-20 with a small, but increasing number up to 30. Reservations may be made directly with the property. Note: The distinction between a "B&B" and a "B&B inn" is not readily apparent, except with regard to building usage.

Country Inn

A business offering overnight lodging and meals where the owner is actively involved in daily operations, often living on site. These establishments are, in fact, B&B inns which serve at least one meal in addition to breakfast, and operate as "restaurants" as well as overnight lodging accommodations. Modified American plan (MAP) country inns serve dinner to overnight guests only, and the cost of dinner and breakfast is generally included in the room rate. A country inn with a full-service restaurant serves these additional meals to the general public. To be a country inn, a property does not have to be located in a rural area. Room numbers tend to range from 6 to 30. To understand bed-and-breakfast/country inn in the context of other properties that are confused with bed and breakfast, the following definitions are included:

Bed & Breakfast / Self-Contained Cottage

A detached building affording privacy and seclusion to guests, with owner providing minimal services. Breakfast is either delivered to the room, taken with others in a central dining room or placed prior to arrival (or upon daily cleaning) in the cottage kitchen facilities. Owner is usually available for questions, but generally guests choose this style of B&B when they want little help. Certain geographic regions see this type of lodging more than others. The light personal touch and memorable B&B decor further distinguish this genre from the vacation rental/condo.

Bed & Breakfast Hotel

These are 30+ room historic properties offering breakfast that can only be considered hotels. Only the historic structure, and perhaps some decorating components and breakfast provide the B&B feel.

Summary

Although all of the above categories view themselves as providing the below-listed characteristics, in reality, the larger the property—and particularly if the owner is not actively involved in daily operations and guest interaction—the property moves rapidly into the "hotel" perception in the minds of the traveller.

- Generous hospitality and personal attention to guests
- Architecturally interesting or historic structure
- Owner involvement in business
- Clean and comfortable ambiance and surroundings
- Individually decorated rooms

Topics Addressed in Q&A Section

Information about Q&A Section

All answers refer, specifically, to smaller bed and breakfast (approximately 2-8 rooms/suites) or historic inns (approximately 9-25 rooms/suites). For easier reading, the term "inn" is used in reference to each, with clarifications made as needed. The questions are topically arranged, and the responses are divided into 2-4 parts (*only selected ones include quotes from innkeepers and "inn tales from inn trails"):

- Brief response to question

- An "expanded" answer

- *Quotes from innkeepers in direct response to question

- *An "inn tale from the inn trail" relating to the issue

Notes: *The B&Bs and historic inns shown in this section have been reviewed or recommended in The INNside Scoop's bi-annual B&B newsletter during the past few years. Each is an "Editor's Favorite," based upon discerning criteria, and represents a sampling of the types of inns reviewed and recommended by The INNside Scoop. The photographs are randomly placed and do not, necessarily, relate to the juxtaposed questions addressed. The name, location, and Web site address of each inn is noted below its photograph. More information about these inns may be found on The INNside Scoop's Web site at* **innsidescoop.com,** *where an archive of all past newsletters is also found. A free e-subscription is available by sending your e-mail address to* **nlsub@cs.com.**

To receive a 3 year subscription
to the bi-annual *INNside Scoop* B&B newsletter,
(published each January and July)
send a check made payable to SSD, Inc.

**INNside Scoop Newsletter
22 W. Bryan St.—PMB 202
Savannah, GA 31401**

M/C and VISA orders may be placed by calling
1-888-717-4040
and
Online charge and PayPal orders may be placed at:
www.the-innside-scoop.com/subscription.html

Be sure to indicate to whom the newsletter
should be sent along with their mailing address.

If you enjoy this "Innformation for Inngoers" section, you will love **INNside Scoop: "Everything You Ever Wanted to Know About Bed and Breakfast Inns"** by Maxine Pinson. Published in 2002, the book includes over 60 "inn tales" plus dozens of "inntertaining" vignettes and anecdotes. For more information about this unique book, visit www.the-innside-scoop.com/IS.html; the site includes the book's Table of Contents and a Listing of Topics addressed in the book. An autographed copy of this book may be orderd by calling **1-800-871-8977** (see page 222 for a special offer).

Kilburnie, The Inn at Craig Farm
Lancaster, SC
www.kilburnie.com

Basic Differences Between Inns
and Traditional Accommodations

Q: What are advantages of staying at an inn?

A: The defining uniqueness is found in the distinctive characteristics each individual inn promises to provide. Inns are as different and individualistic as the innkeepers who run them, and they lack the sterility often associated with more traditional types of lodging. Personal service and guest pampering are trademarks of the inn industry. A stay at a bed and breakfast or historic inn is likely to be far more memorable than staying at a motel or hotel.

Many inns are located within historic dwellings and provide an opportunity for personally experiencing fascinating homes in a way many would be unable to do otherwise. An inn provides an ideal setting for meeting and interacting with interesting people from all areas of our country and abroad. For those desiring privacy in their own zone, there are inns that are totally secluded. See "How I Got Hooked on B&Bs" (p. 176).

One innkeeper presents a challenge to travelers: "Try going back to an inn for a second time and compare your treatment to what you receive when returning to a chain hotel." Another innkeeper relates, "I have started having more guests coming just to get gardening and/or decorating ideas. I know one caterer who frequents inns for recipe collecting."

Q: What are differences distinguishing the inn experience from a traditional stay at a chain hotel or motel, especially one which refers to itself as an "inn" and includes breakfast with the room?

A: The human factor and personal touches. Attention-to-detail. Having an opportunity to meet and interact with other guests. Memorable, home-cooked breakfasts—not pick-up items from the neighborhood donut shop or styrofoam coffee cups with stick stirrers. Most inngoers can tell you the names of the innkeepers at their favorite inns long after their visit at the inn. Many times, they can name new friends or acquaintances met while there. As far as distinguishing between breakfasts at a traditional chain hotel/motel and the morning repast at an inn—well, there simply isn't a comparison. Breakfasts at inns vary as much as the inns serving them. The meal may be simple, plentiful, or a grand 3-course feast.

Q: How can I find an inn that suits my individual needs as well as my budget?

A: There is a bed and breakfast or an inn to suit every taste, budget, and personality. When you are ready to travel, spend some time checking out different inns on the Internet until you find one that appeals to you. Five good Web sites to begin with are:

innsidescoop.com
This site is less expansive than the others, but it includes a listing of outstanding inns (each personally experienced by the editor) in 35 states and British Columbia.

BedandBreakfast.com
inns.com
TravelGuides.com
BBonline.com

Each of these sites can also direct you to specific types of inns and help you locate B&Bs within a requested proximity of a particular city.

Q: Are inns more or less expensive than traditional motels/hotels?

A: Many people think inns are cost-prohibitive. Not true. It is true that inns, especially larger historic inns, can be quite pricey. Inns located in popular tourist areas will always be more expensive than ones located in smaller towns or areas with fewer attractions, but some of these off-the-beaten-path inns are true gems. If you compare the price paid with the benefits received, you will discover inns are more affordable than you might suspect. Inns range from rural to urban, historic to modern, elegant to practical.

Expensive inns often offer special packages and a wide range of rooms at varying prices. Some offer special rates to civil servants. Even the big chains, including ones promising to "leave the light on for you," aren't that cheap anymore. I consider the majority of inns fairly priced, considering their offerings and services. I feel some inns are worth more than they charge, while some are over-priced. If cost is a concern, clarify the details of what you will be receiving when you make your reservations.

Q: Are walk-ins accepted at inns like at traditional motels/hotels? Sometimes, when traveling, I like to remain flexible and plan my trip as I go.

A: Typically, hotels and motels have a staff member on duty round-the-clock. Most inns do not. Rooms are limited at inns and sometimes reserved far in advance. However, if a "walk-in" arrives during an inn's standard check-in time (usually between 3-7 p.m.) when there is availability, most innkeepers will gladly accept the guest without a reservation.

Finding availability at an inn is much less likely on week-end nights or during a high-season period. Of course, cancellations can always occur at the last minute any day of the week or time of year. It is not advisable to start looking for an inn when you are tired of driving and ready to stop for the night. There are no billboards, along expressways, telling you where the next inn is located. Even if there were, just popping-in and finding a room available is less likely than at chain-type lodgings.

Not all innkeepers are keen on accepting guests without a reservation. One innkeeper explains why: "Some inns promote having fresh flowers and/or fruit in a guest room upon the arrival of a guest. This is not always possible with a walk-in or a last minute reservation." Once again, it depends upon the policy of the inn and the innkeeper.

Q: Are most inns open year-round like traditional accommodations?

A: Yes. However, some inns close during seasons when few visitors come to their area, such as during the months of bitter cold in certain parts of New England. This information is usually posted on an inn's Web site. Larger inns (especially ones with a staff) are usually open year-round. Smaller ones usually close on Christmas Day so the innkeepers can spend time with their family. Sometimes a small inn closes for a month in January (or several weeks at another time during the year) so the innkeepers can have a break or make repairs (usually done in January). It varies with the inn.

Q: What did the majority of innkeepers do in "their other life?"

A: There is no stereotypical innkeeper any more than there is a stereotypical guest. They come from all walks of life, and their backgrounds run the gamut from A - Z.

Q: How about inngoers. Is there a profile for them?

A: They, too, come from all walks of life.

One innkeeper says, "Generally speaking, B&Bs attract guests who are more educated and sophisticated than average."

The Importance of an Inn's Affiliation with a Professional Organization

Q: How important are ratings (such as AAA and Mobil) of inns?

A: With so many inns from which to choose, ratings help narrow the focus by letting one know the quality or service they may expect from a specific inn.

I have personally discovered unrated inns which I consider superior to some of the inns I have visited with a high rating from a prestigious organization. Even though Mobil and AAA are usually reliable in their ratings, just because an inn chooses not to be rated—for whatever reason—is not a reason to avoid going to it. Sometimes an excellent inn has not been in business long enough to undergo the inspection required for a rating.

A long-time innkeeper, owner of an established and successful inn, raises an important point. "It is important to remember that the ultimate test of an inn's quality is experiential. Owners of older establishments, under the same ownership for several generations, may not feel compelled to pay the fees of joining certain groups, even though they may meet or exceed the criteria of the various standards of the inspection." Another experienced innkeeper states, "Many of their requirements are not necessary. In some cases, they can actually detract from an inn's uniqueness."

Q: How important is an inn's affiliation with a professional inn group, and what are some of these established organizations an inngoer should know about?

A: Very important. Affiliation with established associations provides assurance to the inngoer that certain basics (such as cleanliness, food codes, and safety) have been met and approved. But, keep in mind, the quality of an inn is not a prerequisite for becoming a member of state bed and breakfast associations, PAII (Professional Association of Innkeepers International), or similar type organizations.

Most state associations set standards that must be met, including periodic inspections. Inclusion in a bed and breakfast directory (online or in most travel guides, unless stated otherwise) requires nothing more than payment for inclusion. Some private groups are more exclusive than others and issue invitations (with a hefty fee) for membership.

Prior House Inn
Victoria, British Columbia
Canada
www.priorhouse.com

Amenities and Services

Q: What is the difference between amenities and services at an inn?

A: In the May 2002 edition of *Innkeeping*, published by The Professional Association of Innkeepers International (PAII), amenities and services are addressed. "Some innkeepers use a limited definition of amenities that includes only items guests can carry away with them: fragrant soap, wrapped in the inn's private label, would be an amenity; the Jacuzzi in the room would not. At the other end of the spectrum, some innkeepers—in keeping with AAA categorization—might label room décor, such as elegant draperies or marble bath counters, amenities. Services, as well as objects, can be amenities."

Q: What types of amenities may I expect at an inn?

A: The extent of amenities varies with the inn and may be restricted to the basics or exceed the bounds of one's imagination. Amenities at an inn may include: clock radios, televisions/VCRs, CD players (sometimes with CDs), terry cloth robes (sometimes slippers), an array of toiletries (shampoo, conditioner, body lotion, make-up remover cloths, etc.), hairdryers, an iron and ironing board, working fireplace, whirlpool tub, European showers, heated bathroom floors, heated towel racks, wireless and/or high-speed Internet service, in-house theaters. The list continues ad infinitum.

One creative innkeeper tucks fresh lilac into a roll of lavendar-colored netting, tied on the ends with lavendar satin ribbon, between the pillows at turn-down. She sprays the bed linens, when ironing them, with a lavendar spritz made with vodka.

Safety Issues

Q: Is it safe for a woman, traveling alone, to stay at an inn?

A: Very. It is probably the safest place a woman traveling alone can stay.

As a travel writer, I often travel alone when reviewing inns. I have never experienced an inn where I felt safety was an issue of concern.

Bush River Farm B&B
Clinton, SC
www.bushriverfarm.com

Children and Pets

Q: Are B&Bs and inns appropriate for children?

A: Most are not, even though they may be accepted at a certain age. Children are much happier at a family-oriented type of lodging. Inns do not cater to children, and sometimes their behavior causes discontent with other guests.

A gourmet breakfast, along with interaction with other adult guests, can be ruined by a crying baby or an ill-mannered child. Many couples go to an inn to get a reprieve from children.

One innkeeper says, "I don't think a couple on honeymoon would appreciate toddlers running around on hardwood floors above their honeymoon suite. Older children often find breakfast conversation, considered an integral part of the B&B experience by some, to be boring."

Q: Do B&Bs object to guests bringing pets to stay in their room with them?

A: Most inns do not permit pets. Inns allowing pets usually have a notice posted on their Web site. Some inns offer barns for equestrian travelers who travel with their horse(s) in tow. As always, whenever in question, just ask. But, do not expect most inns to accept furry friends.

Special Needs

Q: Are most inns set up for guests who are physically challenged in some way?

A: More and more inns are offering special accommodations for physically challenged guests. If there is a possibility you might encounter a problem at the inn, because of a physical situation, be sure to discuss it with the innkeeper when you call to inquire or make a reservation. They will be able to provide the assurance you need or help you find another place better suited for your particular needs.

Inn tale: When it is time to shower, make sure you are not wider than the stall. One inn guest got stuck in a shower stall in Georgia and couldn't get out. He was traveling with a friend, who had a room across the hall. When his friend heard the yelp for help, he performed a successful rescue operation—with the help of a bar of slippery soap and some hefty tugging.

Business & Corporate Travel

Q: Do inns cater to business and corporate travelers?

A: Most definitely. Some inns have mini-suites, complete with a kitchen, for regulars who stay a week or more at a time (usually at a lower rate). Inns catering to business travelers customarily offer fax and copier services, private telephone lines, wireless/high-speed Internet service, and an early breakfast option. Some even have a mini-office set up for business guests.

Most innkeepers do not object to faxes being sent to their guests within reason. Sending lengthy documents is not acceptable. One innkeeper tells the story of a thousand page deposition faxed to an attorney staying at her inn. Not to be done!

Commodore Joshua Barney House
Savage, MD
www.joshuabarneyhouse.com

Q: Do inns accept long-termers?

A: Some inns prefer long-termers, such as individuals in the military. Individuals training or relocating to the area are also welcomed while waiting for housing to become available. Long-termers are usually given discounted rates and sometimes given special privileges (i.e., use of the laundry facilities). In exchange for the lower rate, breakfast and daily clean-up may not be included.

Inn tale: I have an innkeeper friend who caters to long-termers, especially military personnel. Whenever she gets a new military guest, she welcomes him or her by placing a special alarm clock under their bed and setting it to activate the next morning. The clock is a replica of a drill sergeant, and it "activates" by the drill sergeant playing a bugle and yelling, "Get up!" Get Up! Good morning." Imagine the surprise of a guest hearing that first thing in the morning and then finding that loud-mouthed, bossy sergeant under their bed!

Different Types of Inns

Bear Mountain Inn
Waterford, ME
www.bearmtninn.com

Q: Does B&B always stand for "Bed & Breakfast" in the travel industry?

A: "Bed and Breakfast" is what B&B traditionally refers to in the travel industry. However, all kinds of adaptations have evolved: Bed & Biscuits, Bed & Bagel, Bed & Basket, Barn & Breakfast, Bed & Boat. There is one inn named "Bed, No Breakfast."

Inn Tale: A typographical blooper once advertised a unique "Bed & Broad." One inn reports that after a man reserved a room for a night (in a state where prostitution is legal), he asked the innkeeper, in all seriousness: "Does a girl come with the room?"

Q: What is considered a traditional B&B and what characterizes traditional innkeepers?

A: A long-time innkeeper verbalizes the basic framework upon which a "traditional" B&B, operated by traditional innkeepers, is recognized. She states: "At a traditional B&B, guests are treated more like house guests or personal friends than a boarder. The atmosphere experienced and hospitality received is more like one would find at the home of a favorite friend or relative. The majority of innkeepers at traditional inns are seasoned in the art of hosting, and their primary concern is the comfort and enjoyment of their guests. These innkeepers are usually accessible and guest-oriented. Initially, traditional B&Bs refrained from putting TVs and telephones in guest rooms to protect guests from interruptions of the outside world during a getaway. However, that trend is changing. More and more B&Bs now have telephones or TVs (even VCRs) in their guest rooms, especially the larger ones."

Selecting an Inn

Q: I have found that inns do not always measure up to the glorious images they portray in their brochures or on their Web sites. How can I know whether what I see in print (or online) is what I will find on-site?

A: Not finding on-site what is promoted online (or in a slick, glitzy brochure) is my greatest pet peeve of the industry. Of course, this is not something limited to B&Bs or inns. I prefer selecting an inn whose Web site or brochure shows as many photographs as possible (guest rooms, dining area, common areas, outside areas). I also like to have an idea of what the physical surroundings are like. Virtual tours are excellent as they provides 360 degree coverage of the rooms and surrounding area outside. If an inn's Web site offers one, take advantage of it.

If an area of an inn is blatantly absent, I automatically become suspicious. For example, if there are beautiful photographs of the common areas, but none of the guest quarters—or vice versa. Of course, there are all sort of techniques for improving the appearance of a photograph. Pay attention to the furnishings and decor, if that is something important to you. Also, I find innkeepers who take care to provide a high-quality, informativeWeb site usually run a high-quality inn. Be wary of inns using superlatives and claims with nothing to back them up.

Getting the Best Rates

Q: Do inns offer seasonal rates?

A: This is usually dependent upon the location of the inn and the degree of tourism in the area at specific times of the year.

It is almost impossible to get a room (unless reserved a year in advance or more) in Savannah for the green week of Savannah's annual St. Patrick's Day festivities. However, incredibly low rates (in comparison to the usual rates) are often offered at different Savannah inns during the slower months of January and February. Look on the Web sites of inns for specials offered, or call and inquire if seasonal rates are not noted.

Q: Can I get a room for less if I am not interested in breakfast or clean-up service?

A: Rarely. I have only been to a very few inns willing to reduce a room's rate for guests not interested in the daily clean-up service. This option is primarily restricted to long-termers. Of course, you may always ask—but please respect the policy the innkeepers have decided upon, whatever it may be.

Contacting an Inn

Q: Why is a toll-free and a regular telephone number often listed for an inn?

A: A toll-free number is established specifically for making inquiries, reservations, or cancellations. However, most innkeepers do not object to calls being made on their toll-free line to let them know you are arriving later or earlier than originally scheduled.

It is not acceptable to leave an inn's toll-free number with your children, a baby-sitter, or anyone else for the purpose of contacting you during your stay at the inn. Neither is it acceptable for a personal message or greeting to be delivered to you via an inn's toll-free line.

Q: When is the best time to call an inn?

A: The best time to call smaller inns is between 11:30 a.m. and 5 p.m. local time (never during the time breakfast is being prepared/served or late at night). Larger inns, with a staff on duty, may receive calls until 10 p.m—especially in vacation cities. Restrain from becoming annoyed if an answering machine picks up instead of a real, live person—especially if the inn is small and does not have someone to mind the phone round-the-clock. For most innkeepers of small inns, a wireless phone is like an extra appendage. However, innkeepers are not always available to answer phone calls. They do have shopping to do and personal business to tend. When calling an inn outside your locale, it is important to be aware of the inn's time zone.

Making, Securing, and Canceling Reservations

Q: Do most inns offer online availability and online reservations for guests?

A: More inns are now offering online availability and online reservations. Some inns provide an online room chart indicating which rooms are available on which dates. This service provides a valuable convenience for both inngoer and innkeeper, in addition to minimizing telephone calls and costs. Online availability shows which rooms are available, at that moment, so online reservations may be made and secured.

A disadvantage of online reservations is that it eliminates valuable discourse between an innkeeper and a potential guest. Engaging in a one-on-one conversation, with an innkeeper, allows the inngoer to get a feel for an innkeeper's manner and style. This is important since an inn is, in essence, a reflection of the innkeeper who manages it. Smaller B&Bs are likely to require a phone call follow-up so the innkeeper can also get a feel for the type of inn the guest is seeking. This way, the guest is more likely to get the property best suited for specific desires and needs.

An innkeeper says, "We update our online availability manually, and so it may not always be current. If *no availability* shows, it is best to call the inn just to double-check for accuracy."

Q: Do inns require reservations to be guaranteed?

A: The majority of inns do require reservations to be secured by a credit card and usually have their policy stated on its Web site or brochure.

Many inns require an advance deposit. Be sure to find out if they are just holding your credit card number or actually charging your card. Smaller B&Bs (and even some medium-sized historic inns) are not set up to accept credit cards and require payment with cash or check. The standard requirement is full payment for one night; however, it may be more for extended stays, during a "high season," or times of special events.

Q: What if I need to cancel my reservations at an inn?

A: If the need for cancellation arises, call the innkeeper as soon as possible. Most innkeepers are willing to accommodate whenever they can, but revenue from the renting of rooms is what keeps inns in business. Cancellation policies vary; however, most inns have their specific policies posted on the inn's Web site and adhere to them. Sometimes an inn will provide you a gift certificate (usually valid for one year) to use when the visit can be re-scheduled.

Smaller inns often fill up far in advance during special seasons or local events. When there is a last-minute cancellation, the room is more difficult to fill since many would not expect the inn to have an opening. Above all, respect the inn's cancellation policy, and most innkeepers will work with you in working out arrangements mutually satisfactory.

Q: Are inns willing to rent out their entire facility to a group?

A: Many inns (small B&Bs as well as larger ones) rent out their entire facility to wedding parties or private groups. Because of the home-like atmosphere of B&Bs, they provide an attractive option for a variety of private functions.

Zero Water Street B&B
Charleston, SC
www.zerowaterstreet.com

Arriving at an Inn

Q: Is there a procedure I should follow if I need to arrive before or after regular check-in times?

A: You simply do the same as you would want an expected personal guest to do if visiting in your home. You call and let the innkeeper know when you will be arriving, and you call again if that changes. To do otherwise is rude.

The innkeepers of smaller inns often have no outside help, and it is thoughtless to keep a busy innkeeper waiting for hours on end for a late arrival. Sometimes they arrange their schedules specifically for the arrival of a guest. It is equally ill-mannered to arrive hours in advance of the agreed-upon time of arrival. Most innkeepers, I know, are caring individuals who worry when guests have not shown up or called hours after they are expected. I hear more complaints about early and late arrivals, from innkeepers, than all other grievances combined.

Q: Will I have to listen to the history of an inn, or go on a grand tour of rooms and grounds, before being shown to my quarters?

A: "Orientation time" varies from inn-to-inn, and it is a requirement of some organizations to which inns may belong. However, most innkeepers realize that guests—especially those who have travelled a long distance—are anxious to be shown to their room so they can get situated. Often an innkeeper will ask if you'd like to see the inn "now" or "later." Usually, "later" is the wiser answer. On warm or cool days, an innkeeper may offer you something hot or cold to drink upon your arrival.

Q: If I feel I have legitimate complaints about the inn or the innkeepers, is there someone with whom I may register my concerns?

A: Check the inn's Web site or brochure to see if the inn is affiliated with a state organization or PAII. If so, contact one of these groups about the problem. If you would like to address the innkeepers directly, kindly refrain from addressing your grievance in front of other guests.

Q: When do I pay for my room at an inn?

A: This varies with the personal preference of the innkeeper. Some innkeepers prefer getting "the unpleasantries" over and done with at the beginning; others prefer waiting until check-out time, especially if they anticipate additional charges being added to your account.

Bathrooms at B&Bs

Q: I stayed in B&Bs in Europe, and I often had to share a bath with other guests. I do not like sharing a bath with strangers, and so I do not go to inns anymore.

A: Almost all American B&Bs have private baths for *each* of their guest rooms—and I would say 98% of them are adjacent to the bedroom. If a bath is shared, it is usually located between two rooms rented by guests traveling together. An inn's Web site and brochure indicate whether its accommodations include a private bath or not.

Occasionally, a room has a private bath, but it is located across the hall. When this is the case, a robe is usually provided for the guest, and a sign is posted that the bath is a private one (reserved for guests staying in a particular room). In older structures, finding a way to provide an adjacent bath, for each guest room, often provides a challenge—one which sometimes escapes a satisfactory solution.

Gratuities and Additional Charges

Q: Are there any other charges I might incur while staying at an inn?

A: Not usually. If there are, it is usually at the larger inns. If you feel there might be, just ask when you make reservations if there are additional costs involved (such as a service charge or state room tax).

If you need to make local calls or go online, check to see if local calls are free. Typically, there is an information book in each guest room at an inn with basic information. If there is a charge, it will probably be noted in this book. I have never stayed at a B&B where there is a charge for local calls. However, sometimes larger inns charge up to 75 cents per local call. This is not customary at an inn presenting itself as a B&B—a fact I always make a point to bring to the management's attention.

Q: Is there a standard tipping policy at inns?

A: Just as each B&B is different, so is the issue of tipping. Whether you stay in a B&B, inn, motel, or hotel, it is courteous to leave $3 to $5 per night for the housekeepers; I usually leave the money on the dresser. The exact amount varies with the length of the stay, the price of the property, the size of the room, and the services rendered. If the B&B is quite small, and the owners do the housekeeping themselves, no tip is necessary. Since many people are unaware of this practice, many innkeepers have taken to leaving tipping envelopes as a gentle reminder to guests, although there is no obligation to leave anything, especially if the housekeeping is not up to par. Personally, we don't much care for the practice, and would prefer a no-tipping policy, with the housekeepers paid a good wage, but recognize that that's not always possible. If you're not sure, it's always okay to ask. Last but not least, remember that inns which include accommodations, breakfast, and dinner in the rates typically add a 15% service fee to the entire amount. (*Reprinted by permission of Sandra W. Soule, Editor, BedandBreakfast.com*)

Songbird Prairie B&B
Valparaiso , IN
www.songbirdprairie.com

Breakfast Time at Inns

Q: When staying at a B&B, am I expected to eat at the same table with other guests?

A: Some inns have individual tables where a single traveler or a couple may eat alone. This is especially true at the larger historic inns. But, at a typical B&B, expect to share breakfast at a table of strangers who, chances are, will become friends before the meal is over.

As a rule, I have found guests at inns to be friendly folk whose company I thoroughly enjoy. Sharing breakfast with guests has become part of the B&B experience that I look forward to each morning.

Q: What kind of food is served for breakfast at inns?

A: Everything imaginable: simple, Continental, deluxe, a full country breakfast, a gourmet breakfast, a 3-course feast (which usually begins with a fruit dish, followed by a breakfast entrée, and finished off with something sweet). Larger inns sometimes offer a menu, but it is unusual. A few inns provide a menu selection, the night before, from which breakfast selections may be made. Most innkeepers will ask, sometimes when the reservations are made, about food allergies or restrictions (dietary, religious, or other). Some innkeepers creatively post the breakfast menu the night before.

Q: What time is breakfast usually served at B&Bs?

A: It varies with the inn. Some innkeepers just have one seating, but most offer a time span (such as 8:00 a.m. until 10 a.m.) during which breakfast is served.

Most innkeepers are willing to accommodate their guests however they can. If a guest has an early flight or an early business meeting, an early breakfast can often be arranged if requested in advance.

Q: When eating at a communal table, must I wait until everyone is seated before I may begin eating?

A: Absolutely not. For the most part, the modus operandi at inns is very laid-back and amazingly casual—much more than people might realize or anticipate.

Q: Do innkeepers usually join their guests at breakfast time.

A: Some do, but most do not.

Q: If I finish eating, before the other guests, may I excuse myself and leave the table.

A: Certainly.

Q: Is it necessary to get dressed for breakfast at an inn?

A: Even though you may feel quite at home at an inn, especially a smaller B&B, it is not appropriate to show up for breakfast in your nightie, robe, stocking feet, or barefoot. Even though bare feet are not acceptable, bare heads (no baseball caps or curlers, please) are preferred. Other than that, as long as you are dressed decently, almost anything goes. There is no right or wrong dress code at inns, and most people dress casually. I do not see a problem sauntering down, for a cup of early morning coffee, in a cover-all robe. I often do this myself.

One innkeeper says, "the tone of an inn sets the stage for appropriate dress."

Q: I am sometimes uncertain about the correct silverware to use or other dining etiquette. If extra spoons and forks are at my place setting, how do I know what to use and when to use it.

A: Not to worry! If it would make you feel better, refer to the Table Manners section on pages 204-205. The best thing to do, when uncertain about which utensil to use, is to observe which one someone else is using. Of course, they may not know either and might be waiting to see what you do!

Some inns set formal breakfast tables with fine crystal and sterling silver. Others serve breakfast down-home style. If you should slip up and make a faux pas, don't worry about it. You'll probably never see any of the folks at your table again anyhow. If the silverware is turned down on the table, it is being done in the European style.

Q: If I am engaged in a conversation with other guests after we finish eating, does the innkeeper expect us to move to another area?

A: Most innkeepers are delighted when they see guests enjoying each other's company and establishing new friendships. However, I have heard some innkeepers comment that they would prefer guests visiting elsewhere so breakfast clean-up can be completed.

would be best to find another spot. There are usually a number of places, at an inn, where guests may talk and visit. At more formal inns, fine china is used at breakfast time and must be washed by hand. This is time consuming, and innkeepers are usually anxious to clear the table so they can move on to to the next item on their never-ending daily agenda.

Q: Is it okay to request an inn recipe?

A: Most innkeepers are happy to share their recipes. Some inns have compiled cookbooks, with favorite recipes of their guests, which they sell at their inn. Others have print-outs of their recipes available upon request.

Q: Are meals other than breakfast offered at B&Bs?

A: Not often, but sometimes. Some inns, especially larger ones, may offer a prix fixe dinner. Inns sometimes offer to prepare dinner, with advance notice, especially when local restaurants are limited or not available. However, the food offered is usually limited. If you are interested in having all meals available, a "country inn" or an inn resort is more in line with what you are seeking.

Palm House B&B
Bay St. Louis, MS
www.palmhouse.org

Telephones, Fax Machines, and Internet Access

Q: My work requires that I travel with a laptop and have online access. Is this available at most inns?

A: The majority of inns now have a telephone/modem in each guest room, and the larger ones often have private guest lines (sometimes with an answering machine or voice mail). More and more inns are now providing wireless and high-speed Internet services as well.

Smaller inns are less likely to have telephones in guest rooms. Those that do not have phones in guest rooms usually have a guest phone (set up in a private area) or a cordless phone that can be taken into one's room. If there is a telephone in your room at a smaller inn, make sure that using it for Internet access will not interfere with business calls to the inn or disable other guests from using the phone. When a telephone line is shared by guests, an innkeeper will sometimes post "Internet guidelines" for usage. You will also need to check to see if a "9," needs to be dialed in order to get an outside line.

Q: Should I give the inn's main telephone number as a number where I can be reached while staying there?

A: Calling a guest on a business line should be reserved, primarily, for emergency calls. If you anticipate receiving calls during a visit at an inn and do not have a cell phone of your own, ask the innkeeper (before arriving) how you may be contacted. If you will have a private line in your room, the innkeeper can give the number to you in advance.

Smoking and Alcoholic Beverages at Inns

Youngberg Hill Vineyards & Inn
McMinnville, Oregon
www.youngberghill.com

Q: Do most B&Bs have a no-smoking policy?

A: Yes, and most inns strictly adhere to and enforce their no-smoking policy. No exceptions. Some innkeepers require guests to sign a statement indicating they understand the no-smoking policy of the inn and agree that they (and members of their party) will abide by it. The statement forewarns guests that if they do smoke inside, a hefty fine (usually $200-$500) is added to their bill for the extra cleaning required. An innkeeper may also ask a guest, who violates the no-smoking policy, to leave the premises without a refund.

Inn Tale: A sign at one inn reads: "If we see you smoking, we'll assume you are on fire and will take appropriate action."

Q: Is there a policy concerning the use of alcoholic beverages at inns?

A: The use of alcoholic beverages varies with the inn and the legalities of the area where the inn is located. Many inns offer wine (at an afternoon wine reception) and/or cordials at turn-down. However, the availability of hard liquor at inns is not customary. Again, this question/answer section is referring, specifically, to smaller B&Bs or historic inns, not country inns. A few innkeepers do request no alcohol at their inn (customarily noted on the inn's Web site and brochure), which is also usually their home. As always, the policy of an inn should be respected and abided by.

Checking Out and Settling Up

Q: What is the standard check-out time at B&Bs?

A: The check-out time at most B&Bs is 11 a.m., and it is important that guests check-out on time. Preparing rooms for the next guests takes time, especially when the innkeepers do not have outside help. Some small, family-run B&Bs have an earlier check-out on Sundays so the innkeepers may attend a worship service. Certainly, this should be respected.

Q: If I need to extend my check-out time by an hour or two, is that a problem at a B&B?

A: Yes, it usually is a problem for the reason given above. However, if it is mid-week and new guests are not expected that day, you might be able to extend your stay by an hour.

Q: Do I pay my bill when I am ready to check-out?

A: The bill is usually paid at check out. However, some inns prefer handling the financial part at check-in. It depends upon the policy of the inn.

Q: If I decide that I would like to extend my stay at an inn for one or more days, is there any procedure that needs to be followed for an extension? Would it be inappropriate to ask to move into another room?

A: Just let the innkeeper know, as soon as possible, that you are interested in staying over. If there is availability, there should be no problem. If you decide to stay over and would like to move into another room, most innkeepers will not mind as long as the one you want is available. Of course, if your new room costs more than your original one, you will be expected to pay the difference (unless you are able to work out the difference due to your extended stay).

Weddings, Receptions, and Honeymooning at Inns

Q: What is the appeal of having a wedding or reception at a B&B, and what are things I need to be aware of when planning an inn wedding or reception?

A: Inns are favorite spots for weddings and receptions because of the elegant facilities, picturesque settings, and attention-to-detail they offer. Inns specializing in weddings and receptions may offer special wedding packages (including catering and set-up). Most inns, specializing in weddings and receptions, are also able to suggest photographers, florists, catering services, music accompaniment, etc. Sometimes suppliers will work harder to please an innkeeper, than an individual, since they know an innkeeper will provide repeat business. Expect to pay an extra charge for outside services, a percentage to the innkeeper who makes the contacts and arrangements, and (possibly) a damages deposit.

If an inn is small, the wedding party (usually in range of 10 or more) may be required to rent the entire inn for a minimum of 2 nights.

Q: When weddings and/or wedding receptions are held at a B&B, are rooms also rented to individuals not connected with or attending the wedding?

A: Some inns require the hosting group to pay a flat fee (which covers booking the entire inn), before they agree to having a wedding reception at their inn. Other inns will continue renting rooms to guests not connected with the wedding. A wedding reception is, in essence, a big party which often becomes disruptive for other guests—especially when the reception is held after 8 p.m. It is unfair to the non-wedding guests when they are not free to use the facilities and grounds for which they pay.

Some inns will not agree to hosting wedding parties, even though they have the facilities and space. The noise factor is usually the reason why. They do not want their clientele deprived of the peace and quiet they are paying to receive.

Black Horse Inn
Warrenton, VA
www.blackhorseinn.com

Q: Do most inns have a honeymoon suite or a separate cottage catering to honeymooners?

A: Most of the larger inns do have a honeymoon suite or a separate cottage designed for honeymooners. However, even the smaller B&Bs usually have a room (or suite) they refer to as their "honeymoon suite."

Q: I would like to spend my honeymoon at a B&B, but I do not want to eat breakfast with a table of grinning "well-wishers."

A: Innkeepers are respectful of the privacy desired by newlyweds, and they are willing to accommodate their wishes however possible. If you would like to have breakfast alone, ask if you may eat at a separate table (perhaps in another room, porch, or garden) or if breakfast could be delivered to your room. This is something that needs to be discussed when the reservations are made.

Et Cetera

Q: Are guests ever served breakfast in bed at a B&B?

A: This service is usually limited to honeymooners, even though I once received breakfast in bed (as a non-honeymooner) at a B&B. If you are visiting an inn where breakfast in bed is offered and you wish to take advantage of this service, please be wearing something when breakfast is delivered. Simply being draped, with a top sheet, is insufficient.

Inn Tale: It was not a Kodak moment when an innkeeper delivered breakfast to newlyweds on their first morning as husband and wife. Awaiting their delivery of breakfast, they were propped in bed, au naturel, under the covers. When the husband (a rather prosperous gent around the middle) leaned forward to accept the breakfast tray, the bed collapsed and food flew everywhere. Not knowing what to do, the innkeeper also took flight, leaving the couple nude with their food.

Q: Is there an online message board where I can exchange information with other inngoers about B&Bs?

A: I consider the state-by-state message boards found at www.bedandbreakfast.com the best available online. At the top of the home page, click the "Resources" tab (far upper right corner). When the drop-down menu appears, click "Message Boards." A listing will appear of locations world-wide; select the area where you wish to check-out inns and click the appropriate link. For example, if you wish to read what has been posted about inns in Georgia, then click the "United States" link—a list of all states comes up. Then simply click "Georgia" to see postings about Georgia B&Bs. Access to the Message Board is free and available to all, but establishing a personal login (user name and password) is a prerequisite. However, the sign-up process only takes a few minutes and is time well-spent.

Online message boards, newsgroups, and forums provide an excellent way for travelers to exchange information. The last time my husband and I went to England, we needed accommodations close to Gatwick. I posted a notice, outlining what we desired, on a British Travel Forum. Within 30 minutes, I had the information I needed. Use the message boards for receiving and sharing information, but please do not use them as a way to "trash" inns or innkeepers. If you have an unpleasant experience at an inn, you can relate this without going into damaging (or even libelous) details. If someone submits a message that the board monitors consider inappropriate, it will not be posted.

Q: When staying in a cottage (separate from the main B&B inn, but a part of it) where breakfast is provided, is a guest expected to wash and put away the dishes used?

A: Sometimes instructions are posted letting guests know what the innkeepers expect concerning clean-up. Whenever I am staying in a B&B cottage, where I prepare my own breakfast with stocked items (cereal, toast, coffee cake, yogurt, fruit, coffee), I usually wash the dishes and put them away. However, as long as the dishes are rinsed and stacked, I think that is sufficient. It is not acceptable to leave dirty dishes sitting out or scattered about the place. Whenever there is a coffee pot in my room, I always rinse out the pot and toss out the coffee filter with the used grinds.

Q: I love candles and incense and often travel with my own. Is it acceptable to burn candles at an inn?

A: Always ask for permission before burning candles. Incense is best left at home. It travels through an inn's heating/air-conditioning system, and its aroma is not appreciated by everyone. Open flames often violate an inn's insurance coverage.

Be aware that "blackening" the wicks of candles is the proper way of displaying them. It does not provide license for burning the candles.

Q: If I am flying in, is it appropriate to ask the innkeeper to pick me up from the airport?

A: Not unless they promote a pick-up service, which only a few do.

Q: Should I call the innkeeper by his or her first name?

A: In today's more casual society, this is the preference of most innkeepers. And they will probably call you by your first name, as well, unless you indicate otherwise.

Q: I enjoy picking up memorabilia from inns I visit. Do inns ever offer, for sale, special items reminiscent of their inn?

A: Definitely. Small corner or "cupboard" gift shops are frequently found in inns, and they often offer a wide variety of items with the inn's name or logo. Items include mugs, terry cloth robes, artwork, cookbooks, Christmas ornaments, "Do not Disturb" doorknob hangers, magnets, and a host of other things to remind you of your stay at the inn.

My home study is dotted with mementos from visits to inns, special mementos given to me by innkeeper friends, and keepsakes I have picked up when visiting favorite B&Bs.

Q: What if I have an accident while at a B&B (soiled sheets, become ill, etc.)?

A: Even though accidents are embarrassing, the innkeeper (or housekeeper, if there is one) needs to be notified as soon as possible. Accidents happen, and it is better for the innkeeper to hear about it from you—especially if it involves breakage or a stain that needs immediate attention to keep from becoming permanent. If the damage is significant, then offering to pay for its repair or replacement is the least you can do.

Q: Is it acceptable to ask an innkeeper to do my personal laundry or to request permission to use the inn's laundry facilities?

A: No. There is a distinct difference between service and servitude. An innkeeper's charge is to provide the former, not the latter. However, an inneeper may offer the use of the laundry facilities to long-termers. If so, provide your own laundry supplies.

Q: What is considered a "suite" at a B&B?

A: I define a "suite" the same way the dictionary does: "a series of self-contained, connected rooms used as a living unit." However, I have found the term used loosely in the lodging industry, including B&B inns. Even if a room is large enough to be five rooms, yet it is just one open room, I consider it a "large room"—not a suite. Spacious rooms, including a sitting area and/or a kitchenette, are often promoted by inns as "suites." However, unless the rooms are separated by dividing walls, I do not categorize it as a suite.

If you are unable to differentiate between rooms and suite online, contact the innkeeper and inquire about the specifics.

Q: Is it okay to take food into my room at an inn?

A: Avoid taking in "fast food" or pizza into inn rooms. Doing so can result in stains, an offensive lingering smell (which can float into other rooms), and result in problems with rodents and/or ants.

However, if a snack is provided at the inn, innkeepers usually do not object to you carrying it to your room. Just make sure not to put wet-bottomed glasses onto stainable wooden furniture or marble tops. Always use coasters, when provided.

One owner of an upscale historic inn tells about how the doorbell rang one night around 11 p.m. When she opened the door, she was greeted by a pizza delivery guy who handed her a pizza and a bill with the name of a guest staying at the inn. The owner did not say anything to the guest at the time, but she told me later that she regretted allowing a $10.95 pizza to be eaten in a $375-a-night antique furnished suite. Fortunately, no tomato sauce stains were left anywhere, but the area smelled like a pizza hang-out for days.

Lampstand B&B
Ft. Mill, SC
www.lampstandonline.com

Q: *What should I do if I leave something at the inn? Will the innkeeper be willing to mail it to me?*

A: Most inns have a "lost and found" box. Just call and let the innkeeper know what you left and the general area where it might be. Chances are, you are more likely to have it returned than if you had left it at a motel or hotel. However, it is the responsibility of the guest to pay for the postage and handling of a returned item.

Q: *Is it okay to make suggestions, face-to-face to an innkeeper, concerning how I feel their inn could be improved?*

A: Most innkeepers are appreciative of helpful suggestions. Just remember, an innkeeper's inn is their "baby," and sometimes suggestions are not wanted or appreciated.

Unless I am specifically asked for recommendations by an innkeeper, I usually do not offer them. When grievances are voiced, always express them to the innkeeper privately. PAII (Professional Association Innkeepers International) often reminds innkeepers: "A Complaint Is a Gift," which is also the title of a book addressing this issue.

Q: *When I would like to express gratitude, in a special way, to an innkeeper for extra kindnesses extended me during my visit, how can I do this?*

A: Just a hand-written thank-you note, expressing your gratitude, is always appreciated and cherished by innkeepers. If the inn has a special theme or the innkeeper is a collector of a specific item, send a surprise gift that can be displayed in the inn to remind the innkeepers of how their efforts are appreciated.

One of my favorite "inn tales" is related by an innkeeper who has been a recipient of suprise gifts from guests whose first visit brought more "surprises" than she ever anticipated. Listen to her story:

A man called and reserved a room for two nights to celebrate a wedding anniversary with his wife. When he asked if he could stop by early to drop some things off in their room, I told him that would be fine. After he arrived and paid for the two nights, I gave him the key to his room.

After he left, I went to the room to deliver some drinking glasses. When I opened the door, I could not believe the scenario before me. A path of rose petals led from the door to the bed, and a circle of rose petals (about 2 feet in diameter) were meticulously arranged on the bed. A black leather whip had been placed in the middle of the circle of petals, and a set of black leather handcuffs were attached to each corner of the antique iron bed. Next to the bed, sitting on top of the bedside table, sat a bowl of bananas, grapes, a can of fruit cocktail, a jar of cherries, and a can of whipped cream topping. A skimpy, string-type nightie was lying on the floor, and a huge boom box was sitting on the desk—along with other things I dare not mention (and mostly stuff I'd never even seen before and have no idea what they were).

Closing the door to the room as fast as I could, I ran outside and hollered for my husband. "Johnny, Johnny! Get up here quick. Real quick!" As soon as he heard me, he came running up from the barn.

It didn't take but one quick look at that room before Johnny told me to call Bubba, our son-in-law and a law enforcement officer, to hurry over to take a look at the situation. So, I called Bubba.

"Bubba, you need to get up here right now! I think we may have a real problem here."

I guess Bubba could sense the panic in my voice, so he didn't even ask for details. Within a few minutes, Bubba was driving up to our B&B in his police car. By the time he arrived, all sorts of terrible thoughts were running through my mind. So, as soon as I showed Bubba the room, I started pounding him with one question after another.

"What is this stuff? What's gonna happen in this room tonight? Is he going to beat her? Am I going to come up here tomorrow morning and find my expensive white bedspread ruined with blood stains? I have a big name Christian musician staying here this week-end. What's he gonna hear from that room? Can't I just write this man a refund check, pack up his things, and put them on the porch for him to pick up?"

Bubba was amused. He answered, "Well, they're gonna have a good time tonight, that's for sure!" He then informed me that when someone rents a room, they have the legal right to do whatever they please in the room as long as they do not disturb the peace or break the law. Well, all I knew was that my peace was already disturbed!

That couple might have had a rollicking good time that night, but I didn't sleep a wink all night long. However, I must admit, I never heard a sound even though my bedroom was located directly over their fruit-laden "rose petal" room.

Since that never-to-be-forgotten visit, the occupants of that room have returned to the inn twice as guests. Each time, they have brought me a nice gift. But, to this day, they have no idea how they contributed to my "education" on their first visit to my B&B! I doubt they ever will.

Thematic Inns

Q: I have heard about inns which revolve around unususal themes. What are examples of these?

A: A "thematic inn" is one that revolves around a particular theme or motif, particularly in its decor or focus. The theme can be determined by the inn's location, the original use of the building, or something of particular interest to the innkeeper. A few examples of thematic (or unusual) inns include inns incorporating the theme of other countries, romantic cities, a specific time period, famous movies, storybooks, the seashore, specific sports, or a safari. B&B accommodations are available on old Southern plantations and aboard tugboats, paddle-wheel steamboats, and yachts. They can also be found in old carriage houses, jailhouses, smokehouses, barns, school houses, medieval castles—more to be discovered in former slaves' quarters, treehouses, lighthouses, cabooses, Sunday houses, haunted homes, cliff dwellings, and even beagle-shaped inns! Some inns are actually located underground or underwater. As long as the theme is not overdone, a visit to a theme-based inn can be a fun and enjoyable experience—especially for adventuresome, young-at-heart travelers! For more information about unique getaways, go to: **http://bandb.about.com/od/uniquegetaways** (also see the ones on page 203).

B&Bs are Endless in their Uniqueness

Butler Greenwood Plantation B&B
St. Francisville, LA
www.butlergreenwood.com

Henderson Village
Perry, GA
www.hendersonvillage.com

Jail House Inn
Preston, MN
www.jailhouseinn.com

Red Horse Inn
Lancaster, SC
www.theredhorseinn.com

and last, but far from least...

The Red Caboose B&B
Sequim, WA
www.redcaboosegetaway.com

Basic Table Manners

The understanding and application of good table manners makes a statement about one's background and experience. Some regions and individuals are more manners-conscious than others, and cultural differences must also be considered—especially when traveling abroad.

Whether having a country-style breakfast at a casual B&B, a lavish morning repast at an historic inn, or a sumptuous dinner at an upscale restaurant, good manners are important. Knowing which utensil to use when, as well as other basics, enables one to avoid being uneasy or self-conscious during mealtime. However, the most important "table rule" is mealtime pleasantness and consideration of those with whom the meal is being shared.

A brief overview of dining etiquette is bulleted below. Excellent Web sites are available providing detailed information on dining and social etiquette. Suggested links are listed on page 205. A reliable etiquette book (such as *Emily Post's Advice for Every Dining Occasion* by Elizabeth L. Post) is a must for every home library.

- After being seated at the table, place the napkin in your lap. After the meal is over, leave your napkin placed loosely next to your plate. It should neither be crumpled nor left on the chair.

- A correctly set table has utensils arranged in the order they are to be used—from the outside to the inside. For example, the outer fork is the first fork used (usually for a salad or an appetizer). This same rule applies to the spoons and knives (located on the right side of the plate). Glasses are placed to the right of the plate since the majority of folks are right-handed.

- Food is served from the left side, and plates are removed from the right side. Likewise, when passing food at the table, it is served to the right (received from one's left).

- When someone requests that the salt be passed, it is passed along with the pepper. While en route to the person making the request, it is not to be used by others.

- Straw-sipping is fine at fast-food restaurants, but straws are only to be used for stirring at nicer establishments.

- Unless you are adept at using chopsticks, only use one utensil at a time (except when cutting, simultaneously, with a fork and knife). The empty hand is placed in the lap, *not* on the table.

- Once a utensil has been used, it must never touch the table again.

- A spoon is the utensil-of-choice for most fruit-type dishes (often the first breakfast course at inns).

- After eating food served in a compote or bowl, placed upon a plate, the spoon is placed on the plate (not left in the fruit or dessert dish).

Table Taboos

- Talking while food is in the mouth
- Talking on cell phones
- Blowing on hot foods or beverages
- Sopping bread into gravy or sauces
- Smoking
- Nose-blowing
- Picking teeth or using a toothpick
- Slurping soup
- Plate or bowl clanging (trying to scoop up last bites or drops)
- Putting elbows on the table or feet in the chair

Et Cetera

• Beepers and cell phones should be silenced during meal time at a restaurant or an inn. Many restaurants now request this courtesy.

• Even though requesting a take-home bag has become common place and acceptable at most restaurants (except for the most exclusive), this is not an appropriate request at an inn.

• In consideration of other paying guests, crying or misbehaving children need to be removed from a public dining area.

When finished eating, place your knife and fork in the position shown above. This signals that your plate is ready to be removed from the table.

Related Web Links

www.westernsilver.com/etiquette.html
www.cuisinenet.com/glossary/tableman.html
www.unlv.edu/Tourism/etiquette.html
www.ryangrpinc.com/table_demo.html

These Lowcountry oaks were once just two little "nuts,"
but they "held their ground" and survived the fury of Hurricane Hugo.

Meet the Authors

Our Story

Mother and Daughter—
Partners and Friends

Malyssa and Maxine Pinson
Mother's Day 2001

It is not who or what we were yesterday that matters.
It is who and what we are today,
and the hope of who and what we may become tomorrow.

From Feisty Foes to Forever Friends

by Maxine Pinson

Twelve years ago it would have been disastrous for my twelve-year-old daughter, Melissa, and me to have been left alone in a dangerous place like a kitchen. No doubt about it, one of us would have whopped the other one over the head with a frying pan within a matter of moments. The only uncertainty was who would get the first blow and who would win that day's battle.

If Melissa and I had to travel together, I sat behind the wheel up-front, and she sat in the mini-van's way-back yonder spot. The tension between the two of us was so caustic that we would not even sleep in the same room if we had to travel together. I would pay extra just to have a wall between us. Whenever I was home with Melissa alone at night, I slept with my bedroom door locked and a motion detector on. She did not have to worry about me going up to her room. It was such a disaster, I would not allow the exterminator to go into the sty for two years. Melissa and Myra, her guinea pig, lived like two little rats in a room that was knee-high with impossible-to-decipher stuff.

Eight years ago, when Melissa was sixteen-years-old, I no longer had to worry about what would happen if we were left alone or daily battles. Melissa had become a teenage runaway. For two-and-a-half unbearable years, we had no clue where she was. There were times when we did not know if our daughter was dead or alive. Both possibilities were real, and each was haunting. Meanwhile, my husband, Bill, and I were facing another crisis. Our twenty-one year old daughter, Celia, was dying of a rare form of non-Hodgkin's lymphoma—mycosis fungoides. There were many days, during this time, when I was convinced I had died and gone to Hell. When I realized I was still roaming planet Earth, I decided Hell would probably be like a five-diamond resort in comparison. There were times when I wanted to die, prayed to die, asked others to pray for me to die. It was just that bad. I had neither the desire nor the energy for living a life that had become so painful.

More than anything in my life-to-date, Malyssa represents, to me, the manifestation of hope fulfillment and answered prayer. I am grateful that the many prayers (by me and so many others) for Malyssa's safe return and restoration were answered; I am thankful the prayers (prayed to a merciful God of love and grace) for my demise were unanswered.

Today I cannot imagine life without Malyssa, and I look forward to our time together. Seldom does a day pass that we do not see each other, chat by phone, or correspond by é-mail. Without Malyssa's support, encouragement, sensitivity, intelligence, sense-of-humor, keen eye-for-detail, affirmations, and confidence in my ability, *Lowcountry Delights* simply would not be. I love you, 'lyssa!

In 1999, shortly before her twentieth birthday, Melissa decided to change the spelling of her name to *Malyssa*. I sensed her desire to adopt a new spelling of her name was a statement of the "new" person she had become. I understood the message I felt my daughter was trying to convey, and I respected her decision to do so. The road Malyssa traveled was a difficult one, but I feel it has made her a stronger and more compassionate human being. She has become a woman I am proud to call "daughter" and "friend."

Malyssa and I worked, diligently, on the first edition of *Lowcountry Delights* for nine months. During these busy months, Malyssa and I spent much time together (usually with Barrister and/or Chymarra napping nearby) collecting recipes, testing recipes, typing recipes, editing recipes, *screaming* at recipes. After being involved in publishing for almost twenty-five years, I understood the basics. However, compiling a cookbook/travel guide, as inclusive as *Lowcountry Delights*, entailed far more than I anticipated. By the time we went to press, I felt like a baby had been delivered. And, yes, all of our "labor pains" were negated by the overwhelming excitement of what we had jointly accomplished and the enthusiasm we received from others.

As we spent time working together on *Lowcountry Delights,* there were times when each of us inevitably did things annoying to the other. Yet, not once was a cross word or look exchanged, not even when we were working under a tight deadline and totally exhausted. Our relationship was tested in swirling waters and survived. Not only did our relationship survive, it flourished and became strengthened through our valuing of each other's gifts and goals.

In spite of the long hours and frustrations involved, neither of us would trade our experience of creating *Lowcountry Delights* for anything. Not all of our work was difficult, by any means. Our visits to delightful Lowcountry inns and restaurants provided the extra fuel we needed to keep on keeping on; the memories created, while on these trips, provided refueling when we needed rejuvenating.

Traveling together, one of us would drive while the other did cookbook work on one of our laptops. Unlike ten years ago, we both sat up front. We even enjoyed listening to the same music—well, most of the time. No more staying in separate rooms; in fact, we sometimes shared the same bed. During and after dinner each evening, we relaxed and enjoyed each other's company. Whether sitting in a back corner of an earthy-type eatery or on the upper veranda of an antebellum plantation home, we spent time sharing, laughing and talking about things of importance in our lives. During these times, I feel we learned a lot from each other, and we became closer than I ever thought possible.

So, what's the next chapter in our story? The completion of *52 Scrolls*. Malyssa's name will appear first on this book, because she is the one who conceived and initiated it. Her part is already complete; she is now sitting in the editor's chair reminding me of my deadline. The story behind *52 Scrolls* is one difficult to hear while remaining dry-eyed. I respect and appreciate Malyssa's courage and willingness to share her part of our story with others. Each of us hopes our experience will provide encouragement and hope for other daughters and mothers going through difficult times.

As far as we know, there is no book comparable to *52 Scrolls* in style or content. It is slated for release in 2006. Until then, Malyssa and I will continue making up for the years we lost by savoring every moment of the time we have together now.

"The present is a *gift*, and that is why it is called a *present*." This saying may appear trite, but it is full of truth.

Chymarra   Barrister

Learning to Cook

by Malyssa Pinson

*T*hree years ago, it would have been nearly impossible for me to do any real cooking in my closet-sized kitchen. I lived in a studio apartment where everything was designed to fit into a small space. There is nothing wrong with that—I did not mind pulling down my Murphy-style bed (from its storage spot in the wall) each night. It did not bother me that I never had to tell company which door lead to the bathroom—it was the only door, other than the entrance door to the apartment. However, the kitchen was almost non-functional and provided little incentive for trying to cook anything.

The mini-fridge, wedged into my kitchenette, had a small compartment that someone named a "freezer." The tiny cubicle was not large enough to even store an individual-sized pizza. The burners on the stove were so close together that I didn't think two of them could be used safely at the same time. When I did cook something simple, like a bag of rice or brownies out of a box, the entire apartment filled up with so much smoke I longed for more than one window in the place to provide ventilation.

All of this, along with the fact that I did not have much experience cooking in the first place, made me a pretty unlikely candidate for co-authoring a cookbook. I thought my mother had lost her mind, for sure this time, when she initially told me about her cookbook idea. Yet, in spite of some of her crazy-sounding ideas, Mom has an uncanny knack for sticking with them and making them work. Her track record leaves little room for me to think, "That's not such a great idea!" I've learned to trust her on these things and see what happens.

This particular thing, producing the first copy of our cookbook/travel guide, happened pretty fast. Since my kitchen was so small, all the testing for the first edition of *Lowcountry Delights* was done in the kitchen of my parents' home. It was there, with my mother, that I learned most of what I now know about cooking. In fact, we *both* learned a lot by testing the recipes contributed by different inns and restaurants in the area—ones we personally experienced, enjoyed, and selected.

When my mother's "idea" developed into a joint success for both of us, I found myself the co-author of a real cookbook! Not only had I learned how to cook, but before long, I had a kitchen I could enjoy cooking in. That's right, I left the studio apartment for a bigger place with a real kitchen and lots of windows!

Eight months later, when it was time to start working on our book's revised edition, I was able to do some of the recipe testing, on my own, at home. The first recipe I tried was one for pecan pie. Mom thought it would be a good one for me to start with since it is one of the cookbook's easier recipes. I just needed to pick up a few things at the store—Karo syrup, pecans, sugar—and I would be all set. I already had eggs. Well, actually, they were Egg Beaters I had in my freezer. Before leaving for the store, I placed the "eggs" on the kitchen counter to thaw.

I knew Karo syrup was a corn syrup, so I assumed it would be shelved with corn oil, vegetable oil, and other cooking oils. I was wrong. Instead, it was sitting on a shelf with Aunt Jemima's maple syrup and other pancake toppings. I searched down quite a few aisles before I figured out that one. But, I knew I'd have no problem finding the next item on my list: pecans. Obviously, they would be with the almonds, peanuts, macadamia nuts, and other kinds of nuts. When I got home, much to my annoyance, I discovered I had bought salted and roasted pecans—the type used for snacking. I did not think that was the flavor I wanted to create in my Southern pecan pie! At that point, I decided to call it a night and bake the pie the next day.

The next morning, after returning from the grocery store with the right pecans, I realized the Egg Beaters were still sitting on the kitchen counter from the day before. I felt absolutely ridiculous. I realized if I returned to the grocery store a third time, it would almost be like making a separate trip for each ingredient called for in the pie. I was just *not* going to do that. So, I used the well-thawed "eggs" I already had. Later, when I removed the pie from the oven, it was an evenly-colored charcoal black; I knew it was not going to make any difference if the eggs used were good or not. I would not be serving that pie to anyone—not even my parents' dog.

Hey, I never claimed to be a gourmet cook! But since "charcoaling" my pecan pie, I have tested lots of recipes in my new kitchen that have been edible. Not only have they been edible, but they have also been delicious. Right after the first edition of our cookbook came out, I invited my parents over for dinner on Father's Day and impressed them with an especially complicated-looking recipe. The recipe calls for two things I had never used before: a mandoline (used to cut potatoes into waffle-style chips) and a grill. I side-stepped using a mandoline, which I didn't have, by substituting frozen "waffle-fries." I learned how to use my hand-me-down grill as I prepared the steaks on it. After assembling the filets, spinach, and waffled potato-fries, I was so pleased with the attractive presentation that I almost didn't want it to be eaten. But it was eaten, every single bit of it. I thought maybe I could pass for a gourmet cook after all!

Now it is almost time to send the second edition of *Lowcountry Delights* to press. Not only can I now find my way around the grocery store, but I feel much more comfortable in the kitchen—and it isn't just because I have enough space to turn around without bumping into something. With such wonderful restaurants around, like the ones we have selected for this book, I can understand why cooking at home is becoming a dying art. But, I, for one, hope it survives. I promise that most of these recipes can easily be prepared at home, even by a novice cook. I know first-hand.

The first edition of *Lowcountry Delights*, our first book and venture as partners, will always spark special memories for my mother and me. My first-try pecan pie, the first recipe I tested for the second edition of our cookbook, does not provoke such a positive memory! Yet, just like my first-try pecan pie was a learning experience for me, the first edition of our cookbook/travel guide proved to be a significant learning experience for both of us. Now as we go to press with the revised edition, I feel our second edition of *Lowcountry Delights* is comparable to the filet mignon I served so proudly. I think you will see why!

Malyssa prepares another dinner for her dad, on his birthday, using a recipe from *Lowcountry Delights*.

Moving On...

When we began working on the first edition of *Lowcountry Delights Cookbook & Travel Guide* in September 2001, we had no idea that we would be sending our third edition to press in September 2004. The response to the first two editions of our book has far surpassed our expectations, and our "cookbook experience" has been a rewarding one in more ways than we ever anticipated. It has also proven to be an invaluable learning experience for each of us. We marvel when we think about the multitude of individuals who have contributed, in some integral way, to this project. There is no doubt about it, we could not have accomplished what we have without the help of each of them.

Our third edition of *Lowcountry Delights* will also be the final edition of our cookbook/travel guide "trilogy;" each of us is now ready to move on to other pursuits, joint as well as individual. Since this will be our last edition, we are having a greater number of books printed so it will be available for awhile longer. As we are also the publishers of the book, taking care of the business end of our venture will continue keeping us busy as long as our book supply lasts.

So, what's next? Just *what* are we planning to "move on" to? Well, our next mother-daughter project will be co-authoring *52 Scrolls* (see page 215). This book has already evoked much interest because of the issues addressed. If all goes as scheduled, we hope to have this next book completed by the end of 2006. We will also continue hosting Savannah Restaurants Online (www.eatinginsavannah.com) and keeping that Website current.

In addition to handling the marketing and sales of *Lowcountry Delights*, Maxine plans to remain actively involved in the bed and breakfast industry. She will continue visiting B&Bs (throughout the U.S. and Canada), editing and publishing *The INNside Scoop* B&B newsletter, writing a column for *The B&B and Country Inn MarketPlace Guide*, posting online commentaries about inns she visits (for inngoers to read on the B&B message boards sponsored by BedandBreakfast.com), and hosting The Food Scoop: "Where to Eat on the B&B Trail" (www.thefoodscoop.com). However, once she completes her contribution to *52 Scrolls*, her major focus will be writing a book (see page 215) involving concerns of a more serious nature than writing about bed and breakfast inns. This book will expand upon some of the issues referred to in *52 Scrolls* as well as introducing new topics.

Malyssa traveled to many inns and dined at dozens of restaurants with her mother during the past three years. Yet, it is Malyssa's personal journey that makes her Mom smile even more than having her daughter join her for a trip to a favorite B&B or dinner at a choice dining spot. Malyssa was actively involved in the production process, recipe testing, and varied clerical duties with the first two editions of *Lowcountry Delights*.. However, shortly after the second edition of the cookbook came out in July 2003, Malyssa decided to continue her education. The next month she enrolled in a local community college. Between hostessing at a local restaurant, attending college, and a renewed interest in playing the piano, Malyssa had less time for the production process of the third edition of *Lowcountry Delights*.

As we send our last edition of *Lowcountry Delights* to press, Malyssa has just finished her first year in college with a 4.0 average and is preparing for a career in physical therapy. Malyssa began working as a physical therapist's aide, in the physical therapy department of a local hospital, the week she turned twenty-four (April 2004). Like her mom, Malyssa places a high value on relationships and makes time to nurture old friendships while cultivating new ones. Always an animal lover, she also relishes time spent with her 2 cats, Chymarra and Jubal—and, of course, Barrister (her parents' retired greyhound, which she takes care of when her Mom and Dad are able to travel together).

Fortunately, Malyssa was having a break (between summer and fall quarters) just in time to do a final proofreading of *Lowcountry Delights'* third edition. Maybe she just has the advantage of younger eyes or a less cluttered mind, but her keen "editor's eye" found more typos than her editor/mother likes to admit. So, even though Malyssa spent less time testing and typing recipes for this edition, her input was still significant.

We do not know where the paths of our lives will lead us in the years ahead. However, our prayer is that we will each follow God's plan for our individual life, and that we will fulfill those plans in ways making us worthy of the bountiful blessings God's grace has bestowed upon us—including the restoration of our relationship and the strong mother/daughter bond which has become such a vital part of each of our lives.

Maxine and Malyssa Pinson
September 2004

Moving on to higher octaves...

Forthcoming Books

52 SCROLLS

The story of how two head-strong women, Mother and Daughter, Rebuild their shattered relationship in a special way.

Malyssa Pinson
Maxine Pinson

The heart-wrenching and tumultuous journey
which follows the spontaneous combustion
of a mother undergoing a "mid-life crisis
as her younger daughter struggles
with the crises of a troubled adolescence—
and the poignant experiences re-uniting them into a close, loving,
and accepting relationship cherished by each.

*A must-read for any parent needing hope and encouragement
during years of teen-age turbulence.*

(*52 Scrolls* introduces issues which are expanded upon in *A Toxic Legacy*)

"I will no longer allow my wife to be subjected to this type of abuse," my husband Bill, a seasoned trial attorney, informed the moderator/pastor at a call meeting of our church's governing body. Standing up, Bill continued in a tone punctuated with credibility and finality. "I resign my position as a member of this Session, and my resignation is effective immediately." As the group responded with looks of disbelief and a deafening silence, I walked out of the inquisition chamber with my husband. Before I went to sleep that night, I vowed I would never permit myself to be devalued, tyrannized, stifled, or muzzled again.

It was May 1989 when I received a "summons" to appear for questioning about what I considered to be cultic methodology, spiritual/power abuse, and hidden agendas at a well-known historic church (see www.the-innside-scoop.com/spirabuse.htm). As if I were in a preliminary hearing, I was questioned to determine whether or not a church court was needed to further examine or discipline me—a middle-aged matron who refused to play "follow the leader" in spite of "either-or" proclamations from the pulpit.

After answering each question asked, I was found guiltless. However, still convinced that I was "wrong, wrong, wrong" for questioning and disagreeing with one of "God's anointed," the young, first-time pastor launched into a lengthy diatribe against me. Appalled by what was transpiring, a senior member of the group objected and said, "I thought we agreed that we would not conduct a kangaroo court here tonight." The protest was ignored by the pastor, and he continued interrogating me until my husband stood up and resigned from the group he had twice chaired.

The following week, Bill submitted his resignation to the Session (as several other members had already done), and he requested a copy of the proceeding's tape. His request for the tape was denied, and the tape mysteriously disappeared a short time thereafter. A few months later, we followed the lead of a number of other long-time members, including highly respected community leaders, and moved our membership to another church.

A book about Overcoming the Poisonous Effects of Abusive Domination within Family, Religion, and Society

I never dreamed that my 1989 "star chamber" proceeding, as Bill calls the event, or the events leading to it would later prove to be an evolution of blessings which would change the entire course of my life in a multitude of enriching ways. During that time, through experiential learning, my scope of understanding broadened and became more focused. For the first time in my life, I became cognizant of the differences between healthy spirituality and unhealthy religiosity. In addition, I became aware of the toxic legacy I had inherited from my own family-of-origin—a legacy which played an integral role in my vehement reaction to a new regime's controlling manipulation, intimidation, subjugation, and demand for blind obedience/allegiance at my former church home. Most importantly, I learned that until toxic situations or legacies are recognized and confronted, they cannot be broken or overcome. After years of being urged to tell my story, I am now ready to do so in hopes that it will provide insight, hope, and courage for countless others whose lives have been adversely affected by abusive forms of domination found within family, religion, and society.

Index of Recipes

French Toast/Blintzes/Crêpes, Pancakes/Waffles

Fruit Dishes

Main Dish Casseroles & One-Dish Meals

Meats
Beef

Ham, Pork, and Sausage

Lamb

Poultry

Veal

Pastas

Variations of Recipes Referred to in Editors' Notes

Vegetables and Side Dishes

Helpful Information

Sources for Ordering Difficult-to-Find and Specialty Food Items

True Grits
912-234-8006
(sells and ships stone ground grits)

www.nueske.com
(sells/ships apple-wood smoked bacon, country hams, andouille, tasso, pancetta, rack of lamb, and other quality smoked meats)
1-800-392-2266

www.MaineLobsterDirect.com
(sells/ships live Maine lobster, most seafood called for in LCD recipes, as well as seafood stocks and bases)
1-800-556-2783

Note: For other difficult-to-find or specialty items (i.e., specialty mushrooms, truffles, stocks and broths), check **www.thefoodscoop.com/specialtyitems.html** or do an online search through a search engine.

Online Cooking Sources

www.epicurious.com
(click "The Food Dictionary" link on home page—includes over 4,000 cooking terms)

www.foodsubs.com
(includes pictures, descriptions, pronunciations of foods and offers suggested substitutions)

Basic Recipes Called for in Recipes Included in This Book

Crème Fraîche
To make your own Crème Fraîche, simply combine 1 cup whipping cream and 2 tablespoons buttermilk in a glass container. Cover and let stand at room temperature for 8 to 24 hours until very thick.

Basic Roux
Melt 4 cups butter (fat or oil) in a heavy bottom pot over moderate heat until butter starts to foam. Sprinkle in 6 tablespoons flour, stirring constantly, and cook until a light gold color is reached. To use, stir roux into soup or sauces (adding a little at a time) until correct consistency is attained. Leftover roux may be frozen in small portions (or in ice-cube trays) for later use.

A Simple Preparation for Grilled Fish, Chicken, or Pork

2 teaspoons ginger, finely minced	2 tablespoons fresh lime luice
2 teaspoons low-sodium soy sauce	2 teaspoons ground cumin
1 pinch Kosher salt	2 tablespoons extra virgin olive oil
2 teaspoons lime zest	2 cloves garlic, finely minced

Mix all ingredients for marinade. Place fish filets in a zip-lock bag, cover with marinade, and refrigerate for 20 minutes. Marinating fish filets too long will make them mushy, but chicken needs marinading longer. Heat grill until hot. Once hot, oil the grill and place filets flesh side (the "presentation" side) down and the skin side up. Grill for a couple of minutes and then turn (one-fourth turn) for a couple more minutes to create "grill marks." Don't fuss with it, or it will stick to grill. Carefully turn filets over to cooler side of grill and cook till done. Fish should be firm to touch. If preparing pork, substituting the lime juice with orange, pineapple, or apple juice is recommended.

The above 2 recipes provided by Frank Ciccone, food consultant for Lowcountry Delights Cookbook & Travel Guide.

Helpful Cooking Tips

Frank Ciccone
Food Consultant

Concentrating on Low-fat and Low-carb Cooking

Substitutions may be made to help lower saturated fats and carbohydrates in some recipes. For example, when sautéing or frying, canola oil may often be substituted for butter. Fat-free/low-fat yogurt, sour cream, mayonnaise, and cream cheese may also be integrated into some recipes in place of their high-fat counterparts. Using *Splenda* sweetener, instead of sugar, will reduce the carbohydrate content of some recipes as well. Experiment and have fun!

Things I've Learned

• Invest in a set of measuring spoons, dry measuring cups, and something else for measuring liquids. (1 quart and 2 cup sizes are particularly handy).

• Ovens vary widely, especially as they age; don't depend upon the oven dial for total accuracy. Instead, use an oven thermometer to verify operating temperatures and adjust as needed. When pre-heating an oven, allow 30 minutes (or more) for oven temperature to stabilize before using.

• When baking, exact measuring of recipe ingredients is essential for success. For example, when measuring flour or sugar, slightly overfill measuring cup and then level off with a straight edge. Pay attention to types of flour used and check your pantry before starting. All-purpose flour, cake flour, bread flour, and self-rising flour all have different qualities which give different results. Use the type of flour the recipe calls for.

• Invest in a heavy, stainless steel skillet or sauté pan with an oven-proof handle. Unless you are cooking large amounts at a time, a 10-inch size should work. A heavy pan retains and distributes heat evenly (I prefer uncoated stainless steel to the non-stick types).

• Invest in a decent quality chef knife as well as a paring knife. Most required cutting, slicing, dicing, mincing, etc. can be done with these two tools. Keep knives sharp and always use them on a wood or plastic cutting surface; anything else will dull and ruin their edge. If you must keep your good knives loose in a drawer, wrap each blade in a cloth towel or use a plastic knife-edge protector. A serrated 9-inch bread knife (for slicing breads, cakes, etc.) is also handy.

• A stainless steel hand whisk, large wooden spoon, spatula, vegetable peeler, and a fine mesh strainer round out the basics.

Frank Ciccone, food consultant for Lowcountry Delights Cookbook & Travel Guide, retired from IBM in January 2002 after spending 39 years in the corporate world. A few months later, he and his wife Rose went on an "Inn to Inn Cooking Tour" in New Hampshire. Classes from that trip sparked a further interest in the culinary arts which led Frank to enrolling in "Culinary Boot Camp—Basic Training" at the world-renowned Culinary Institute of America (CIA) in Hyde Park, New York. After completing the basics, Frank moved on to the next level by enrolling in CIA's "World Cuisines." Though not a full-time student of the CIA, Frank continues taking on-campus classes as part of CIA's continuing education program. He has taken several programs (on Mediterranean Cooking, Fusion and Eclectic Cuisine) at Johnson and Wales in Rhode Island and assisted with kitchen demos for food and wine pairings at a local wine shop. The Ciccones live in New York's Hudson Valley.

How to Receive Answers to Questions About Recipes Included in This Book

Send specific questions you may have, about an ingredient in or the preparation of any recipe in this cookbook, to: lcdelights@cs.com(FC). Your question(s) will be answered, as soon as possible, by *Lowcountry Delight's* Food Consultant, Frank Ciccone. However, as the Ciccones are frequent travelers, he may not always be able to respond immediately.

Order Form for

Lowcountry Delights Cookbook & Travel Guide—3rd Edition

by Maxine & Malyssa Pinson

"Featuring Recipes from Favorite Lowcountry Inns & Restaurants"

(in Savannah, GA—Selected Barrier Islands in GA & SC—Beaufort & Charleston, SC)

www.thefoodscoop.com/lcd.html (links to a printable order form)

Please send me _____ copies of *Lowcountry Delights* @ $19.95 each _____

Shipping & Handling: Add $4.95 per book _____

GA residents add 6% sales tax _____

TOTAL _____

VALUE PACK

Purchase **4** books for *$72.00* _____

Shipping & Handling *$10.00*
(sent to 1 address) _____

GA residents add 6% sales tax _____

TOTAL _____

_____ **I would like the book(s) autographed to:**

_____

_____

_____

_____

Fill Out Form below and Send By Mail or Fax

Send payment (check or a charge order) to:

SSD, Inc.
22 W. Bryan Street—PMB 202
Savannah, GA 31401
(Make check payable to SSD, Inc.)

Fax order form to:
(charge orders only)
912-232-8550
or order online
(using M/C, VISA, or PayPal)
www.thefoodscoop.com/shoppingcart.html

Charge to: M/C or VISA (circle which) _____ Exp. _____

Cardholder's Name _____ Signature _____

Ship To:

Name _____

Address _____

> Charge orders
> (M/C or VISA only) orders may
> also be placed by calling:
> **1-888-717-4040**

City _____ State _____ Zip _____

Telephone _____ E-mail _____